Call me Li Nana

Memoirs of a foreigner in China

KAROLINA ACHIRRI
Kalahari Press

ISBN: 9781532993800

Proofread by: Emilia Balcerzak
Content consulted with: Sherie C.
Images by: Karolina Achirri & Yunqing Xia

For Ishmael, who helped me believe
that my stories are worth telling ♥

CONTENTS

WHY I WROTE THIS BOOK

I went to China as a 20 something young girl and left it as a 30 something woman. I transitioned from being a Polish girl outside of Poland, to being a citizen of the world.

This book has always been in me. It was just waiting for the right time to come out. All the stories depicted in this book happened to me or someone close to me (who gave me permission to share them here). Living in China often felt like living in a war zone. No matter how close relationships one developed with the locals, no matter how good Chinese one spoke, and no matter the length of one's stay, I never felt like a part of a community. I made lifelong friends and even gained a Chinese brother and sister, but China always kept me at a distance. I was always the other, the foreigner, the anomaly.

William Faulkner once said: "If a story is in you, it has got to come out". That's why. I never saw myself as a writer, but a reader instead.

When I first moved to China, I didn't know a word of Chinese. I quickly and painfully discovered that learning Mandarin Chinese would save me a lot of trouble. I wouldn't need anyone to go shopping with to help me read off the labels, I would know which bus to take without having to decipher its stops, I would be able to learn so much more about the Chinese culture if only I spoke the language. Every day in China became a story.

I experienced a lot, learnt a ton, cried more times than I can count but also laughed till I couldn't breathe. I felt at home in China. I miss China every day. Hence, I had to tell my stories, with hope that those who are thinking of braving the mystical Middle Kingdom could use them for guidance, caution and reflection. China awaits those who are adventurous, those who are curious and those who are brave. This book is my own take on China and its multiple cultures. It offers an outsider's inside view on life there. It both informs and narrates, trying to depict my dear China in encouraging light. I might have failed at times to stay objective, but I tried to keep my subjectivities to a bare minimum. After all, it is my life this book encompasses.

If you, my dear reader, have ever thought about going to China at least for a split second, stop thinking! Go! China will change your life, if you stay prepared, open-minded and ready to absorb all it has to offer. And trust me, that's more than you have ever imagined.

Karolina Achirri

Introduction: My first letter from China.

My first letter after a month in China...
Nimen hao! 你们好 ! Witajcie! Welcome!

After almost three weeks of my staying in this country, here I find myself desperately wanting to share!

China shocks wherever I go. Supposedly, cultural shock, which I am now experiencing, should last a couple of months. God have mercy:)

Everything here is different from Europe.

To begin with, the weather. Daily temperatures of 35-40 degrees and humidity at 90% make one feel like being in sauna 24/7 (July). Adding to that, I'm right in the middle of the rainy season, which means it is chucking down almost non-stop. And I do not have my wellies.

Then, the language. Before I came I had been of an assumption that people in China COULD generally speak English. I could not have been more wrong! Need to undergo a crash course in Chinese... taken from daily life experiences. So far, I've succeeded in saying that 'I don't understand'. When I am getting in a taxi, I've got to show the driver the desired address on my phone's screen. :)

Thirdly, chopsticks and weird food. First day killed me with its frogs and snakes available on some traditional menus, mainly in traditional restaurants from the 80s and 90s. Up till now, I have not compelled myself to try a snake, but seaweed doesn't seem to be so bad. The art of using chopsticks seems like a mysterious version of and advanced culinary skill which I clearly have not yet obtained. Imagine Chinese people's fun when observing a foreigner chasing their food on the table. It's almost like a battle for the last piece of sustenance on Earth. At work, I am trying to follow suit and eat whatever others are having. I'm also trying not to ask too many questions about the details of my meals☺.

The biggest amazements so far:

1. The special pants for kids, with the opening right between their legs. They basically pee wherever convenient and required, even on the bus.

These days such garment serves as an emblem of being a villager here, as my friends tell me. Thumbs-up to the open-crotch piece of clothing!

2. Some Chinese people (especially in Guangdong or Hongkong) believe that human foetus is extremely healthy to consume or that it even holds healing attributes. I have heard that it is possible to buy it straight from abortion clinics, which, btw, are to be found here in large numbers. The foetus is later cooked and consumed. Guangdong Province and Hong Kong are infamous for this kind of practice. No comment needed here, I assume.

3. Everybody commutes on bikes here. E-bikes, to be more precise. Regardless, there are absolutely no rules being obeyed, hence I started calling them 'crazy bikers' already. In cities like Hangzhou, it is free to use a public rental bike if one has a citizen's card. I was told that e-bikers are not held responsible for their involvement in traffic accidents, only car drivers are.

4. Found one church. Saturday evening seems to be the time for the English mass. Joined their choir and Bible Study as well. Home reminiscence. Luckily, the church-goers include many people from all over the world. Thanks be to God, as I'm sure I'd have gone insane by now without them.

5. I have huge cockroaches at home. It shook me up at first, but now I kind of warmed up to them. They don't even bite. It's just this uncomfortable feeling when they crawl over me at night.

6. Before I came to China, I had been convinced that I'd be stunned by the locals here, but quite inversely it's me who shocks them. Being stared at non-stop, on the bus, on the street, in a shop. Once a guy almost lost his life while commanding a view of me on the pavement.

7. Hot and lukewarm water. Despite the scorching temperatures, nobody here drinks icy water. Again, hot and warm water is supposed to be very therapeutic.

I have been living here, on the seventh floor, for a month now. Outside there is a construction going on, so they are hammering day and night. It is all hugely gripping. People are friendly and overly nice towards foreigners here.

That's it for now. Will stay in touch. K.

CHAPTER 1

THE CHINESE CREDO

*Beliefs have the power to create and the power to destroy.
Human beings have the awesome ability to take any
experience of their lives and create a meaning that
disempowers them or one that can literally save their
lives.*

(Tony Robbins)

But there is no racism in China.

Once I was asked to teach a VIP couple for a very prestigious training school in Hangzhou. I hadn't even started yet but was warned that they were extremely discriminatory. Apparently, when the school sent an American (black) teacher there, the woman refused to even attend the class. Then, the clients asked for a new teacher but also demanded to see his or her photos beforehand. The manager sent it over but since the girl (from Britain) was black too, they refused to have classes with her as well. I was the only choice left and when they heard I'm white, the photo requirement was instantly ditched. This is when I ditched them as students, too. So much for a developing mind in a developing country.

I will never forget when my husband came to visit me one year and while photographing the mesmeric West Lake, lots of people around us were actually taking photos of him instead. He, being a happy-go-lucky and lax as he is, didn't even comment on that, but I started thinking. Living in China makes one think about varieties of topics that wouldn't even cross my mind elsewhere. Should racism be re-defined in China? Surely everyone can agree that a standard definition of it does not apply to the curious Chinese.

In China, race is a matter of status. In such society, where order goes vertically, rural people are perceived differently from city dwellers, ordinary blokes do not match the level of officials and white, yellow and black people fall into three different sorts. If a Chinese girl is dating a white foreigner she is socially climbing the ladder, while the one dating a black is stepping down.

I heard lots of stories from other teachers who were discriminated at work. At their job interview, some of them were told: *Sorry, we are looking for professional teachers. The parents won't accept your looks. We only need native speakers* (to a black guy was born and bred in the US).

I also heard from my Chinese female friends that they were told by their own parents that marrying a black person is out of discussion and in case they disobeyed, their parents threatened to disown them. Some of the people I met in China even believe that every black person comes from Africa, which in their mind is one big country.

This all happens not because Chinese people are mean. They

aren't. They are the most hospitable nationality I have ever met in my life. However, for thousands of years Chinese citizens of lighter skin looked down on those of darker skin, usually farmers. If you walk into any drugstore in town, you'll see a wide range of whitening products being hit sales. White is beautiful. No one can argue about that with any Chinese girl who wants to be fashionable.

Minorities are also experiencing racism. A lot of them would be recognized as 'backwards', obsolete and behind the contemporary world. Children's tuitions would be higher and sometimes they wouldn't even be allowed in schools due to a lack of 'hukou' (a Chinese registered permanent residence).

Three years ago, my Polish friend came to visit me in Hangzhou. The first night I took him out to dinner to a little café near my house. I knew the owner and was confident that the food would be tasty there. As we walked and sat down, another customer, a middle-aged Chinese man, also entered the restaurant. We were chatting in Polish and having a wonderful time while he called the waitress and asked her why foreigners were in this place. *Isn't this a Chinese restaurant? Why do they need to eat here?* I heard every single word because he wanted me to. He fussed about us for a while longer and five minutes later, he stood up and ostentatiously left, slamming the door behind him. When I explained to my guest what happened, we had a good laugh about it.

Every foreigner is pointed at, taken photos of, talked about, called 'the other' or 'the outsider'. Every time someone calls me a 'laowai' (which translates as a foreigner), I riposte: *Wo shi Zhongguoren* (which means: I'm Chinese), just for giggles. I don't think any foreign visitor, regardless of the number of years spent in China and the level of their Chinese, can ever be seen as one of them, the Chinese. We will always be the others, as the cultural and geographical chasm is beyond belief in the Middle Kingdom.

Guangzhou is locally called 'Chocolate City' due to a vast number of foreigners from Africa there. There are multitudes of African cuisine restos, African-owned businesses, even shops selling fufu (a mash of starches served as an addition to meat soups) and waakye (a popular dish from Ghana of cooked rice and beans). Little Africa, they call it. It is a convenient place to ship products back home, and hence the growing black population there (100,000 Africans right now and counting).

One black guy I know was approached by a young Chinese girl in Shanghai once and asked if he had any drugs. She was trying to convince him she's got money. We, who were listening to his story, asked him whether he took the money and ran. All of us were in stitches.

Funny thing happened in Kenya two years ago. A Chinese restaurant in Nairobi put up a sign saying: *No coloured allowed*, banning Africans from entering after 5pm unless they were in a company of a Chinese, European or Indian friend. When asked about it, the owner was trying to use a 'security threat' excuse. I don't assume their business is booming these days. Who would like to eat there? No matter their skin colour.

I could go on hours on end with stories of such kind. The bottom line is: black or white we are all people and we should be treated as such. Let me finish with a quote from H.G. Wells: *Our true nationality is mankind.*

Spit on my shoes and I'll know who you are.

There are certainly many pet peeves one can easily develop in China. Even if you had no phobias before, you'll get infected with anger slash confusion virus. It is omnipresent. This is how it goes. You get up in the morning thinking *I'm going to have a wonderful day.* You leave your flat and the second you step out of your building a crazy biker spits right in front of you, or even worse, directly on your shoes. (I'm not kidding. It has happened to me, I swear.) You continue on, going to work hoping to get there on time because you must punch in (otherwise a part of your salary will be deducted). The bus is swarming with people (the Chinese phrase: *People mountain people sea* couldn't apply better anywhere else). So, before you manage to get on the bus, you get elbowed a few solid times (I definitely learnt my own Art of War from bus rides). While squeezing and praying to arrive at your destination in one piece (some drivers must have dreamt of becoming car racers), you'll be stepped on and punched or sworn at in Chinese (of course). I guess the last one is a perk, though. Then, you finally get there, you can now breathe but hold on there is somebody smoking right next to you, exhaling into your face. I have always thought that smokers must enjoy indulging in this lovely habit and thinking *I know I'm killing you, but I couldn't care less*. Only when you begin to believe your day can't get any worse, do you realize it's only 8am. Later in the afternoon, the food in the canteen sucks and is utterly inedible and you're back to square one when you have to remind yourself that you're in China, a country of contradictions and unexpected twists and turns. Now, embrace it all. If you can make it in China, you can make it everywhere else.

Chinese people have many habits that can shock a foreigner. Spitting mentioned above is a common sight and sound, especially on the taxi. Just when you are about to stop at the traffic lights, you'll often witness a driver rolling down his window just to spit till the Kingdom come. Nose picking and loud eating are other culprits. Well, I get the loud eating by now. It is culturally ingrained to chat over meals, get together with friends not seen for a while, discuss business. But I don't think thousands of years living in China would ever change my attitude towards picking one's nose. It is widespread literally everywhere. Some do it out in the open without shame, some try to hide this nasty habit behind their smart phones, others grow an unreasonably long pinkie nail just for this particular pastime.

Still, my favourite part of an everyday etiquette in China is sneezing aka honking. Some of my Chinese friends told me the way Westerners blow their noses is gross to them. They cannot understand why would someone blow their nose into a handkerchief and then shove it into their pocket. Is this why I see many Chinese blowing their noses right onto the ground? Might be. I have seen, and yes, I admit I stared at, guys who would blow their brains out right next to me in a queue at the railway station.

My least dear obsession has always been smoking. My father was a heavy smoker. Back in my salad days, I would wake up in the middle of the night suffocating in clouds of smoke relentlessly spreading into my bedroom (the flat was 32sqm only). So, I guess I picked up my aversion to smoking quite early. China takes it to a whole new level, though. Smoking is present at almost every business interaction. Thank God, I'm not a man for the sake of this situation. I heard Chinese friends say that if they refuse to smoke they'll not only lose face but also make others lose face. No business deal will be sealed without a ciggie. According to WHO, China is the No 1 consumer of tobacco products in the world. A cigarette seems to be a status symbol, a societal currency unit offered instead of a handshake or a toast.

What puzzles me most are those ones who smoke right outside the lift, standing next to a *Non-smoking* sign. I was unwillingly placed in such situations almost every day. Frequently, in my building I would find myself telling a person pushing into the elevator, puffing away, off. I even noticed that if I'm with a Chinese friend and they politely ask the smoker to leave the cancer stick outside, they would be utterly and bluntly ignored. However, if I ask them to do the same, they would say *Sorry* and do as I please. I guess being a foreigner does have certain benefits in China.

In July 2015, the government tried to implement a ban on smoking in Beijing. This would include smoking near schools and hospitals and would be fined with RMB 200 (around $30). Sadly, this idea never took off. With such pollution issue, we are facing in China right now, I am staggered to see many people not doing anything to stop the smokers from killing their lungs.

I feel like the Chinese are in for an impending rude awakening soon. Regarding *The Lancet* medical journal's findings, if prevalent smoking rates continue, 2mln Chinese will die by 2030. I still hope that one day we will be able to dine in smoke-free restaurants and ride in breezy lifts. 加油 China !

Don't die in China. It's too expensive!

According to *China Daily*, the regular price for embalming one's body is around RMB 300 (approx. $40-45). However, if you are a foreigner you'll be charged RMB 8,000 (which is close to $1200). Even if you could afford that, you'd still face the problem of not being able to be buried on a Chinese soil. It's illegal. There are only a few cities that allow foreigners to rest in their holy land, providing those had contributed to the Chinese society. If you haven't, your family will have to pay around RMB 80,000 ($12000) to get you back home.

Normally, the minute a person dies, their family is given a slip, which needs to be stamped in the hospital (of course) to issue a death certificate. On the way to the counter they are already swarmed with different undertakers offering their services. Never miss an opportunity to do business! Once a deal is done, the body is moved to the undertaker's, usually conveniently located next door to the hospital. Coffin, ashes box, ceremonial clothes are all bought as a part of the deal. The dead person is then changed into their funeral clothes. It is a widespread belief that clothes need to be changed as soon as possible after one's passing to make sure the deceased would enter the next world in style.

Then, they put the corpse into a truck to be taken to the mortuary. All gathered need to bow three times before the truck drives away. As is believed, the house of the dead must stay warm, so the whole family gathers there for the next three days, at least. The undertakers also provide superstitious rituals, such as setting up a photo shrine at home, burning incense and paper money (so that the dead can be rich on the other side). Fruit are also prepared as an offering for the gods. I also heard of paper horses, TVs, cars and iPhones being burnt.

Whoever arrives to pay their respects, must burn an incense stick, raise it over their head three times whilst saying wishes for the deceased's safe crossing to the afterlife. On the actual funeral day, the body is moved to the crematorium and later to the cemetery. Some families carry the urn with ashes only to smash it at the gate of the community, as a symbol of a life's end. I also saw people jumping over a bonfire, made on the ashes, as bad spirits can't go through fire and follow one back to the house.

Later, when cremation is done, the ashes are placed in a tomb at the cemetery. Members of the family are to wear armbands, signifying their relationships to the deceased, which are later burnt in the tomb, followed by more money made of paper.

Again, some families are more credulous than others, so they would hire a Feng-Shui Master to perform lots of crazy-looking rites. One of them would be washing the hands of the children of the dead in *baijiu* (Chinese maize liquor) before handing them the bones. Only the male offsprings are invited to this ceremony.

Some of my Chinese friends told me that the family tombs at the cemetery are already having all the family members' name engraved. So, even if you're still alive you'll see your name next to your great-grandfather, etc. The names of those who are still alive are in a distinct colour, though.

Fireworks are also an indispensable part of the funeral (as they are of most big occasions in China), for they are to scare away evil spirits. Sometimes musicians accompany the dead along with dragon dancers, with the hope of protecting one while crossing over. White is the colour of death in China, so don't dress in black.

Some wealthier families also hire services of professional weepers. There would be ladies bringing livestock and placing it at the feet of the coffin, and sitting around the dead weeping, wailing and making noise day and night.

Lately, China has been running out of space at the cemeteries. Also, new innovative tombstones have been seen in Chongqing. Instead of having an epitaph on them, one would scan a QR code and then read all the information online. Better? Too modernized? Perhaps in the future we will find virtual graves, too.

On the concept of 'face' in China.

Men can't live without face, trees can't live without bark.

(A Chinese idiom)

If I were to recall how many times I must have lost face in China, I'd be buried under a mountain of embarrassment and shame. Gaining and losing face is a serious business in China. Even if you don't care about that, you may unintentionally make your Chinese friends lose face. So, don't take *mianzi* too light!

I have seen friendships broken due to faces being lost. It's not about Chinese people being too sensitive or unable to take criticism, as much as it is ingrained in their culture. It's a society that values harmony and generally avoids criticism. A Westerner doing business in China and speaking his or her mind like nothing else matters will be considered rude and overbearing. That's also why the Chinese barely ask questions in classes or during meetings. They simply don't want their teacher or boss to lose face.

Renowned writer and translator Lin Yutang (1895-1976) claimed *mianzi* 'cannot be translated or defined'. He only managed to characterize it as "abstract and intangible, it is yet the most delicate standard by which Chinese social intercourse is regulated". A few other scholars went on a limb and translated it as *pride*, *prestige* or *dignity*. However, it is so much more than that. This social phenomenon has a lot to do with Confucius's teachings. He taught that if you lead people "with excellence and put them in their place through roles and ritual practices, in addition to developing a sense of shame, they will order themselves harmoniously." China is a shame-based culture. It has been one for centuries. I often wondered why Chinese students behave so well or why there are no hearings of riots on the streets of Shanghai or Beijing. It's surely not because we live in a perfect country. Until I realized that they "behave properly" to avoid shame and out of fear of losing face, in which case, if they are not caught red-handed, anything goes. For shame is not just a personal affront, is extends to the entire family, neighbourhood, society. You would never see anyone's dirty laundry to be aired on talk shows or even discussed with acquaintances in China.

When one looks at ethics, the ethics known in China have never been based on what's right or wrong. Again, it was their great teacher Confucius who instructed people to treat others differently, depending on your relative status with them. Even the concept of truth is not black and white. More focus is placed on what an actual situation needs rather than digging to the bottom of the matter. Therefore, lying is one of the biggest cultural differences between the West and China. Every time I ask my students to explain to me what a 'white lie' means, they would answer: 'a good lie'. I laugh and think to myself, is there such a thing? A typical Chinese person will do whatever it takes to protect their holy face, even if it means lying blatantly. And that's acceptable. Oftentimes, however, both sides can read between the lines and know that the truth is being twisted to help save face. Hotels are infamous practitioners of that. You might be told that there are no vacancies whereas it is really a cover for 'No foreigners allowed'. Or, as it happened to my close friend, you'd be told your country is on a special list of countries not allowed in that place. Having worked in China for almost six years, I noticed that even employers try to steer clear from foreigners. It is to avoid potential situations where losing face would be inevitable. Lots of Chinese friends of mine are also highly concerned with preserving national face. They care what we think of China. Whenever they ask you *Do you like Chinese food?* it is because they really want you to say *Yes, it is indeed the best cuisine in the Universe.*

How to give face? Well... Praise your Chinese friends or colleagues as much as you can in public, especially during meetings. Evaluate services highly on the feedback forms in hotels and restaurants, particularly teachers you work with. Give an expensive gift and leave the price tag on. Treat them to a luxurious dinner.

How to avoid losing face? Hmmm... Do not criticise anyone openly, especially in public. Don't call their bluff. Don't get angry with them, it causes both of you lose face. Don't turn down an invitation, but instead say *maybe, I'll think about it, I'll do my best*, etc. If you're late, make sure your excuse is solid. Lastly, don't ever ridicule anyone's English ability.

In one of the schools I previously worked for, we noticed a problem with our students' hygiene. They were either not showering at all or very rarely. Our manager, also a foreigner, tried to address the issue during parents meeting explaining that the kids will go abroad in a year's time, so they should know about the importance of not smelling bad. This completely backfired. None of us knew we were not supposed to challenge the kids directly, let alone to their parents' faces. All parents complained about it to the Chinese management of the school. It happened in a year when the Internet exploded with this buzz phrase: *ren shen jian nan bu yao chai chuan*, which in English means *Life is so hard, don't hurt me with the truth.* Go figure, eh?

My second year in China, someone told me a story of an old married couple. Apparently, they never argued with each other and were never seen in conflict. They were named as the most harmonious couple anyone had ever seen. People were convinced these two lovely elderly people must have been as happy as a clam. How far from the truth! Since their wedding day they had not slept one night in the same bed, and never expressed their true feelings to one another. Yet, they were so concerned about saving face that they continued living a lie till the day they died.

To conclude, I often read or hear of the inscrutable Chinese face expression. It is, nonetheless, mentioned as a compliment to be able to read true feelings of a Chinese person. Poker faces? Well, I must admit it isn't easy to deduce what my Chinese friends truly think. Since eye-contact is widely avoided in China, how otherwise can a foreigner read their Chinese conversation partner?

As I see it, the only way to comprehend the *mianzi* idea is to observe this society closely and avoid mishaps. I often ask my Chinese friends what is acceptable or assumed of me in a situation I feel like a fish out of water. They always patiently and eagerly explain it to me. But let's keep balance in our dealings. After all, as Ralph Waldo Emerson said: *To be yourself in a world that is constantly trying to make you something else is the greatest accomplishment.*

I will give you some colours 'to see see'.

I adore Chinese idioms. They are just so much fun. Like this one when one's angry with someone they'd say: *I will show you some colours* (给你点颜色看看 = *gei ni dian yan se kan kan*). Colours in Chinese culture have their profound meanings and purposes. The five main colours are ranked in gradation: red (红 = *hong*), yellow (黄 = *huang*), blue (青 = *qing*) (including green), white (白 = *bai*) and black (黑 = *hei*). According to geomantic theories these colours are linked with the Five Elements ideology (explained at length later in this chapter): green with wood, red with fire, yellow with earth, white with gold and finally black with water.

Let's start with the grand red. It is the symbol of joy and is always used for all festive times of the year in the Middle Kingdom. It is supposed to mean the sun, the provider to all life on Earth. Its significance is reflected in an old saying: *The sun rises and all life comes out* (日至而万物生 = *ri zhi er wan wu sheng*). It is a prerequisite to wear a red wedding dress as well as be wished 红红火火 (*hong hong huo huo*), which means a thriving life. During Spring Festival (Chinese New Year) people hand out red envelopes with money (红包 = *hongbao*) and stick red couplets on their doors called 红对联 (*hong dui lian*) for good luck. Red stands for auspiciousness and good fortune. It also signifies fertility for new mothers give out hard-boiled eggs dyed red to all their friends. They believe this symbolic gesture passes their fertility onto their friends. Red is also seen as a weapon against evil spirits. Every year a different animal takes over the nation and the Chinese believe that if you were born in the Year of the Monkey, then every Monkey Year is considered extremely dangerous to you. So, to protect yourself you should wear bright red underwear all year round or a thin red bracelet on your wrist.

Moving on to yellow, the national colour, which was sacred to the Emperor, and hence only reserved for him and his sons. In Chinese mythical stories, 黄帝 (*Huang di*), the Yellow Emperor is the great father of all indigenous ethnic groups in China. Yellow indicates neutrality and good luck. In Buddhism, priests are buried in yellow as to depict freedom from worldly cares. Monks' garments are yellow and the most important parts of temples would also be painted in yellow. As opposed to the Western belief, yellow is associated with heroism. According to the Five Elements philosophy, each colour links with a different direction: green with east, red with south, white with west, black with north and yellow with the centre. That's why the king, as a ruler of the nation, would always sit in the middle. I once received a charm against the evil spirits written on a yellow paper with a black ink. The person who gave it to me explained that I'm supposed to paste it on my doorframe. The paper contained four characters which were to protect the house and keep away all malignant forces. I was glad to receive such a thoughtful gift, especially that the giver had made it himself.

The next colours in line are blue and green. Traditionally both colours would be grouped together under the name of 青 (*qing*), mentioned above. This one is connected to nature and means renewal, spring, vigour and vitality. Green itself represents health and harmony. Funnily enough, if a man receives a green hat, it makes him a cuckold. Mind you, the same goes for calling someone a turtle! The first colour that successfully decorated porcelain was no other but jade-green, which is supposed to depict the blue sky after rain. Admittedly, green was also the colour of the painted board, shamefully carried in front of a criminal going to be executed in the bygone era.

As for white, a token of moral purity, it symbolizes fulfilment and brightness. This colour embodies cultural differences between China and the West. White is the colour of funerals. One can see lots of white flowers and wreaths decorating funeral homes, and white flowers are given to the family of the dead. Remember not to give a white flower to your sick Chinese friend! Many Chinese ladies wouldn't wear anything white in their hair either. Only wearing white is considered unlucky and might bring about someone's death. The ancient expression 红事白事 (hong shi bai shi) refers to red events and white events, so first weddings and then funerals. On a Chinese stage of Peking Opera, a white face denounces a treacherous hypocrite. If you find someone ungrateful you'll most likely call them 白眼儿狼 (bai yanr lang), which translates as a white-eyed wolf.

Finally, the black colour. While it means solemnity, and is commonly worn at official events, it also stands for winter and the unknown. It connotes with darkness and secrets, that is probably why it is seen in phrases like 黑钱 (hei qian), illegal money or 黑工 (hei gong) for illegal work. It is one of the Yin and Yang unity. In the past, some kinsfolk would wear black clothes to one's funeral but only if they were not immediate family.

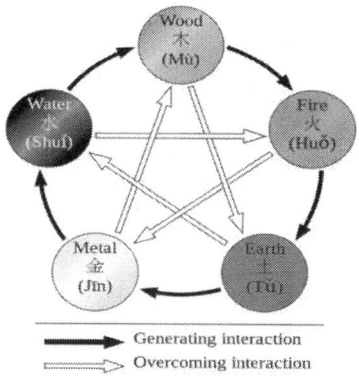

Image by Yunqing Xiang.

Before the Five Elements Theory was established, Taoists strongly believed there were only two colours, opposing one another: black and white, *yin* and *yang*. The Western beliefs of what each colour means are certainly challenged in China. Red no longer represents love and passion, yellow - cowardice, green - luck and jealously, blue - sadness, white - angels and peace and black - power and death. Don't be afraid to experiment with colours. Just make sure you won't offend any of your Chinese friends.

There's luck in odd numbers.

I will always remember my first trip to a local store in the middle of a scorching summer in Hangzhou. I only needed a couple of bottles of chilled water, but when it came to payment, I could not, for the love of mine, understand what the seller was showing me with his fingers. Apparently, I was supposed to pay RMB 6, but thought he was 'rocking out' with his twisted fist. That was the day when I learnt how to gesture numbers the Chinese way.

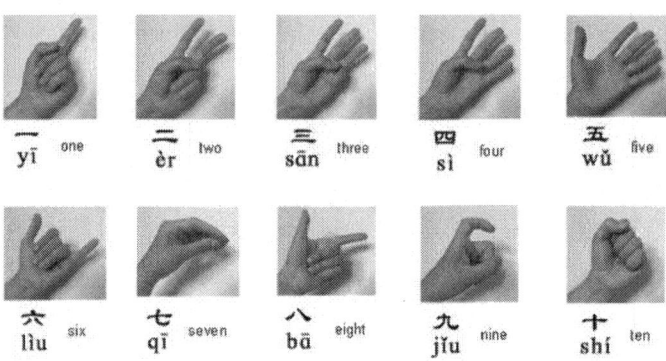

Numbers shown by hand. Image by Yunqing Xiang.

To start with, a lot of places still use the abacus to perform calculations. It is a common belief among the shopkeepers that it's unlucky to use this instrument in the early morning. After a day's work, it is violently shaken with the hope of casting out demons. No customer can touch the abacus or it will be perceived as the beginning of a jinxed day.

Furthermore, numbers in China have unique meanings and are often associated with superstitious beliefs. Firstly, the infamous number four (四 = si) comes to mind. This number is widely avoided as its pronunciation is close to the one of 'death' (死 = si). While Western hotels steer clear from using 13 as a floor or room number, one will seldom see four used in these instances in China. When a car is purchased, a number plate is scrutinized for the presence of four. It is also seen as ominous to have this digit in one's phone number. By the same token, variations with 4, like 14 or 44, are to be inauspicious and hence shunned. On a lighter note, this integer has often been depicted in literature or traditional proverbs. To illustrate, the expression 四世同

堂 (*si shi tong tang*), which signifies an ideal family of four generations under the same roof, is a title of one of the best-known novels in China.

Moreover, six (六 = *liu*) is a favourable number in the Middle Kingdom. It stands for happiness and is pronounced like fluid (流 = *liu*). Smooth running of water links with good business dealings. As opposed to the Western concept of 666 connoting with the devil, living in a house with this number would be deemed as triple happiness and luck. There are lots of Chinese idioms which use this number, such as 六亲不认 (*liu qin bu ren*), which indicates a person who is not willing to use their status to grant favours to relatives. Also, 六路 (*liu lu*), representing six directions: left, right, up, down, front and behind, is a part of a commonly used idiomatic phrase 眼观六路, 耳听八方 (*yan guan liu lu, er ting ba fang*), which carries the meaning of an agile person who makes well-rounded observations. Many couples choose to be married on the sixth of June, as double six is believed to be fortunate.

In addition, a phone number with 8 (八 = *ba*) in it can cost an arm and a leg. This digit is a homophone for 发 (*fa*) meaning 'good fortune' or 'making good money'. Since most businesses hope to thrive in the new year of the lunar calendar, they would resume work on the eighth day after the holiday, with one thought in mind, making money: 发财 (*fa cai*) in Chinese. By and large, China recognizes eight grand cuisines (八大菜系 = *ba da cai xi*): Shandong, Sichuan, Cantonese, Fujian, Jiangsu, Zhejiang, Hunan and Anhui. A very sustaining congee is usually eaten on the 8th day of the 12th lunar month, celebrating 腊八节 (*la ba jie*), a festival when Buddhist temples make this porridge as an offering to the gods. Even the eminent Taoist symbol of *yin yang* (阴阳) ☯ consists of eight trigrams, reflecting the principles of its philosophy. Don't call anyone a 八卦 (*ba gua*) because that would mean they are a gossip.

Almost every number has a story in Chinese culture. Some groups of numbers need a second look, as they can be offensive in certain situations. 38 (三八 = *san ba*) is a perfect example of that. If you use it with a relation to a woman and address her as *san ba,* you basically call her a bimbo. Another one to avoid is 250, 二百五 (*er bai wu*), especially used on a man. It practically means a moron, idiot, twat. Once my foreign friends decided to test if this insult really works and when leaving a taxi said it to the driver. I have never seen anyone running away so fast! The driver was fuming and chased them for quite a few blocks. I was in stitches.

In my opinion, the best and easiest way to learn numbers in Chinese is to pronounce them closely to another word you know. For instance, 1 sounds like *want* and 9 sounds like *alcohol*. Never knew that numbers could be so much fun.

Are you patting a horse's butt[1]? - On animal symbolism.

One must love oodles of Chinese fables involving animals. Through the adventures of animal characters, you are taken into a magical world full of great moral lessons. I guess the most commonly known idiom is 卧虎藏龙 (*wo hu cang long*), which translates as Crouching Tiger, Hidden Dragon. It refers to undiscovered talents.

Dragon, 龙 (*long*), stands for authority and symbolizes the emperor. That is why parents who hope to raise a successful child are often called 望子成龙 (*wang zi cheng long, literally "long to see one's son become a dragon"*). Along with phoenix, 凤凰 (*feng huang*), they account for two most often depicted animals in Chinese literature and art. Dragon is seen as strength and goodness while phoenix is considered the Emperor of all birds, the most honourable one. Both are most likely to be seen at weddings, the dragon embodying the groom and phoenix the bride. Some families still embed a set of silk beddings with both animals on as a gift for the newlyweds. Most wedding halls are named after the two creatures. Following one Chinese fable, a dragon can reduce itself to a size of a silkworm so that it can fill the space of Heaven and Earth. The Chinese strongly believe in the existence of this mysterious creature and see themselves as descendants of it. It is present in their ancient history, Buddhist legends and Taoist tales. It is a part of Chinese identity. Similarly, phoenix supposedly appears only in times of prosperity and peace. It is the second among the four supernatural creatures, the dragon being number one, followed by the unicorn and the tortoise, respectively. It symbolizes the sun and the warmth

---

[1] *Pai ma pi*, literally "to pat a horse's butt"- the art of flattering oneself.

associated with summer. It is the most decorative emblem for sophisticated costumes, affordable mainly to the affluent.

Next comes the tiger, 虎 (*hu*), famous for its power, courage and fierceness. It is linked with the military. In times of Qing dynasty, only highly ranked officers could wear robes with tiger's image, when out of their uniforms. If you see a painting of a tiger in one's corridor, you can be sure you entered a house of a military official. An idiom, 骑虎难下 (*qi hu nan xia*), means it is difficult to get off when riding a tiger. It is mostly used when a person is in a tricky situation and cannot give up but must continue till the end. Also, a stocky man would be typically called 虎背熊腰 (*hu bei xiong yao*), which literally means he's got a back like a tiger and a waist like a bear. One legend states that a spirit of a victim eaten by a tiger makes it guzzle others. And, as a widespread belief goes, those who suffered a pugnacious death stand a chance of returning to this world.

A horse, 马 (*ma*), one of the Seven Treasures of Buddhism, cannot be omitted. It stands for speed and perseverance. It gives canvas to a lot of phrases and idiomatic expressions in Chinese language, like 马马虎虎 = *ma ma hu hu*, literally "casual, so-so". For the longest time, it has served as the main form of transport. My personal favourite is the equivalent of the Western *when pigs fly*: 猴年马月 (*hou nian ma yue*), *monkey year horse month*, word by word. Having been in China for a few years, one tends to get tired of hearing 马上 (*ma shang, literally "on horseback or right away"*), meaning *promptly*, especially when its meaning extends to half an hour or longer while waiting for things. There is this ancient story describing an old man who lost a horse and was pitied by his village only to learn later that the same horse brought back a more valuable one. Villagers congratulated him, but the man only pondered over the events. Later in the story, his son rode the horse and broke his leg. The pity party repeated itself until his son was the only young man not enlisted for war due to his injury. Commiseration again changed into praises. The story went on and on and every time the wise man only ruminated on the status quo. From there, a Chinese *blessing in disguise* formulated: 塞翁失马 (*sai weng shi ma, literally "the old frontiersman losing his horse"*).

Thinking of animal symbolism in China, it is important not to call a man a turtle/tortoise, 龟 (*gui*), or he'll be convinced he's two-timed by his wife. Turtles can be found everywhere on the street available for purchase for both petting and eating. The record turtle's age limit is reported to be 1,000 years; hence these animals are symbols of longevity for Chinese people.

In addition, bats, 蝙蝠 (*bian fu*), can be spotted in jewellery designs, especially in jade pendants. Because the name sounds like luck, 福 (*fu*), commonly worn gold charms display the mammal, too. In China, nobody detests bats, which is quite common in Western cultures. They denote happiness and longevity. So do cranes, 鹤 (*he*). These are often seen in brush paintings and statues made of bronze in traditional gardens. Quite commonly placed next to a pine tree which also symbolizes strength and robustness. A figure of a crane is sometimes seen on the centre of a coffin at a funeral. It is believed to be delivering the soul of the dead to Heaven. Talking about birds, Mandarin duck, 鸳鸯 (*yuan yang*), can't be forgotten. It is highly associated with both weddings and anniversaries, hence seen as a decorative element on dishes. Mandarin duck's special green-blue head and brown-black feathers make it a great detail for ornamentations. Not only their plumage but also the belief that they die once separated from their partner, make them a perfect emblem of conjugal fidelity. It is understandable that a newlywed couple would use them to depict their own love for each other. I remember getting a pair of those, porcelain ones, as a wedding gift from one of my Chinese students. I was told they make a perfect wedding gift in China. They are to represent a couple's lifelong commitment to each other.

Furthermore, everyone in China knows the importance of the fish, which Chinese name 鱼 (*yu*) makes a homonym for 余 (*yu*) which means *extra*. It makes many people believe that keeping fish at home will miraculously supply some extra money. Almost every restaurant keeps multicoloured shoals of fish in tanks by the entrance, from which customers are welcome to choose their desired victim for dinner. There is even a special type of goldfish (usually displayed in shops' windows for prosperity) called *get rich fish*. Their orangish looks abundance (connotation with gold), making a perfect blessing for Spring Festival: 年年有余 (*nian nian you yu, literally "may you have abundance year after year"*), teeming with extra luck. During a Chinese New Year's feast, fish is indispensable. In the past, families who could not afford to buy fish, would normally place a wooden one on the table instead. Today, fish and rice make the staple food of almost every Chinese family. Once I saw a few lucky fish in a gigantic aquarium in one of the restaurants in Hangzhou with a tattoo on their bodies. The characters were 发财 (*fa cai*), which spell out as *get rich*. The best part was that the tattoos were fluorescent so the fish glowed in the dark. According to Buddhist beliefs, fish designates freedom from all limitations. Just like a fish moves swiftly and freely in water in all directions, the same way a Buddhist should face life obstacles. Also, the carp is admired as a fighter against the current, so it embodies perseverance in Chinese culture.

I have always loved to look at toads, 蟾蜍 (*chan chu*). And so, when I came to China I was elated how easy they are to be seen. It is customarily believed that a spawn of the frog (the Chinese do not differentiate between the two) fell from Heaven with the dew so they started calling a frog a *heavenly chicken*. Following the legend, with its warty appearance, a toad is mostly seen during the eclipse, when it swallows the whole moon. Hence, it symbolizes the unreachable. Many places in contemporary China keep statues of toads perched on counters. It is usually sitting on a heap of coins, exemplifying great wealth. There is a story of Liu Hai, a Minister of State in the 10th century A.D., who was an expert on Taoist magic. He managed to capture a three-legged toad by luring it to tons of gold coins. Presumably, the animal was to convey him to any place he wished to go. The toad's draw to money led to its loss of freedom and ultimately served as a warning for men against greed.

Finally, a few more idioms related to animals. If you're considered *as strong as an ox*, you can be called 气壮如牛 (*qi zhuang ru niu*, literally "fierce as a bull"), including cattle which stands for strength and persistence. Another idiom, where cattle plays a role, is the one describing someone who is *blowing their own trumpet*. In such case, we say 吹牛皮 (*chui niu pi, literally "to boast, talk big"*). There are a few animals that typify negative characteristics, such as a pig, 猪 (*zhu*), which indicates stupidity, and 耍猴 (*shua hou*), a monkey trained to entertain others. I learnt the meaning of the latter the hard way when one of the schools I worked for wanted me to become it☹.

Finally, a man's best friend: dog, 狗 (*gou*). This one is a bit tricky. Have I seen dog's meat in restaurants? Yes. Have I tried it? No. Am I tempted to try it? Not at all! Here I'll only mention that using 'dog' in any Chinese phrase brings about a very negative meaning, such as when reading a bad piece of writing one can say it's 狗屁不通 (*gou pi bu tong*, literally "unreadable rubbish"), mere trash.

"An apple a day keeps the doctor away" – The role of fruit in the Chinese culture.

Rambutan fruit, photo taken in Dali, Yunnan Province by Karolina Achirri.

As one of the Chinese proverbs goes: *The best time to plant a tree is 20 years ago. The second-best time is now.* Fruit play a key role in Chinese culture. They are not just random food, they bring meaning to the table, so to speak. The ones that represent best wishes cannot be missing from Chinese New Year's family dinner table.

APPLE 苹果 (*ping guo*)

An apple is a symbol of peace and safety in China because its name is homonymic to 平安 (*ping an*), which means safety. People like to eat apples especially in winter. Every Christmas time I receive tons of them with a stamped name of peace, oftentimes in an electronic version (through We Chat). It is kind of an equivalent of *Peace be with you*. It's become an essential Christmas tradition in China. Families prepare big plates of apples for Spring Festival time as their presence frees the household of troubles and conflicts. Traditionally, an apple was an emblem of feminine beauty.

CHERRY 樱桃 (*ying tao*)

More than the fruit itself, China appreciates cherry blossoms. They signify power, sexuality and delicate feminine beauty. Many poets wrote about cherries due to their rich ruby colour evoking imagination and leading to artistry. Every April till early May thousands of curious tourists take photos of cherry blossoms in Chinese parks.

GRAPE 葡萄 (*pu tao*)

I love grapes in all shapes and colours. But I was shocked to learn that in China I must peel them before eating. The first time I saw one of my colleagues peeling each grape, I laughed. She didn't know what I found so funny. Yet, I must also say that a Chinese brand wine tastes just awful. I'm no epicure but it's like drinking a mixture of bleach and fermented fruit juice. Normally, grapes are used in art as a border pattern or a background symbol.

MULBERRY 桑树 (*sang shu*)

Now, this wine I can drink hours on end. It's delicate and palatable. Berries are also quite tasty. The bark of mulberry serves as a great material for paper, its wood is excellent for carving. In a traditional Chinese culture, a person mourning their mother would carry a branch of mulberry tree, while bamboo for a father. Its symbolism is depicted in a legend where the sun is shown as a three-legged Sun Bird. The bird perches on a mesmeric mulberry tree, which is a link between earth and the Eastern heaven. Also, another fable portrays a first bow, which was made by Emperor Huang Di to defeat a tiger who had chased him into nothing else but a mulberry tree. The tree symbolizes the archer.

ORANGE 橙子 (*cheng zi*)

It is one of the auspicious New Year symbols in China. It represents immortality and good fortune. Its peel is used as a sedative. After the peel is collected and dried by boys or women, it is being sold to the pharmacists. People in the past used to make sacrifices to Heaven at the beginning of every New Year using this fruit. When you give someone oranges you wish them abundance of prosperity and happiness. Its bright colour symbolizes gold, hence its relation to wealth. You might also see potted oranges and tangerines in the halls of hotels or offices, just to make sure the places are teeming with non-stop business.

PEACH 桃子 (*tao zi*)

Also known as the Fairy Fruits, peaches supposedly originated in China. Locals believe peaches are one of the healthiest fruit as they will expand one's lifespan significantly, if eaten on a regular basis. They symbolize longevity. So, if you wish an older person long and healthy existence, then give them a present of peaches. On the other hand, however, apricots and plums are considered very harmful, according to a folk tale which says: "Peaches nourish, plums harm, and apricots bury"! Not many people actually know that peaches heal coughs and rheumatism. I also met some Chinese doctors prescribing them as a sedative. Apart from the long life, peaches are also seen as an emblem of marriage and immortality. They often evoke pictures of springtime. Watch out for their branches when in fever though, as a more superstitious person might strike you with them to cast out the evil spirit. I absolutely love the season of peach-blossom in China (March). Parks smell so luscious and photos get an amazing background, too.

PEAR 梨子 (*li zi*)

The name sounds like *separation*, so pears are not so appreciated, especially at weddings. I have seen so many strange versions of pears, from The White Pear through The Fragrant Pear to The Snowy Pear. Because the pear tree bears fruit when 300 years old, it is a solid sign of longevity.

PERSIMMON 柿子 (*shi zi*)

I admit that I had not had the pleasure of encountering this fruit before I came to China. They call it a *date plum* or *China fig*. After it gets exposed to frost, it becomes lush and juicy as well as full of nutrients. Due to its festive colour (from yellow-orange to dark-red orange), it simply represents joy. To me, it looks like a weirdly coloured tomato.

POMEGRANATE 石榴 (*shi liu*)

Its many seeds naturally symbolize fertility in China. Before one-child policy was implemented, it had been a common belief that having many offsprings is a blessing. But not just any offsprings. Preferably those behaving in a virtuous and filial manner only. Pomegranates are often used in Buddhist temples as offerings as well as gifts for the newlyweds.

Apart from common fruit, China is abundant in the weird ones too. Durian takes the pedestal. Looks innocent on the outside, but one needs to put up a real fight to overcome its pungent smell before tasting. When I travelled in Yunnan Province one year, I came across a rambutan. The vendor taught me to peel off its hairy skin and after that it was all sweetness and freshness in my mouth. Also, my school has a habit of giving us a bag of fruit every Monday. There's usually langsat in there, whose fruits are often called duku. My Chinese colleagues showed me the ritual to twist both my thumb and index finger to crack it open. Still, once I found jackfruit crisps in a supermarket, they have become my ultimate favourite. Never actually tasted the real fruit. I read that it is super heavy, though, as it can weigh up to 80 pounds (approximately 26kg for those who go by European metric system, like myself). The crisps look like banana or plaintiff fritters and taste like heaven. One of my best-loved fruit is dragon fruit. They do remind me of dragon flames on the outside, whereas resemble white kiwi on the inside. Taste mild, a bit bland really. But anytime my stomach cannot handle any more of Chinese spices, I reach for a dragon fruit, which is an emancipator of digestive problems. Longans are also quite affordable at any local market. They are sometimes called "cat's eyes" because their seeds are round, shiny and black. I've seen them mostly in Chinese desserts. Have you ever heard of pomelo? I substitute lemon with it for my daily tea intake. Its yellowish-green skin makes it look scrumptious, but its weight can go as high as 5 pounds (over 2 kg). As I began to read some Chinese characters, I have also discovered kumquat. It resembles an orange to a certain extent but it is smaller and oval. Most popular are jellies and marmalades made of kumquat. I will finish off with the fruit I called a hedgehog before I learnt its actual name, which is waxberry (*yang mei*). Not only is it sold on the street, fresh, but makes a predominant ingredient for *baijiu* (Chinese liquor).

In China, you're 1-year old when you are born☺.

Once in my first job, one of the training schools in Hangzhou, we forgot a colleague's birthday. Things were hectic that week as it was getting closer to Christmas, and hence our school's 'Christmas around the world' party. When we realized her birthday had passed, we asked her out to dinner and KTV the following week. As we tried toasting to her, she explained that the Chinese do not celebrate their birthdays after the fact. They can only have a party before or on the actual day. It was strange to us, clueless foreigners, to hear that belatedly organized party brings bad luck.

In Chinese culture, a new born baby is already one-year old. That's why every time I look at my hospital ID card something isn't right. I'm a year older and registered under my Chinese name (李娜娜 = *li na na*). There are also certain birthdays that a woman wouldn't memorialize. The 30th birthday is one of them. To steer clear from danger and uncertainty (which is what being 30 signifies), Chinese women choose to stay 29 for one additional year. My favourite custom comes on the 33th birthday, though. A woman must buy a piece of meat, place it behind the kitchen door and chop it 33 times to cast away bad spirits. When the same woman turns 66, her daughter is expected to chop the meat, this time 66 times. If a woman does not have a female offspring, her closest female relative takes over. As for men, they do not tend to celebrate their 40th birthday, because this age is perceived as unforeseeable.

While most Western traditions require a cake for birthday, China can't go without noodles. Due to noodles being so long, they symbolize long life. So, a birthday boy or girl must eat a bowl of uncut noodles on their actual birthday. It is also very important not to cut them with your chopsticks. Only when you have run out of space in your mouth, can you bite the noodles off. Some families also practise a custom of slurping noodles on behalf of another celebrant (family member), especially if they are far away.

Usually every ten years birthdays are considered significant in China. As turning 18 marks entering adulthood, most people would only have a festive meal with their family on that day.

The funniest thing is that some Chinese people I know celebrate their birthdays according to lunar calendar (which changes the date every year), some follow the Gregorian one while others sneakily do both. I always have to ask my Chinese sister, Sarah, *so when is your birthday this year?* It cracks us both up.

In my country, when a child turns 1, the parents would place a few objects in front of him/her and then wait and see which object their baby picks up. If the baby picks up money, there's fortune waiting for them in the future; if a book, they might become a teacher; if a vodka shot-glass, they might even become alcoholics☺. I was surprised to learn that China has the same custom. It is called 抓周 (*zhua zhou*).

To sum up, as a Chinese proverb goes: *Men grow old, pearls grow yellow. There is no cure for it.*

Gift-giving in China.

As much as I enjoy giving gifts, I think since I came to China I must have received more presents than have given out. Being a foreign teacher in China makes Chinese students admire you and hence often bestow varieties of objects on you. One thing an expat should bear in mind is that we are not supposed to open gifts in front of the giver. It should be done in private later. If you open your gift too eagerly, you will be perceived as a greedy person. Another thing is the price tag. Leave it on for people to know how much you paid for it, assuming it cost you an arm and a leg. This is something I had troubles adjusting to as in my culture letting the person know how much money I spent on their present makes me look vain and smug.

I've decided to split this section into three categories. The first one will introduce gifts that are most appreciated and most common in China. Then, I'll move on to talk about the no-nos. And finally, I'll steal some of my partners' in crime (i.e. other foreigners') ideas of what to bring back home from China.

Let's begin.

If you're visiting someone's home, it's good to bring along a basket of fruit. This idea also works for someone you're visiting in the hospital. If there's a hostess, she'll appreciate some flowers or anything that can be useful in the household. I remember my mum complaining year after year, when people would always buy pots and frying pans for her Name Day. She wanted something for herself, so that she could appreciate the gift's beauty, not its usefulness.

Yet, since we are in China, tea is always a safe bet. If there's a toddler in the house, you should consider buying a small toy for him or her as well.

When it comes to weddings in China, that's a long story. To put it in a nutshell, red envelopes (money placed in actual red envelopes) beat anything else. Depending on how close your relationship with the couple is, the expected amount of money increases. Oftentimes the newlyweds would use all their collections to cover some wedding expenses or to sponsor their honeymoon.

If you work in a company, you have probably noticed that your boss might have brought some local specialties back from his/her business trips. It is also worth mentioning that whatever you prepare as a gift, its number should never be odd; that's bad luck. Even numbers symbolize harmony and wholeness.

Generally speaking, staple food from local places (such as a hairy crab from Shanghai in the fall), hard alcohol of an expensive brand (especially *baijiu* which compared by its volume <40%> can match only vodka) and cigarettes that cost through the roof are absolute favourites. When Mid-Autumn festival approaches (normally somewhere between mid and late September), everyone can be seen walking home with boxes of moon cakes. I am not a fan, just because the first time I ate them nobody warned me they were filled with minced meat. That killed my zeal to try those "cakes" ever again. For those who don't know what moon cakes are, a word of explanation. They are round pastries with varieties of fillings. The sweet ones would have lotus seed paste inside, but as I said there are also those with all sorts of weird meat mixtures; impossible to distinguish just by looking at them. I think the priciest set of moon cakes I have ever seen had shark fin and birds' nest filling in them. It cost over $15000. Some boxes are also made of gold. What's more, lots of people I know like to give nicely wrapped imported liquors to others. Funnily enough, barely anyone would drink them. Instead, they would put them in the most visible place in their home for display, to boast about their material value. When it comes to cigarettes, most men love them (as most of men in China smoke). I heard a saying from northern China: "You are not a man if you don't smoke". If you want to buy some for your Chinese friends, make sure you understand the hierarchy in China. First, the brand matters a lot. If the occasion is extremely important, go ahead and splash out, but when it's just a common gift exchange situation do not go too crazy. The most popular brand (as I was told by those who whiff) is called *Zhonghua*, or *China*. It ranges from $50 to $300 per carton. You'd need that one if you're asking your friend for a big favour. It is said that "people who buy *Zhonghua* don't smoke it, those who smoke it don't buy it". If you decide to give those cancer sticks, remember to do it in twos (two cartons of them). I was often puzzled at Chinese weddings. I have been to a few and every time the couple prepares cigarettes for their guests. They always look expensive to me and, as I don't smoke, I do not take them. I was told the remaining packets would be deducted from the wedding cost.

As far as gifts not to give go, clocks hit the charts. The Chinese phrase *song zhong* (*give someone a clock*) sounds exactly like *attending someone's funeral*. Once Angela Markel, German Chancellor, gave a clock to Hu Jintao during a state visit. It was an international faux pas. The next ones not to bother with would be fans and umbrellas. Even opening umbrellas indoors traditionally invites bad spirits and misfortune to the room. When we look at the words here, umbrella-*san* and fan-*shan*, they are close enough to *scatter* or *split up* in Chinese. No wonder nobody wants to receive such message. Also, believe it or not, chopsticks are not too hype. Especially when you are considering giving them to a pregnant woman. The name *kuai zi* sounds in Chinese like *soon son*. Chopsticks are just not posh enough to be given to others. Knives and scissors might slice or cut your friendship. A green hat means you are being cuckolded. Finally, shoes signify you want someone to *zou kai* (*get lost*).

And here we are at the GIFTS FOR PEOPLE BACK HOME section. Of course, if you're not a superstitious person, go ahead and buy whatever catches your eye. Since everything these days seems to carry a tag saying: MADE IN CHINA, you shouldn't have a problem finding a 'typical' Chinese gift for your folks. My sister bought it all. From chopsticks, silk garments, traditional Chinese shoes, to magnets and can openers with the photo of the Great Wall. Seems now like she might have done it all backwards, huh? I'd say an unusual Chinese musical instrument (such as *pipa* or *hulusi*) is always a great fit. I saw many foreigners buy the *Little Red Book* and fortune frogs. Chinese batik might be worth a look, if you're planning to use the gift on your friends. Since I'm from Poland, *baijiu* is a must for all the uncles and male friends. Traditional clothes (such as *qipao* dress) can be troublesome as they are usually tailor-made, hence require specific measurements. My winner, however, is.... Chinglish T-shirts. You cannot get them anywhere else except for China. They'd make a great gift to someone who appreciates a good joke.

Chinese beauty standards.

*"The beauty of a woman must be seen from in her eyes,
because that is the doorway to her heart, the place where love resides"*
(Audrey Hepburn)

China disagrees with Audrey Hepburn. In China, everything is about the way you look. If you want to make it, you've got to fake it. Most of it stems from vanity, not only on the female side, I'm afraid.

In China having the right looks is perceived as an investment. It is commonly believed that only the ones fitting 'the right beauty standard' have a shot at landing a decent job. Nobody says it openly, but candidates are judged on their height, face shape, complexion shade and even the size of their hands. In one of the schools I've worked for, a girl (a potential assistant to the director) was turned down because she was considered 'ugly'. The boss couldn't show her off to his business partners so she did not get the position despite her evident qualifications. The person who did get the job couldn't even spell her English name right.

Chinese women take beauty very seriously. They see it as a project, which (if successful) can help them find their Mr. Right, get that dream job, be discovered. The way you look is your personal asset, which you can easily convert into financial capital. Hence, the whole quest for beauty.

Women are willing to go to great lengths to achieve their goals. The most popular alterations are skin whitening, double-eyelid surgery, a nose job and breast enlargement. They are willing to spend thousands on a renowned surgeon in a fancy clinic. Sadly, many charlatans take advantage of their insecurities and lack of self-confidence and oftentimes leave them scarred for life. In Chinese culture, one must have small mouth, teeth and chin to follow the beauty trend. What can you do, if you inherited protruded ears and hooked teeth? Go under the scalpel.

When it comes to skin whitening process, I experienced it first hand when during my visit to the drug store I couldn't find any face cosmetics that would not try to make me look like a vampire. Despite the clerk's assurances that this cream would make me look beautiful and cool, I left the shop empty-handed and in despair. How on Earth was I going to buy face creams now? *Taobao* and my Chinese colleague came to my rescue. Dark skin signifies manual labour, so it places one in a low social stratum. The minute first rays of sunshine start to break through the clouds, umbrellas are being open to shield those who carry them. While in the Western countries women pay top dollar to get tanned (either naturally on the beach or artificially in a salon), even women on their e-bikes and bikes protect themselves from the sun by holding an umbrella in their hand (and when in the driver's seat, in their other hand they often hold a mobile phone!). Being pale means you're posh, sophisticated, not worn out by outdoor work. It means you have value.

Next comes the body shape. Ever since I came to China, I kept hearing "you are too fat" in shops and markets. "Nothing will fit you here". I was considering feeling insulted, but then I realized having a normal body form is indeed fat. I let this one slide. Chinese women are petite and the way they dress doesn't help with figuring out their real age. Some over-the-hill ladies look like 18s from behind, in their miniskirts and long leather boots. Lots of Chinese women go for a painful leg lengthening procedure as well as a boob job. They think by doing so they "westernize" themselves, which in fact only deepens a vicious circle of insanity. It is estimated that the number of plastic surgeries in China rockets by one million every year. It might be quite difficult to differentiate "real" from "fake" soon.

In 2004 someone had an epiphany and created a special beauty pageant called 人造美女 (*ren zao mei nv*), which briefly translates as "the man-made women". A bold 18-year-old, who got disqualified from the real pageant due to her beautifying, saw red and started that show. What's alarming is the fact that the majority of clientele of plastic beauty salons are teenage girls. Three of my former students went to Korea to get their eyes done. When asked why, they all said it was cheaper and better quality, and made them look less Asian. I asked one why she did it and she surprisingly replied that she herself did not want to, but her mum kept telling her that she was ugly and if she didn't do it she would never find a husband. Sad case but not a singular one, I'm afraid.

Talking about body shape, being chubby in China is no walk in the park either. Media have called it "obesity epidemic". I don't think they've seen a really obese person, though. Whoever is bigger than size 8 is considered obese, which seems crazy to any Westerner. But China hasn't always been obsessed with thinness. In ancient times, women were depicted as plum. Since poverty was widespread whoever looked bigger was considered wealthy, because they must have had enough money to buy a lot of food. These days bigger sizes are usually blamed on driving, taking a bus or taxi instead of walking or riding a bike. China's current prosperity allows people to be picky about their food. More people can afford meat, dairy and oils.

What's more, I have met Chinese women who took acupuncture treatments to lose weight after their pregnancies. I have also worked with a colleague whose (I am not joking) looks reminded me of a concentration camp survivor. I was always asking why she is so thin and was always told: "That's beautiful". Well, to my mind, bones sticking out everywhere and tiny clothes hanging on a woman like a rag - that's not beautiful or sexy, that's common and plain. I come from a culture where a woman must have curves and certain measurements to be considered sexy. Otherwise what's there for a man to love? – quoting my grandmother.

Ironically, with China's fear of fatness, I kept coming across ladies (be it my colleagues or students) who are constantly on a diet. They don't even eat rice during lunch because it will make them fat. Seriously, girls! Meanwhile, the same girls present the weakest stamina I have ever seen. Menstruation period is like a terminal disease which leaves many of them completely unfit to function.

Over three million people a year undergo plastic surgery in China. Alarmingly, in the past 10 years only about 50% of these procedures were successful. The remaining half left patients permanently damaged. The best example of a knife-job-gone-wrong is a 15-year-old Li Enxi. It's hard to say whether her popularity on *Weibo* brought her fame or shame, but she did go for a full-body work-up. Now, she's spending most of her time uploading selfies and trying to rebut her followers' comments. She claims in this day and age if you don't follow the times, the times will overtake you and you will be lost at the starting line. Also, a 50-year-old woman in Korea died on the table last year. Her heart simply stopped and her brain suffered death. The clinic that killed her is now closed. But these are just a few drops in the ocean.

If you step into any *Sephora* in China, you'll immediately notice crowds of girls surrounding make-up shelves and stylists like vultures. An average woman spends 30% of her income on cosmetics. Naturally, foreign brands are favoured, especially Korean and Japanese ones. Herbal beauty products also share several fans as they are linked with

TCM (Traditional Chinese Medicine) and hence considered healthier.

If you want to be perceived as beautiful in China, you've got to go with the flow, wherever it takes you. For some girls, that's the only ace they might have up their sleeve and they know it. For others, the game isn't over until it's over, which means they would even spend their last penny if it brings them closer to a more Western nose or less Asian eyes. Beauty is a concept that cannot be boxed in. Every culture has its own conceptions and taboos. Everyone is perfect in their own way. No matter what the size of your thighs or the length of your nose are, feel good in your own skin. That's the only way you can maintain your appeal.

On Confucius.

"Life is really simple, but we insist on making it complicated."

(Confucius)

I read most of Confucius' writings the minute I got my hands on their English versions. I wanted to get to know China's most prominent philosopher and the secret behind the figure who has influenced and is still influencing generations of the Chinese.

A lot can be said about Confucius, as he was a Jack-of-all-trades of his times. An educator, philosopher and politician were just a few of his societal functions. To put his ideas in a nutshell, I'd say he focused on moral values in both personal and governmental dealings. He valued justice and sincerity. His aphorisms are endless. He emphasized tradition, family bonds, worship of ancestors and respect for elders. He also implemented a Bible based idea of not doing to others what one wouldn't like to have done to themselves (己所不欲，勿施于人 = *ji suo bu yu, wu shi yu ren*). I won't even try to write about his work, as the day isn't long enough. I will, however, look at how much of his teaching survived and is visible in the contemporary Chinese society.

Confucius' schooling laid foundation for the moral code back in Han Dynasty (4th century BC) and still impacts modern culture in China by keeping people in line and maintaining order. It was no one else but Kong Zi (孔子 = his Chinese name) who brought about filial piety concept. Anyone who has lived in China and observed his or her Chinese friends must have noticed their devotion to family, respect for parents and their opinions. Many families still have three generations living under one roof. What's more, the broadly spread preference for a male child also stems from the Confucian credo. This one has certainly given rise to some negative attitudes. With most of the society hoping to give birth to a male heir, the abortion rate rises rapidly and does not even pose a moral dilemma. Filial piety also contributes to a largely believed opinion that it is a son's duty to take care of his parents in their old age. So, whoever has a daughter is considered a loser in a societal game of power, as she will tend to her husband's parents in the future. Of course, Confucius is not to be blamed for the situation, he couldn't have known his ideas would spill over decades.

A nationwide consumerism is one phenomenon that seems to be pushing an old wise man's concepts away, though. Chinese tourists (which equals shoppers) are infamous for fighting over luxurious brands and buying them like maniacs. I even heard of a woman who called her husband from one very respected handbag shop in Italy reporting on a beautiful bag she found and considered a bargain. The minute the man heard the price, he ordered her not to buy anything and leave immediately. According to him the price was far too low (even though it exceeded $1000). The Cultural revolution (文化大革命 = wen hua da ge ming) between 1966 and 1976, made Confucianism and traditional moral values its main targets to destroy and turn upside down. Since then people who don't appreciate politeness or social principles have been on the rise.

According to Confucius' ideology, there are Five Constants (五常 = wu chang) which are to be strictly followed by all citizens. These are xin (信) which means integrity, zhi (智) which stands for knowledge, li (礼) for etiquette, yi (义) representing justice, and ren (仁) meaning humaneness. The Party has been trying to revive these values in recent years, after Mao had tried to forbid them. I see some of Confucius' 5 Constants in my middle-aged Chinese friends, but I certainly fail to notice them in my students (who are shaping the future of China).

Harmony is one of the strongest points of Chinese culture. It is not only understood as harmony and peace in society but also inside families and the entire nation. Confucius claimed everyone should know their place in each hierarchy and act accordingly. It also meant a complete lack of open criticism as this led to losing face. Following this notion, Chinese media often filter negative news, seeing it as shame for the whole country. Accidents are held off and foreign news are depicted as something evil, where one can only see massacres and disasters. A sort of warning for the Chinese: *See how dangerous the world outside is? Stay in China. It is safe here.*

My favourite part of Chinese culture is the idea of *guanxi* (关系), which can be briefly explained as interpersonal relationships that can be used to one's advantage. I remember a similar mindset in communist Poland, hence my appreciation of it. It's important whom you know and whom you don't. It's also important to keep your options open, so never burn any bridges with anyone. If you have *guanxi*, you are likely to gain anything you desire. *Mei guanxi mei qian* (没关系没钱) means no connections, no money. I have experienced this concept on my own skin. It wasn't until I'd worked there for a few years, and made friends with people from all walks of life, that I could actually pick and choose jobs. It was all about who knew me or rather knew of me and told someone else about me. *Guanxi* might look like nepotism, unfairness or corruption to those who were raised in Western cultures, but in China it's just normal.

Chinese culture is famed for its collectivism. The "collective I" notion has been running this country for generations. Nobody in particular and everyone overall is responsible when things go astray. One should sacrifice their individual needs to the greater good of a group, be it a team at work, a family, a community or even a company. Even with such strong consumerism and vivid selfishness (especially amongst the one-child generation), the group mentality still perseveres.

One of Confucius' renowned work is 'The Analects' (论语 = *lun yu*). They played a very important role in civil service exams. If one can pass them, it's the highest achievement possible in a society followed by general respect and pride. Today, also the notorious university entrance exam, called *gaokao* (高考), holds similar stature. With fierce competition, students need to work extremely hard and diligently to be able to secure spots in top China universities. Being a studious child is what all parents dream about, not only to boast about to their friends but also to maintain the echo of Kong Zi's teachings.

What are proper standards of behaviour in the 21st century China? Keeping up with appearances, for sure. Maintaining one's face ranks top among all others. Whatever you do, when you fail, don't let anyone see you fail. Keep a heavy mask on. Don't let them know what you truly think or feel. It will make you exposed and vulnerable. It will make you flop. Keep your individualism to yourself. The society doesn't like 'different'. I find these truths very hard to accept. Not because they are complete opposites of the way I was raised, personal views aside, but mainly because they create a culture of 'fakeness', where one needs to second-guess every relationship and think twice before making any statement. It must be extremely bewildering to survive where only the fittest (meaning the best actors) achieve something!

THE SUN SQUABBLE

When Confucius was traveling in the east of China, he came across two children in a heated discussion. Intrigued, he couldn't pass on asking them what the hassle was about.

I think the sun is near to us at daybreak and far away at noon, said the first kid. *I disagree*, another one stated, *the sun is far away at dawn and close by at midday.*

The first one replied: *When the sun comes, it's as big as the canopy of a carriage, but it shrinks and becomes the size of a bowl at noon. Isn't that true that objects far away seem smaller than the ones nearby?*

No, negated the other, *when the sun comes out it's very cool but it gets scorching hot at midday. It feels like putting your hand in boiling water. Isn't that true that what is nearer to us seems hotter?*

Confucius was puzzled and not able to solve the kids' dilemma.

The children laughed at him: *And who says you are a learnt man?*

I asked my students what in their opinion is the moral of this story. They all chorally replied that *Nobody knows everything*. I added: *Children never pretend and if they stay curious they can see through even the wisest man.*

On cultural differences.

"To become a true global citizen, one must abandon all notions of 'otherness' and instead embrace 'togetherness'."
(Suzy Kassem)

China shocks. No amount of reading or research can prepare one for what he or she is to experience after moving to China. But a shock doesn't need to be a negative thing. It can make one more open-minded and tolerant if we let it.

Basically, a cultural difference seems to me an image in one's head (pictured by one's home culture). If what you see is different from that particular image you've been carrying around your entire life, you'll find yourself in a clash of cultures. For instance, joking about death or dying is inappropriate in China and even uttering the word 'death' is considered a bad omen, for that matter. In the West, there are tons of jokes that start with: "So and so died and went to heaven...". Having a different sense of humour with your Chinese friends is inevitable. Another example can be a concept of personal space. People can get extremely close to one another at the bus stop, on the bus, in a queue or even in a supermarket. At first this bothered me a lot. In Europe, we grow up being used to having our own area where no one can breach the perimeter. Even after six years in China, I still get agitated when someone elbows me at the counter, steps on my toes on a bus or simply touches my shoulders like we're the best of friends (when indeed we are pure strangers). Chinese culture is relationships oriented, whereas my culture tends to be more time oriented. To the Poles, too long of a socializing would be seen as a waste of time which could be spent more productively elsewhere. Perhaps that's why my work efficiency has been admired by my Chinese colleagues so much. The Chinese see spending time with others as a chance to build relationships, establish *guan xi*, make a useful move which might come in handy in the foreseeable future. It derives from the fact that everything is done in groups. The importance of team work is stressed, which allows for collective accountability and simultaneously serves as a great hiding place for those who find creativity their drawback. Also, table manners and eating habits vary between China and most Western countries. I still remember how startled I was when my first visit to a Chinese canteen ended with a neighbouring customer spitting bones on the floor and waiting for the waitress to pick them up. Surely, it was not the poshest of places, but it taught me of Chinese people's sense of entitlement to having people look after them, clean their messes and take care of things for them. Why would they think of others first if they can and should put themselves first? Sadly, consideration for others is not the strongest Chinese characteristic.

One thing that drew my attention right after I landed in China, was the number of boys holding hands with boys and equally girls holding hands with girls. I even told my sister I thought so many people were gay. But in China, it is a sign of closeness amongst friends. It indicates that best friends are walking side by side. It is also common to see mothers and daughters clung to one another during shopping. At the same time, it is culturally acceptable for boys to wrap arms around each other's shoulders. As opposed to the Western views, it does not diminish their masculinity. So, this is how I learnt that if a person is indeed homosexual, they would be the last ones to expose it to a public eye in China by holding hands or embracing their partner.

I was six years old when I started learning English as a foreign language. When I got to high school and had to communicate with my English teacher, who was in fact an Englishman and the first foreigner I had ever met, I struggled with the concept of a 'small talk'. It is considered polite, especially in British English, to chat about the weather or simply ask someone how they are doing (without caring about the answer most of the time). My culture and language don't have that. We start with a *Hi* and then get straight to the point and to the core of the matter at hand. So, when I was asked in Chinese *Chi fan le ma?* (吃饭了吗), meaning *Have you eaten yet?* twenty times a day by complete strangers sometimes, I was growing weary of trying to answer. Until my Chinese teacher explained to me that no one expects me to actually say whether I've eaten or not. That phrase is more of a *Hello* than an actual question. Since money, politics or religion have been established taboo topics in many societies, it seems safe to ask of one's culinary endeavours instead. Don't get me wrong. I'm often asked: *How much do you make? Are you married?* A small talk is a real talk, getting straight to the important info, such as whether you're worthy of trying to make friends with or not. Your gross annual income would determine that in many cases. However, in China everyone is obsessed with food. My co-workers spend hours on end figuring out what to have for lunch and usually end up ordering in anyways; to save time, ironically. So, if you're ever asked about your last meal, don't try to revise all your vocabulary related to food to give a brilliant answer. Simply say *yes* or *no* and that will suffice. After all, it is just a conversation starter!

The eyes are useless when the mind is blind
– An eye-lid surgery.

One day I was taking a ride in a taxi when the driver asked me which girl, from a line-up standing at the bus stop, would be considered most beautiful in my country. Well, I thought about it for a quick moment and then pointed at the chubby one with the rosiest cheeks and very natural facial features. No additives or colourful ribbons in her hair. Neither did she look like a dyed puppet. He laughed and said nobody would even look at her here.

This got me thinking. The driver went on and on about how 'whiteness' is the key to beauty in China. For me, all the girls he chose as being exceptionally blessed by mother nature looked like they suffered from anorexia or were about to perform in a Beijing opera production; superficially whitened faces and clothes making them look more like tomboys than women. So, I became rather puzzled. What is it about skin colour that makes so many people wonder and discriminate at the same time? How can one be judged by something they had no influence over?

This made me think of another piece of news I had come across recently. Lately, some of my students (girls of 18 and 19 years of age) have been undergoing a painful operation on their eyes. This invention is called double eyelid surgery. Imagine my surprise when some of them tried to explain the main concept of it to me. My eyes (quite ironically) became bigger with every sentence. The more reasonable they were trying to make it sound, the more ridiculous it appeared to me. So, I decided to do a bit of digging on the topic itself.

The official name is Blepharoplasty. The general idea is to add a crease to your eyelids after some not so pleasant incisions. Swelling and bruises stay with you for weeks or months at a time. Apparently, a similar effect can be guaranteed with a piece of tape plastered on one's eyelid, too. The whole craze for enlarging eyes seems to have started in South Korea, but recently China has surpassed it. Diverse sources report various prices of this luxury, ranging from 200 dollars up to an eye-opening 2,000 dollars, all depending on how famous your surgeon is.

My students said it hurt like hell. No wonder, somebody just cut your eyes in half. However, they all said it was worth it. I won't even start to understand the logic here. It's supposed to take up to half a year to start looking natural, but how can an Asian woman look natural with Western eyes? It's like me having only a part of my face turned black if trying to resemble a woman from Africa. Getting the picture here?

Anyways, here are the before and after pics. Judge by yourselves! I simply can't stop myself from pondering: is this what westernization means? Are we all going to slice our eyes in half one day when China rules the world? Certainly, food for thought.

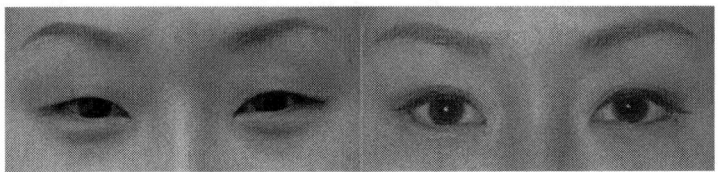

Before and After. Image by Yunqing Xiang.

Feng shui: Good karma for your life.

Feng shui (风水) literally means *wind* and *water*. Its main idea is to balance one's environment to allow for the good kismet to enter your life or business. It revolves around the Five Elements (wood, fire, earth, metal and water), each one representing a different area of life. It focuses on harmony and balance. In practice, it is often used in house design and interior decoration. Some Chinese people take it very seriously.

It is widely believed that every place has special topographical features, which allow the spiritual breath *qi* (气) . These might be natural, such as the shapes of mountains and directions of water flow; or artificial, like forms and heights of buildings or directions of roads and bridges. When natural forms are changed by men, bad luck is welcomed. It also matters where one is buried. It is a heavy burden on each family to secure the most appropriate and auspicious spot for the grave. Otherwise the dead might be affected by evil forces and hence never able to find eternal peace. Ideally, a grave should have a wide river in front, a high cliff behind and enclosing hills on both sides. Both house and graves must face the south and should be ornamented with symbolic figures on top (either gravestone's or a roof) and pictures of spirits on the doors.

Originally, in ancient times, *feng shui* was supposed to identify the best surroundings for farmers to have their crops flourish. However, today it has grown to a profitable business of determining where to open a shop, how to locate offices or which rooms should be used for what purpose at home. The philosophy is claimed to be responsible for one's wealth and prosperity. And as we all know, this is what the Chinese relentlessly seek.

Here are main *feng shui* solutions for your home:

1. Always use your front door to enter a house. It will allow good energy to get in with you.
2. Fix all the squeaks and whining of your door. Oil your door hinges to create more positive energy.
3. Don't buy a house next to a curvy road. It brings bad luck.
4. Don't go for a place which neighbours a building made entirely out of glass. It will reflect into your windows and bring ill fortune.
5. If you have a mirror hanging in your bedroom, make sure it does not face your bed. Similarly, a mirror in a bathroom should never face the door.
6. Leave no space between your kitchen cabinets and the ceiling as it creates stagnant *qi*.
7. If you want to keep your wealth, don't let the water out of your house. Keep your bathroom door closed and your toilet seat down.
8. Don't plan your front door directly opposite your staircase.
9. Don't ever place fake flowers inside your house. Everything in it should bring real life in.
10. If you have a TV set in your bedroom, cover it up to protect yourself from its active energy oftentimes making it difficult to sleep.
11. Put your furniture legs on rugs or carpets.

12. Keep your kitchen clean at all times. It has the ability to attract money.
13. Make everything a double, i.e. place two armchairs in the corner, if you want to start a successful relationship.
14. Paint your walls in red, green or purple.
15. Get rid of all the clutter! Remove everything you don't love in your house.

Many contemporary families in China invite a *feng shui* master to design their houses' decorations. It might seem ludicrous to some, but millions believe that the safety and wealth of their families depend on their front door being widely open. We can see crystals, bamboo flutes or wind chimes hanging from the ceilings to deflect sorrows and woes. Is it the power of luck charms or just a misleading hope for the magic entrusted in other superstitious paraphernalia? I guess it all depends on what you believe in. Also, *feng shui* has become an admired art form over decades called *Asian décor*. Quoting a current president candidate in the US, Donald Trump: "You don't have to believe in *feng shui* for it to work. I just know it brings me money." Go figure!

The five magical elements: 五行 *(wu xing).*

If you attempt to interpret constant changes in the universe and to comprehend the interconnections between different beings, you must read into the theory of the Five Elements: Metal 金 (*jin*), Wood 木 (*mu*), Water 水 (*shui*), Fire 火 (*huo*) and Earth 土 (*tu*). Some people also call it Five States of Change, Five Steps, Five Movements or Five Phases.

According to this theory, these elements mutually promote one another by forming a circle.

Water creates Wood, but destroys Fire;

Fire creates Earth, but destroys Metal;

Metal creates Water, but destroys Wood;

Wood creates Fire, but destroys Earth;

Earth creates Metal, but destroys Water.

That's how the two circles of existence go with all elements being both friendly and antagonistic to each other.

Depending on your year of birth, each element represents a specific personality trait. 12 Chinese zodiac animals (explained in depth in a separate essay) are linked with one element. If your year of birth ends with 0 or 1, you are believed to belong to Metal; 4 or 5 to Wood, 2 or 3 to Water, 6 or 7 to Fire, and finally 8 or 9 to Earth.

Metal = Righteousness

Earth = Honesty

Fire = Propriety

Water = Wisdom

Wood = Benevolence

I feel lucky to be representing Water☺.

When it comes to Metal, its usual cultural connotations include gold or any other distinctive but highly valued colour. When Chinese people see a Western girl with blond hair, they often say 金发碧眼 (*jin fa bi yan*), which means "golden hair and jade blue eyes".

Due to Wood, 木 (*mu*) resembling a pictograph of a tree, a reticent or withdrawn person would be best called 木讷 (*mu ne*), linked to static feature of wood. I think one of my favourite Chinese idioms containing wood is this one: 呆若木鸡 (*dai ruo mu ji*), which translates as "dumb as a wooden chicken". Very vivid☺.

Water, on the other hand, is thought to be the source of wisdom. Most phrases associated with water are positive in Mandarin Chinese. One example might be 行云流水 (*xing yun liu shui*), which describes a naturally flowing style of writing, "floating clouds and running streams".

Fire 火 (*huo*) looks like a flame, doesn't it? That's why it almost always brings a feeling of warmth, when used in Chinese. Hot and spicy, 火辣 (*huo la*), also stands for a sexy lady. At weddings, people often say 红红火火 (*hong hong huo huo*), which means "very happy and prosperous".

When you look at 土 (*tu*), the character for Earth, you must spot its similarity to a shoot of a plant sprouting from the soil. Although earth is the source of all food, Chinese language does not particularly like it. If someone calls you 土包子 (*tu bao zi*), know that it's time to find new friends, as this one means "a clodhopper" or "a country bumpkin".

If you are Wood, you might discover you're impulsive, while being Fire means dynamic and creative. People representing Earth might be seen as changeable, whereas those who are Metal might often contradict themselves. Water is supposed to bring calmness, reflection, observation and consideration. Not sure if that's a hundred percent true in my case, though☺.

Wood is the most human of the elements. It helps one plan, look forward and make decisions but may also turn anger into frustration easily. The colour associated with Wood is green and when it comes to bodily parts: liver and gallbladder are primary here. Spring should be your beloved season.

Fire represents enthusiasm and summer. People who were born under this element are supposedly very warm-hearted and like red most. This element links with one's heart and circulation system.

Earth brings abundance and fertility; hence it's associated with a change of seasons. It is a symbol of great stability and yellow colour. If you are Earth, you should be patient, logical and extremely reliable, as well as stubborn at times. Your digestive system is seen in Earth, especially your spleen.

Metal, although structured, accepts new forms. It is oftentimes compared to a flower closing its petals. It is represented by white colour and stands for a strong, self-reliant, determined and sophisticated person. It is also linked with autumn as it displays a solidifying process. Lungs and nose go in pair with it.

Water has the capacity to flow with power, silence and flexibility. It is ever changing and often dangerous being able to nourish and cleanse at the same time. The kidney is especially related to this element. It is represented by black and blue and winter among seasons.

The transition from one element to another is very smooth, just like changes in nature. Harmony and balance play vital roles in the process of changing. Only through maintaining this order of things can the universe function without obstacles. Following the words of Tom Rath: *Wellbeing is about the combination of our love for what we do each day, the quality of our relationships, the security of our finances, the vibrancy of our physical health, and the pride we take in what we have contributed to our communities. Most importantly, it's about how these five elements interact.*

Can China make you happy?

Leo Tolstoy once said: "If you want to be happy, be". Not that easy, is it? Whoever has lived in China for a while must relate to the struggle of keeping it together from time to time. When I ask my Chinese friends whether they are happy or not, I usually get an awkward moment of silence first (seems to me they are trying to process what crazy concept this crazy foreigner just brought up) and then the answer seems to be very practical. Something like: *I have a good job and I'm making decent money* or *I have a car, a house, a baby and a husband, so I guess I should be happy*, etc. If you asked me the same question, I'd say *I'm being happy*. It is not an everlasting bliss but me and China have our moments.

What does happiness mean to Chinese people? Well, most of the time, a comfortable life. Many youngsters are looking for a better future than their parents' past. They keep their eyes open for business opportunities that would allow them to say: *life is good*. The concept of happiness does not have much to do with a particular feeling in China. It's not about how you feel but about how the things you surround yourself with make you feel. Lots of people complain about losing touch with relatives while being forced to migrate to big cities for work, endless mortgage payments for the apartment they so eagerly bought just before getting married or fierce competitiveness which does not let them sleep sound at night. Some of my students have never seen a truly blue sky in their life. That's why, whenever abroad, the first thing they do after stepping out of a plane is taking photos of clear blue sky. Pollution can make one's hope seem hazy, too. People are forced to move to metropolises if they want to make something of themselves. Rural areas are constantly abandoned by the young workforce and the elderly complain that when they get sick there's no one to take them to hospital. An average income in a big city can surpass that of a small town up to even 20 times. I guess some are trying to stay immune to "urban sickness" focusing on their goal, which is to become rich and to become a boss. Not many know what or whom they'd like to boss around but that does not matter much. Position is power. Power is worth more than all the money in the world. Here comes the never-solved puzzle of whether money brings happiness. As many people as many answers. There's no one golden rule here. Whatever makes one content counts.

As China's economic development progresses, so does the number of social problems. How can I get my kid into the best school? How can I send my kid to the best foreign school? How can I land a secure government job? How can I save enough money for the rainy day? How can I gather enough so that my kid never lacks anything? How can I come across as more cultured and hence save face? These are questions behind life journeys in China. Despite the chances presented by the China's open policy, people are still not happy. According to World Happiness Report from 2015, life in China makes one utterly miserable. The Middle Kingdom placed 84th, emoting the feeling that most citizens (domestic and foreign) hate life in China.

Topics like happiness and values never went well at English corners I used to conduct. People were simply not willing to openly and publicly share their most hidden fears, emotions and ideas. Ultimately, if you say something wrong or different from others, you'll lose face and might never get a chance of regaining it.

How about us, foreigners there? Are we happy? Overall, from my observations the generalization I can honestly make is that there are two types of foreigners in China. The first one suffers from a 'constant whiner syndrome'. Their attitude is so negative that no number of anti-depressants could fix that. They complain about everything, and I mean literally everything. Nothing is ever good enough for them and their home country is always portrayed as the land of milk and honey. These guys feel stuck and their unhappiness permeates everything they touch.

They are the biggest moaners at work. They even create and join WeChat group chats just to vent. Surely, letting it out is an important part of getting closure, but if you dislike it so much, why are you still here? The second lot, would be people who have settled down in China, either got married to Chinese nationals or simply decided to call China their home. These ones are not blind to the problems around (which every country has, by the way) but they are also not trying to be magic fairies and by a touch of their wands transform China into something it is not. These expats are in China because they choose to be there. They stay faithful to their choices and try to make the best of this experience by learning Chinese, exploring Chinese culture and mingling with the locals.

What I'm trying to say here is that it is all in one's attitude. When I came to China, I was overwhelmed. I didn't know anyone, couldn't speak a word of Chinese, felt lost and almost banished. Even though I made a conscious choice of moving to China, I was struggling. Until one day, when I got on the wrong bus for the third time just because I could not read the names of the stops in Chinese characters, I decided to change my approach. China wasn't going to change, so I had to. I went from negativity, disappointment and confusion to openness and eagerness. Today, I can speak (and read!) Chinese quite well, I have tons of friends, I have enjoyed visiting many amazing spots, I have tried most Chinese dishes and I can honestly say that China changed me.

The key is to attune oneself to the situation. Don't allow yourself to feel stuck. Go out there. Embrace the differences. Stop comparing what you see with what you know and feel comfortable in. Go out on a limb and try to listen and observe instead of criticizing and spacing out. Life is China is not easy, but if you allow it to, it will be challenging and adventurous. Who knows, maybe one day you'll be able to call it home, just like I do now. It was George Orwell who bravely said that "happiness can exist only in acceptance". Accept where you are and China will welcome you.

Not everything in life is about money.

I'm not sure if "money makes the world go around", but I'm

positive it does make China spin. If your aim is financial benefits and you have a skill China is looking for, that's the place for you to be. I didn't come to China thinking of money, as generally speaking I don't care about finances so much. I've always thought the more money the more problems☺. However, having lived in China for 6 years taught me that "money talks" Chinese louder than any language.

Life of a foreigner is not easy when it comes to exchanging currency. The government allows to exchange only $500 a day, which means if you need $5000 you will have to visit a bank 10 times. Lately even Chinese citizens started facing restrictions. I used to ask my Chinese friends to exchange Chinese yuan into foreign currency, but most of them had reached their annual limit which is $10000. Sometimes even when I would get to the bank and queue for over an hour (one needs to get the ticket first), the clerk would still tell me they didn't have dollars at the moment. I highly doubted it was the truth, but I understood they were trying to exchange as little as possible to follow central laws.

Funny thing is that except for money, China sees other things as symbols of status as well. First comes a mistress, or mistresses in plural. Highly ranked officials are known for having a harem of mistresses for whom they typically need to provide a car, apartment and luxurious clothes (the record holder is a former railway minister who got caught with 18 mistresses). In my apartment complex, as I was told by the estate agent when I was moving in, one never has to worry about hailing a taxi in the middle of the night. There are plenty of those, waiting at the gate for so called 小三 (xiao san), literally 'the other woman', who are available to their benefactors 24/7.

Then, there's a posh car. Whether one tries to get a wife or woo his society, a real man needs to purchase high class wheels, preferably of German make. Then of course Apple products come to play. iPhones, iPads, *Macbooks* stand for luxury, even though most of them are made in factories in Guangdong. Also, one can't forget to furnish their place with sophisticated pieces. Lots of people hire professional interior designers and decorating companies, in a race of 'who's got more European-looking home'. Lately, playing golf has risen to a status symbol, too. If you want to establish *guanxi* (connections), you'd better learn how to swing the golf club. Finally, purses need to be mentioned, as well as "murses" (man purses). Not just any kind, but those from fancy designers, with huge logos. One who has it all doesn't need to worry about money or "friends".

First time I got a red envelope (红包 = *hong bao*), I was puzzled. It was for one of the festivals and someone at the school I worked for at the time left it for me on my desk. I felt very uncomfortable taking it, when I saw it's full of money, but my Chinese colleagues explained to me that this is the way companies give out bonuses. Later I discovered it is also the most desirable wedding gift, as it helps the newlyweds and their families cover the expenses of a lavish wedding. Also, parents give *hongbaos* to their offsprings for Chinese New Year, making sure the bills are brand new to indicate a clean start. There's even a nursery rhyme which goes like "May you be happy and prosperous, please give me my red envelope" (恭喜发财，红包拿来 = *gong xi fa cai, hong bao na lai*). I asked some of my students what they do with the money (as these days also relatives give them those), and all of them said that it is their parents who keep the money, or if the lucky receiver gets to keep it – they sometimes re-give the envelopes to their younger cousins.

Once a friend of mine received a *hongbao* with a new bank card inside, and a corresponding pin number, where the school (grateful for her amazing care of the kids) deposited quite a handsome amount. It is also common to hand in red envelopes to doctors and nurses, just to assure the best treatment and extra attention. Security guards are also often presented with extra money to keep an eye on a particular car.

What's more, the phenomenon that fascinates me most is the rise of the so called *fu er dai* (富二代), which means "second rich generation". I have had my share of kids whose parents got rich overnight, during the period of societal reforms. These sons and daughters are easily recognizable by their attitude to money. They don't have to work or even think about money, they just need to use it. All they do is go shopping to Europe and bring ultra-expensive products, just so they can show them off on social media. They are the biggest spenders of the 21st century China. They are involved in frequent traffic accidents, where - even having killed someone – they are let scot-free, relying on their parents' reputation or wealth. The reason why *fu er dai* aren't the most popular members of contemporary Chinese society is that nobody clearly knows where their money comes from. Multiple suspicions point to corruption and exploitation. The question is: how long can they put on their show? With the currently decreasing Chinese economy, most people try to figure how to save for the future and not waste the fruit of parents' sweat and blood. The attitude of "second rich generation" kids is also quite obvious in their approach towards studies. I have taught many of them and it often drove me up the wall how little respect for knowledge they had.

Some time ago I had a gripping conversation with a Chinese friend, who is married to a foreigner and currently pregnant. She was complaining to me how hard it is going to be for her baby to grow up in China and how even harder it's going to be for her and her husband to provide all the things current Chinese culture requires for a child. In Chinese society, parents are obliged to work until their kids leave home, which is usually when they get married. They must be able to provide them not only with proper education but also all their demands or needs. There is no option of saying 'no' to your only child, which results in a generation not knowing the value of money. Apparently, there is a Chinese saying claiming that the rich circle in China lasts only for three generations (*fu bu guo san dai* = 富不过三代). Hence, this common and widespread feeling of entitlement to everything. Whatever they want, they will get. One of my students lost his new iPhone last month and refused to participate in class until his mum bought him a new one. Let me be clear, the latest iPhone costs around RMB 6000 (approximately $930), which is an average salary for most Chinese people. That mum, however, drove all the way from another city on the same day with a new iPhone just to calm her son down. This reminded me of Marxism, where family always comes first. A nuclear family is also the most prominent one, no matter what. That friend of mine, mentioned above, was very worried that they didn't have enough money at the moment to buy a new flat for their kid, who wass not even born yet. She said there were 7 people in her family waiting for that baby, all of whom would take care of it. That means constant spoiling by grandparents and not enough time from parents, who will be working double hard to provide. It's so peculiar to observe this society. I wonder what's going to happen to China in 10 years. At the moment, young people seem to have lost the sense of wonder, focused on rote learning and pleasing everybody around. They reflect no dreams or passions. Sometimes they resemble robots. I guess 'robotical society' has become a catch-on phrase for a reason. If anything can be bought, why not everybody?

All in all, money has become a version of a god in China. Everyone wants it and needs it to survive. Was Mark Twain right saying: "The lack of money is the root of all evil"?

Chinese superstitions.

"Superstitions are habits rather than beliefs."
(Marlene Dietrich)

"My mom went to a fortune teller to figure out what to name me" – I have heard many times from my Chinese friends. I don't believe in luck or any sorts of superstitions, but a lot of Chinese people do, so I looked into it.

If you have ever failed to book your tickets fast enough and was stuck to spend Chinese New Year in China, you understand when I say fireworks in all shapes and colours can make one go bananas. At first, it's all cool and beautiful, then it is just annoying, until it finally becomes unbearable as it never stops. I was told the Chinese love to burn firecrackers to chase away evil spirits when welcoming the new year. That's just one of many superstitions I have encountered in China.

Various dictionaries define 'a superstition' as a completely different thing, from an irrational belief through magic to an unsupported idea derived from fear. Whatever it is, it is surely a big deal in China. Before I came to China, I had only heard about 13 or a black cat being unlucky. So, I'm no expert on such theories in the West either. I did learn, however, that in China number 4 (四 = si) is considered jinxed for it's a homonym for "death" (死 = si) . Lots of people I know, even the young ones, do not want to have this digit in their phone number, home address or car's number plate. On the other hand, number 8 (八 = ba) is extremely favourable since it's a homonym for "prosperity" (发 = fa). That is why the Olympics were due on August 8th, 2008.

It's well-known that white colour is linked with mourning so its good fortune directly opposes its Western connotations. I have also read somewhere that if a baby cries alone in a room, a ghost is likely to be present there. From then on, I understood why my Chinese female friends never want to leave their babies without someone's presence, even for a second.

China's superstitions are certainly unique and intriguing, at least to me. A new mother is not to take a shower for a month after she gives birth to her baby. Some ladies also schedule their C-section on an auspicious day. That one seems a bit of a stretch. During Spring Festival, one should remember to sweep the house diligently, keep all windows and doors open at midnight and place red wherever possible, including on oneself. Noodles are never to be cut since they symbolize longevity and always follow *feng shui* as your interior decorator.

I must admit cabbage as a fated vegetable surprised me, to say the least. I've noticed cabbage roots in many places of business, including restaurants and a few Chinese homes, too. Apparently, the Chinese name for 'napa cabbage' (*da bai cai* = 大白菜) is a homonym for 'hundred' or 'wealth'. So, everyone considers it a sign of prosperity and wealth. The same is thought of the money tree which I'd seen back home before but never knew why people placed it on their tables. It's actually the Malabar chestnut tree and came to its fame in 1986 by a Taiwanese truck driver. As the tree grows, its abundant five-leaf stems are to visualize one's financial fortune.

I did receive a Chinese knot a few good times in the period of six years spent in China. Of course, as many others, it symbolizes prosperous life and good luck. It dates to Tang Dynasty and contains a cord, a knot and a tassel, which are characteristically bound by a single piece of thread. An authentic knot must look identical on its front and back side. If you ever wondered what shapes and forms they come in, go to a Chinese supermarket around Spring Festival time, they will make your eyes pop☺.

A chubby laughing Buddha is also kept to help one reach good health, success, and basically abundance of everything. This Buddha is called Pu-Tai (布袋和 = *bu dai he shang*) (which apparently means 'cloth sack') and even though he's an obese man with no hair, his prayer beads are, I guess, what makes people believe he's a lucky charm. Chinese people look at him as a good-natured, kind and loving character, that's why it is a common view to see them rub his belly. He is specifically keen on playing with children and so is often depicted in their presence.

When it comes to plants, bamboo comes in handy. It is a long-believed symbol of strength. According to ancient poets, a true gentleman should be just like bamboo: upright, strong and perseverant. Just like the plant (hollow inside), he should stay open hearted and never give rise to prejudice. Finally, there is fish with its multiple meanings. It is cooked but not eaten at Spring Festival's feast; it grows very old reminding people of long life; and it stands for loyalty and fidelity, since fish often swim in pairs.

If you are living in China, you should also learn what not to do, if you believe in omens. Never leave your chopsticks upright in your rice bowl. It reminds Chinese people of an offering made at someone's grave. Don't flip your fish on the plate. As fishermen in the south of China tend to believe, if they do so, their boat would turn over in the sea the next time they go fishing. Also, don't cut a pear in half and give it to your husband if you want to avoid divorce. Under no circumstances should you sweep or dust on a New Year's Day itself, as you might be sweeping away good luck. Don't buy books on a New Year's Day either or you might lose something in the upcoming year. If you happen to be pregnant, remember never to use glue as you will have a very difficult birth. Don't attend a funeral while expecting, as bad spirits might harm your unborn baby. According to some sources, those mothers-to-be who rub their bellies, doom their kid to become spoilt from the very beginning.

I was, however, fascinated by the phenomenon of fortune tellers in China. 算命 (*suan ming*), or fortune telling, has been present in the Chinese culture for centuries. People use such services to calculate an appropriate time to have a wedding, a funeral, open a business, or start harvesting crops. The most widespread one is 八字 (*ba zi*), which means 8 characters and is used to calculate one's birthday with the precision to the particular hour. This method allows for a personalized horoscope for each individual. If you're still not convinced, there's 面相 (*mian xiang*) as well, which is basically a face reading ritual. With regard to this technique, different parts of one's face are responsible for luck at different life stages. Your nose is the most prominent point as it symbolizes your future wealth and divides your face into feminine (*yin*) and masculine (*yang*) side. An interesting fact is that small ears are viewed as very unlucky as they don't indicate a long future.

When I was travelling in rural areas of Yunnan Province in China, I saw people using long flat bamboo sticks with numbers on them. This rite is named 求签 (*qiu qian*). The sticks are kept in a cylinder and shaken. A person first silently prays to whatever deity they believe in and then asks a specific question they need an answer to. Whichever stick falls out of the cylinder, its number represents an answer to your question. Mostly guardians of the temple are the ones to interpret the result.

The Party officially forbids such practices, but more traditional folks won't stop using them. A lot of people, just like in the West, consult fortune tellers out of desperation, looking for hope and consolation in times of trouble. Needless to say, one person's illusory magic is another person's firm credo.

The Chinese Zodiac.

I have never believed in the power of zodiac signs, neither have I ever been interested in astrology. However, the Chinese Zodiac animals seem intriguing to me. Following a legend, the Jade Emperor (*Yu huang da di* = 玉皇大帝) was told to create a Zodiac of twelve animals. It was a difficult task at hand so he asked his trusted advisor for help: a rat. The rat suggested a race. The first twelve animals to cross the river would be included in the Zodiac. And that is presumably how we ended up with the rat (子 = *zi*), the ox (丑 = *chou*), the tiger (寅 = *yin*), the rabbit (卯 = *mao*), the dragon (辰 = *chen*), the snake (巳 = *si*), the horse (午 = *wu*), the sheep (未 = *wei*), the monkey (申 = *shen*), the rooster (酉 = *you*), the dog (戌 = *xu*), and the pig (亥 = *hai*). Apparently the cat refused to get wet, so when people don't want to reveal their age, they say: *I was born in the year of the cat*, which simply translates as *don't poke your nose where it doesn't belong*☺.

<u>THE RAT</u>

Years corresponding: 1960, 1972, 1984, 1996, 2008, 2020, etc.
Element: Water
Works well with: Dragon, Monkey & Ox
Enemy: Cat
Characteristics: inventive, intelligent, enigmatic, adaptable, quick-witted, charming, artistic, sociable but a bit sly.

<u>THE OX</u>

Years corresponding: 1961, 1973, 1985, 1997, 2009, 2021, etc.
Element: Earth
Works well with: Snake, Rooster
Enemy: Horse, Tiger
Characteristics: strong, reliable, steadfast, trustworthy, thorough, reasonable, determined, happy to spend time alone, but stubborn at times.

THE TIGER

Years corresponding: 1962, 1974, 1986, 1998, 2010, 2022, etc.
Element: Wood
Works well with: Horse, Dog
Enemy: Sheep, Ox
Characteristics: graceful, confident, intelligent, self-assured, but arrogant at times.

THE RABBIT

Years corresponding: 1963, 1975, 1987, 1999, 2011, 2023, etc.
Element: Wood
Works well with: Sheep, Pig
Enemy: Rat, Rooster
Characteristics: trustworthy, modest, emphatic, diplomatic, sincere, sociable, considerate, non-confrontational.

THE DRAGON

Years corresponding: 1964, 1976, 1988, 2000, 2012, 2024, etc.
Element: Earth
Works well with: Rat & Monkey
Enemy: Sheep, Ox
Characteristics: helpful, selfless, charismatic, great leader, admired, lucky, flexible, artistic, spiritual.

THE SNAKE

Years corresponding: 1965, 1977, 1989, 2001, 2013, 2025, etc.
Element: Fire
Works well with: Rooster, Ox
Enemy: Monkey, Pig
Characteristics: philosophical, persuasive, organized, hardworking, intelligent, elegant, attentive, decisive, but sly at times.

THE HORSE

Years corresponding: 1966, 1978, 1990, 2002, 2014, 2026, etc.
Element: Fire
Works well with: Dog & Tiger
Enemy: Rat, Monkey
Characteristics: easy-going, optimistic, adaptable, good-natured, loyal, courageous, ambitious, athletic, with a strong sense of humour, smart, adventurous.

THE SHEEP

Years corresponding: 1967, 1979, 1991, 2003, 2015, 2027, etc.
Element: Earth
Works well with: Pig, Rabbit
Enemy: Dragon, Tiger
Characteristics: happy to be a part of a team, tasteful, warm, elegant, charming, sensitive, calm but crafty.

THE MONKEY

Years corresponding: 1968, 1980, 1992, 2004, 2016, 2028, etc.
Element: Metal
Works well with: Dragon, Rat
Enemy: Snake, Horse
Characteristics: quick-witted, likes to have fun, energetic, charming, lucky, adaptable, bright, versatile, lively.

THE ROOSTER

Years corresponding: 1969, 1981, 1993, 2005, 2017, 2029, etc.
Element: Metal
Works well with: Snake, Ox
Enemy: Sheep, Rabbit
Characteristics: flamboyant, energetic, honest, intelligent, diverse, flexible, confident, likes to show off, often arrogant.

THE DOG

Years corresponding: 1970, 1982, 1994, 2006, 2018, 2030, etc.
Element: Earth
Works well with: Tiger & Horse
Enemy: Dragon, Rooster

Characteristics: reliable, sociable, generous, courageous, hard-working, steady, diligent, adaptable, smart, often puts the needs of others before their own.

THE PIG

Years corresponding: 1971, 1983, 1995, 2007, 2019, 2031, etc.
Element: Water
Works well with: Sheep, Rabbit
Enemy: Monkey, Snake
Characteristics: good-natured, jolly, fun to be around, honourable, philanthropic, determined, optimistic, sincere, sociable, but sometimes lazy and indulgent.

The truth won't set you free in China.

China is a funny country. It's a country where one can get knocked down by a crazy bike rider, spat at by a random passer-by and pointed at by... well...let's face it, basically anybody.

There are so many wall paintings. Not a graffiti type, but the ones placed there by the government to remind people to be kind and polite. Isn't it odd that people need to be reminded by their surroundings to say things like 'please' or 'thank you'? The wall art is usually in a form of a cartoon, I guess the government figured it would appeal to younger audience. They literally remind one to use polite words, not to spit or litter on the street and to give seats to the elderly. The authorities seem to have gone a step further implementing a new law lately that states if a son or daughter does not visit their parents on a regular basis, they have the right to call the police. Seems a bit forced to me.

This brings me to the topic of lies and trust in Chinese culture.

No lie is too big or too small to be told. It reminds me of a game of tennis, where one player needs to respond with even more strength to be able to stop the opponent's attack. Lying is a game and a complex one, too. I have always believed truth will come out sooner or later which discouraged me from telling lies in life generally. I believe in the truth, however relative it might seem. I remember asking my students to explain a 'white lie' to me in class. Most of them shouted: *It's a good lie, teacher.* Hmmm. It's all about the face, losing it, gaining it or hiding it, for that matter. Sometimes young Chinese people will disguise the truth when asked whether they have a boyfriend or a girlfriend, simply saying: *He's/she's just my friend.* Is that a lie? Bending of the truth? I'm not judging here. Just commenting on the status quo.

Lies in business are most common, though. Fake products, beautified ads of things, showing off before closing a deal. These are just a few instances when telling the truth might ruin one. Once a friend of mine wanted to order motorcycle parts from one factory in China. I helped him communicate with the company and we agreed on everything including the price, shipment, delivery costs, etc. When the cargo didn't arrive as scheduled, I phoned them and frantically asked what happened. I was told they had already sent all products we had ordered and that it must be the shipper's fault. When my friend got his parts (a month later), the stamp with the date of a send-off showed just the day I called and complained. Go figure.

Surely, there are a few loopholes and one might argue that there is always room for interpretation, but when it comes to money things should be clear. Oftentimes different languages get blamed, or their translators, if things go south. This creates a very unhealthy social phenomenon, when even Chinese people openly claim that no one can be trusted. According to a survey conducted in 2012, 40% Chinese don't trust more than three people. That's shocking statistics. Many friends of mine tried to explain the concept of friendship in China to me. Almost all of them claimed they called certain people friends or even stayed in touch with them for many years just for benefits. *You know*, one said, *I might need them one day.* When I asked if they trust these people the call friends, all of them said: *No, I only trust myself.*

Personally, I've been lied to a few good times, too. The realtor would lie about the possibility to have something fixed in my flat. A Taobao seller would lie they had the product I asked for and then go and buy it from another seller. My hairdresser lied to me that a haircut I showed him in a catalogue *could* be easily done on my hair (that did not end well!). Even a doctor lied to me by saying my test results weren't "too bad" (when I was on the verge of anemia). One gets used to being lied to in China. Might be little things, but telling the truth is not considered a virtue in the Middle Kingdom.

Although there are prompts anywhere you look, people still behave in a way that leaves one with a lot to think about. Not only does it come across as forced love but also forced civilization and fake manners. Even though many people I've met in China long for real and deep relationships, they would not risk opening up and reaching out. It's just safer to hide behind the lie, even if it's 'white'.

On faith, religions and what's left of 'God'.

"What do you believe in? I believe in myself", said one of my teenage students in China.

Many people imagine most of the Chinese dressed like Buddhist monks, practicing kung-fu on top of some secluded mountains, all balanced and meditating even in their sleep. Couldn't have been more wrong. I think the only time I actually saw a monk was when I went to one of the touristy temples in Hangzhou and he was selling souvenirs at the gate, shaved bald but ready to jump into his jeans and head back to the city the minute he finished his work at 5pm. I was very disappointed.

I have a tendency to ask a lot of questions, which, as I learnt pretty quickly, is not the most appreciated quality in China. Foreigners get away with being curious and inquisitive, though, as locals understand we simply don't know many things about China, thus they are happily ready to explain what's left of their traditional culture to us. Hence, every time I would meet a student with Buddhist beads on their wrist or a taxi driver with a plumb Buddha hanging down from his/her inside mirror, I would naturally ask what it meant to them. Imagine my surprise when most of the answers were just: it's just an auspicious charm for luck, all people have them, I don't know what it means, I just keep it for luck in business.

I began to read about religions in China and I was gobsmacked when I realised that statistics do not reflect the contemporary status quo at all. 70 percent of people might be considered Buddhists but that's mainly because they still follow traditions instilled in them by their grandparents. Once I went to a temple with a colleague, a girl of about 20 years old. It was during the Chinese Spring Festival break. We crowded on the bus for two hours, then an hour more to actually buy a ticket once we got there. She bought incense sticks and told me they were a necessity to pray with. When it was actually her turn to pray in front of what looked like a grill with incense sticking out everywhere, she bowed four times (to all sides of the world), burnt the thing and left. I asked her what she was thanking for and she replied with a glimpse of a shock on her face: What do you mean thank for? We don't thank, we ask for things like a good husband, luck in the new year, health in the family, etc. The whole experience reminded me of a hectic market on a Sunday morning with people frantically hustling around, and a complete lack of intimacy. It was my first and last visit to a temple.

I must say, the Catholic church I found in Hangzhou has been my safe place for the past six years. With all that's going on around, with the crazy situations coming right at you without a shadow of a warning, with the number of decisions and uncertainties one faces every single day, that church has saved my sanity. Christianity isn't popular in China, but I have witnessed it gaining more attention in the past few years. Especially among young people who are curious about Western cultures, so they happily come on Saturday nights more to see and talk to foreigners than actually think about what's actually going on during mass. They also try to practise their English with us. Fair enough. Funnily, I have learnt that Wenzhou, the city which produced the biggest number of current millionaires in China, also holds a population of Christians six times higher than the national average. Some of them believe they got rich because God blessed them, so that's why the pray and that's how the wheels go around. On the other hand, I have met a few nice lads (whose nationality I will not reveal☺), who openly refused to attend services in that little church of mine, claiming it's a national church, so not underground enough for them. They still meet in their homes to pray privately. At times one can hear their loud 'Alleluia' channelling out of the flats on the 26th floor of a skyscraper late at night. Yet, some denominations don't allow Chinese nationals in their churches and others check passports at the door. I have met students torn inside because they wanted to get baptized but the party members approached them and threatened their parents job or public shaming if they went ahead with becoming Christians openly. So, the biggest Christian church in China today is the one full of silent followers, who attend small Bible Studies (often conducted by foreigners who teach at universities at daytime and try to convert people at night), believe in God but can't admit it. My observations are simple. So many Chinese people I've met are looking for something bigger than themselves. They don't believe in the government like their parents did, they might doubt the purpose of earthly treasures and want to find something that would give their lives meaning. Oftentimes, however, they are so conflicted, emotionally split between loyalty towards their ancestors (read: parents) and the promise of freedom that might come when they trust a Higher Power. Comparisons of Chinese Christianity and Polish Christianity proved pointless at very early stages, when I joined a Bible Study group at the church. It was then when I actually opened my own eyes and realized that there is not just one way to believe, nor just one way to pray. By observing brothers and sisters from all over the world, the way they lived their faith and not just spoke of it, made me realize that there's no correctness in believing or practicing one's faith. We are all just looking for something and the form in which we find it does not matter at all.

I also had a real pleasure of meeting pure Taoists, who most of the time would be doing yoga extensively. This philosophy, as I was told, focuses on harmony with the Tao which could be best explained as the driving source of everything. Taoists value simplicity, humility, moderation and compassion. The idea itself stems from *yin and yang* (阴阳), of which I have been a fan for years. It was my acupuncturist who explained the notion of *qi* (气) to me, while fixing my back. These two complete opposites that can't exist without each other, are what many call *qi flow*, which seems responsible for one's both mentality and physique. Meditation is a daily bread for most Tao followers, which keeps them grounded and balanced. These days Taoism is facing a real renaissance. *Tai chi* (太极 = *tai ji*), one of the Taoist arts, is on the rise (especially amongst the elders at 4 am in parks and gardens). In this tumultuous current world, many are seeking to experience a true connection with nature. Even expatriates can be spotted practicing their moves in local parks, of course, drawing tons of attention. The message of being good to one another, getting closer with the Mother Nature and exhibiting balance in everything has certainly been catching on world-widely.

But what about Buddhism (佛教 = *fo jiao*)? Is it completely dead? Is it all just for show? Certainly not. Against what many might believe, Buddhism did not originate in China, it came to China around 202 BC. The Chinese version of Buddhism is also very unlike the Indian one. It is more of a folk belief. Only Tibet keeps to this philosophy's strict rules and follows its core points exclusively. In mainland China it is more of a mixture of the root ethos and Taoism or Confucianism. The borders are very flexible. Everyone seems to be choosing what suits them best and becoming a disciple of their own edition of Buddhism, be it beaded bracelets, jade pendants or statues of a chubby Buddha.

What interests me most are the other gods. One might think that money emerges as the main one. It is true to some extent that materialism has been overtaking any other conviction in today's China. People just figured that money solves a lot of problems and can help one make 'friends'. Without money in this society one can count on no one or nothing. There are, however, still some funny little creatures that some consider gods.

If you've ever been to a tea house, you must have noticed minuscule statues on almost every table or a tea set tray. They all account for having different powers. They are like totems, house gods, making sure you lack nothing. If you happen to see a *pixiu* (貔貅), an offspring of the Great Dragon, bear in mind that this one only accepts only gold and silver as offerings, as it has a huge stomach and amazingly hideous mouth. A pig, represents happiness and endless peace. I was told by a reliable source that a Chinese character for family (家 = *jia*) resembles a pig under a roof. So if you want to stay prosperous, keep a clay pig in your home. There are many more of those talismans to keep you safe, happy, rested, beautiful, slim or even white (skin-wise), but a tortoise and a swan can't be omitted. The first one symbolizes longevity, as it moves so slowly; while a swan's composure reminds one to stay happy and graceful at all times. Among other bizarre gods I have encountered are a god of the bedroom and the one ruling over the bathroom as well as a god of cooking and a god of partying. Most of these gods are highly disposable and can be switched as one wishes.

Even though China doesn't strike me as a nation based on a strong moral compass, it does strive to come across as a devotional place. I have seen people wearing beads up to their elbows and so many jade superstitious pendants than one's neck can barely carry. It is all about the appearances, though. And funnily enough, the ones wearing the most of those pendants are the richest of all. As I was told by my Chinese friends many people got rich by doing business in "grey zones", which means not entirely legal, so they pray for the inner peace from Buddha's mercy or protection to help them escape divine punishment. They even donate huge amount of money to temples, and that's why monks are so rich...

Why does Chinese booze taste so nasty? – Looking into the drinking culture in China.

Born and bred in Poland, I guess I should have expected that Chinese alcohol would burn my throat, but optimistically (thinking I'd tried it all) I gulped it down like a pro. It felt like my entire oesophagus just landed in hell and was being punished for all my sins. Never before had I tried such a mighty drink. *Baijiu (*白酒*)*, a Chinese white spirit distilled from maize or sorghum, really strikes a chord.

In China, booze is commonly exchanged among business partners as a token of appreciation and hope for a productive cooperation. Even Mao Zedong was known for having given Moutai (*mao tai* = 茅台) brand *bai jiu* to Nixon in 1972. Since there is no legal drinking age in China, 51% of Chinese teenagers admit to have tried alcohol, be it beer or wine, before turning 10. Shocking? Ha. Students know barely anything about the effects drinking can bring to one's health. Most of them believe that only cheap booze can be detrimental, not the expensive one.

No banquet goes without liquor. I have attended a few Chinese weddings, where super pricey alcohol was served. My table happened not to drink one particular night, so the bottle was discretely taken back and, as it was later explained to me, the newlyweds got reimbursed for the unopened bottles afterwards. Another example of what can give one 'face'.

If you closely examine some Chinese paintings, you might notice that the image of a scholar rising a glass of wine is omnipresent. Back in the ancient times wise men's drinking would be seen as seeking inspiration, a muse search. The character for alcohol: 酒 (*jiu*) has water on the left and a fermentation of grain on the right. Previously mentioned newlyweds are required to go around their guests' tables and toast with every single one of them. Nobody can reject that drink since it's called a drink of happiness (喜酒 = *xi jiu*). Try doing it Chinese style: 干杯 (*gan bei*), which means "bottoms up"! According to an old Chinese idiom, when drinking with a close friend even one thousand shots do not suffice (酒逢知己千杯少 = *jiu feng zhi ji qian bei shao*). I think from all different makes of slug I've tried in China, 米酒 (*mi jiu*) or rice wine, would be my favourite. It is a bit sweet and thick, so feels more like swallowing a medicine. There are also 黄酒 (*huang jiu*) or a yellow wine and 烧酒 (*shao jiu*) which literally means fire water. The former is also a kind of rice wine while the latter contains a very high alcohol level. While, at least in my opinion, *shao jiu* tastes like medicinal spirit, *yao jiu* (药酒) actually is a medicine. It has berries or herbs inside or, if you're lucky, snakes or scorpions. Even though Chinese language claims that drunk people speak the truth (酒后吐真言 = *jiu hou tu zhen yan*), an inebriated Chinese man held by his friends on both sides is a rather sad view.

So why does Chinese alcohol taste so awful? I'm no wine connoisseur, but reliable sources report to me that even locally-made grape wine tastes more like a detergent than liquor. The simple answer would be, *bai jiu* resembles vodka but with an extra kick. Being razor hot and full of kerosene flavour, it seems to be serving a better purpose as a warming up drink in freezing winter than any recreational choice. In my country, people who don't have money but like to drink buy ethyl alcohol that is actually unfit for drinking but useful for other purposes, such as unclogging a stuck pipe. We call it 'denaturat'. Once a person starts to drink that, it is just a matter of time when they kick the bucket. In China, blue-collar workers prefer 二锅头 (*er guo tou*), which is a cheaper but not any weaker version of *bai jiu*.

To sum up, Chinese *bai jiu* ranges between 40 and 60% alcohol by volume. Basically, start slow and be gentle to yourself. Don't try to compete with your Chinese counterparts as they will not stop until they drop (literally) so as not to lose face. This white devil will leave you with the most unexpected and most uncomfortable hangover the very next day. So, if you don't have a strong head, try some Chinese beers, which in contrast with the pungent *bai jiu*, taste like flavoured water.

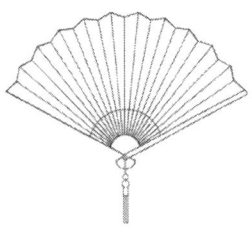

The conundrum of Chinese bamboo.

Bamboo forest, Hangzhou. Image by Karolina Achirri.

It was when I read Coelho's *The Aleph*, where I came across the concept of Chinese bamboo. The author introduces a short fable, which left him puzzled over how one a plant could experience little growth for about five years. You see, the maturation process takes place underground. The system of roots is so complex that only at the end of the fifth year can one shoot out to about twenty-five meters or so. I decided to dig a little deeper into the nature of the plant, following the time-old Chinese proverb: 'When eating bamboo sprouts, remember the men who planted them'.

Apparently, the word bamboo is of Dutch origin (who would have thought?) and is translated into Chinese as 竹子 (*zhu zi*). It can grow up to a meter a day, surpassing all the other plants around it. It quickly reaches for the sky, becoming this magnificent but often intimidating piece of nature.

The growing process has a deep meaning for the Chinese. It signifies a person who is ready to wait for the results of their work. After all, a farmer needs to plant a seed and then water it day by day without noticing any visible changes. It's a clear picture of patience, which we tend to lack nowadays. Life is very much like that. We work, sometimes struggle, often get confused along the way, lose our paths, but those who eventually come out on top are those who patiently wait.

Bamboo has a very important part in Chinese culture and history.

It is the main food for pandas and bamboo-made furniture is commonly seen in China (even bamboo bicycles). Yellow and purple bamboo is also used to make a traditional Chinese gourd-flute (葫芦 = hulusi), which to my Chinese friends' amazement, I learnt how to play a few years back.

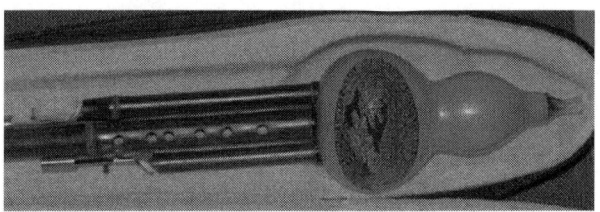

My first bamboo hulusi. Took me a while to master it. Image by Karolina Achirri.

According to Confucius, there are four plants (bamboo, plum blossom, orchid and chrysanthemum = *méi lán zhú jú* = 梅兰竹菊) which represent four seasons and indispensable parts of *jun zi* (君子), the equivalent of an ideal gentleman.

There have been countless poems created through ages to worship bamboo, or rather its features: nobleness, hollow heart, consideration and perseverance. The most famous Song Dynasty literary scholar, who was actually responsible for constructing a pedestrian causeway across the West Lake, Su Shi, wrote a memorable poem entitled *On Qian Seng's Green Bamboo Skin Veranda*, which goes like this:

I would rather eat a meal without meat

than live in a place without bamboo.

Eating without meat makes you lose weight,

but living without bamboo makes you lose refinement.

When a person loses weight, it may be regained,

but when scholars lose refinement they are untreatable.

Others will find these words funny,

seeming lofty and at the same time, crazy.

Ruminate on this carefully if you're wise,

or you'll never ride a crane to Paradise.

There could be so much more said about this enthralling shrub, but I'd like to end with this Zen proverb: *From the pine tree, learn of the pine tree. From the bamboo, learn of the bamboo (chan zong yan yu =* 禅宗谚语).

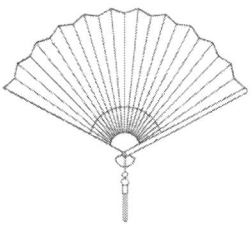

CHAPTER 2

TRADITIONAL SIDE OF CHINA

When a tradition gathers enough strength to go on for centuries, you don't just turn it off one day.

(Chinua Achebe)

"March on!" – China's National Anthem.

Yes, I did learn it. For two reasons. First of all, I felt I needed to include it in my Chinese language learning private curriculum, but also because the school I'm currently employed at performs a flag ceremony every Monday morning (at 7:45!) and I felt stupid standing amongst my students and colleagues silent like a mime. After all, a country's anthem is a door to its patriotic spirit.

It is full of historical victories and melancholic encouragement to always fight for your motherland, even if it means giving up your own life. "March of Volunteers" or "March of the Volunteer Army" (义勇军进行曲 = *yi yong jun jin xing qu*), as its official titles state, was first used on October 1st, 1949, when the People's Republic of China was historically found. Signifying the birth of the new China and encouraging patriots to fight against the Japanese, it quickly spread across the country. It had actually been written 14 years before the PRC's establishment, for a film called "Sons and Daughters of the Storm" by Tian Han. The country's authorities decided to name it the national anthem in 1982, though.

The lyrics go as follows:

起来	qi lai
不愿做奴隶的人们	bu yuan zuo nu li de ren men
把我们的血肉筑成	ba wo men de xue rou zhu cheng
我们新的长城	wo men xin de chang cheng
中华民族到了	zhong hua min zu dao le
最危险的时候	zui wei xian de shi hou
每个人被迫着发出最后的吼声	mei ge ren bei po zhe fa chu zui hou de hou sheng
起来，起来，起来	qi lai, qi lai, qi lai
我们万众一心	wo men wan zhong yi xin
冒着敌人的炮火	mao zhe di ren de pao huo

前进进进   qian jin jin jin

Arise,

Ye who refuse to be slaves!

With our very flesh and blood,

Let us build our new Great Wall!

The peoples of China are in the most critical time,

Everybody must roar his defiance.

Arise, arise, arise!

Millions of hearts with one mind,

Brave the enemy's gunfire, March on!

Brave the enemy's gunfire, March on! March on! March on!

I felt much better when on Monday mornings I could pretend to be one of the builders of the Great Wall☺. Apparently, the anthem can only be performed at chosen arenas, which are vetted and considered distinctive enough by the government. As a foreigner, if you want to impress your Chinese friends (or students), learning this "song" by heart can certainly make it happen.

Beijing Opera.

Simplistically speaking, Beijing Opera （京剧 = *jing ju*） is a form of Chinese theatre which combines music, singing, miming, dancing, acrobatics and martial arts. It pioneered in the 18th century while gained the peak of its popularity in the 19th. I had always been intrigued by it so when I finally made it to Beijing in 2014, I went to see it. I tell you one thing: you have most probably never heard a truly high-pitched voice until you've been to Peking Opera. I thought the roof would be blown away when a lady started singing. Although it makes it hard to sit through it for over two hours, it expresses as much passion as it evokes.

Image by Karolina Achirri.

The Opera has undergone three main stages of blossoming. During Qing Dynasty (19th century), travelling troubadours from Anhui Province came to the capital to perform at the Emperor Qianlong's 80th birthday. The second boom came between 1920s and 1940s, when the art grew to a national scale by applying photography and film making techniques to the performances. Finally, in the 1960s, its revolutionary themes won the audience countrywide, creating a new genre thematically diverse from the original Beijing Opera.

From the very beginning, only men were allowed to perform, pretty much copying the Western notion of women not permitted on stage. In 1772, the emperor made an official ban for females to appear in operas, but his idea slowly faded over the years. It was Shanghai that first employed women to perform in 1894, having been a rebellious city back then. The nationwide ban was lifted in 1911, after the establishment of the Republic of China.

Image by Karolina Achirri.

Interestingly, during the Cultural Revolution, only those pieces compatible with the Party's communist ideals were allowed to be shown. Previous collection of over 1400 shows was cut to only 8, called Eight Model Operas (*Yang Ban Xi* = 样板戏). These were based on stories from the war against the Japanese.

As a synthesis of so many forms of art, Beijing Opera requires a very rigorous training schedule. Draconian methods and corporal punishment to those who did not excel in all walks of the opera, were not uncommon. Before starting, even to this day, artists' capabilities are evaluated based on which their future and unchanged characters are determined. The lead male character is *sheng* (生), who can take on various disguises, including a young man, an old man, a red-faced man, a martial-arts man. As for a woman, the leading role is called *dan* (旦) and can also evolve into other characters, such as a young lady, an old lady, etc. I think the hardest role goes to a painted-face male, called *jing* (净), who needs to perfect all 15 traditional face patterns. As in any good play, there's also a clown, 丑 (*chou*), who can be either military or a civilian. One needs to be extremely versatile to qualify for a role in Beijing opera. Everyone needs to complete a compulsory training in martial arts, which typically takes from 7 to 12 years. The best film to watch for reference would be "Farewell My Concubine" (霸王别姬, or *Ba Wang Bie Ji*) by Kaige Chen, which won the Golden Palm Award on Cannes International Film Festival in 1993.

The stage is fairground, which explains why both orchestra and singers put on a show with such loud piercing melodies. The stage is fairly simple, with one table and two chairs and a curtain hiding the orchestra. I noticed the characters were mainly walking in circles, which (as I learnt later) represents a long journey. If a bard is holding a whip, he's riding a horse. If minstrels' bodies are trembling, they are angry. This form of art is best enjoyed, to my mind, when one has read the explanations of most gestures it displays.

Although the stage lacks props, the actors' richly embellished costumes and colourful masks certainly make up for that. The colours are super bright and each signifies a different thing: yellow is for the emperor, purple for highly ranked officials, blue for low ranked ones; white is for the young characters while brown for the old. The designs of costumes are dazzling, often embroidered with silver and gold. The make-up is also top-notch. It reveals the personality, age, status and the abilities of a character. It is believed to have originated from masks ancient warriors put on when at war, to scare their enemies more effectively. Different colours of the masks carried different meanings as well: red stood for courage, black was always worn by a ruthless character, white by a treacherous one; green meant violence and stubbornness. Masks got replaced with facial make-up with time, which still allows the audience to identify who's the villain and who's the hero in each story.

Image by Karolina Achirri.

Sadly, these days Beijing Opera is not as popular as it used to be. With advanced forms of entertainment popping like mushrooms after rain, it also faces challenges of a prolonged training which puts off many young people from auditioning for it. Even many Chinese people consider it archaic and old-fashioned. When I asked my students whether they've seen it or not, most of them said it's something their parents and grandparents might enjoy, but they have no interest in it whatsoever. Oh well, as any time-honoured type of entertainment, it might need to adjust its ways a bit to appeal to the youth. I really do hope it will see its revival one day.

Chinese calligraphy.

I have been fond of Chinese calligraphy （书法 = *shu fa*) since I saw my dad engraving stamps and making decorative emblems in my childhood. I love letters and writing by hand. I had even insisted on writing this book by hand until I realized it would take me years to actually do so. So, when I had some spare time on my hands, I signed up for calligraphy classes.

Me trying to master the strokes.

There shouldn't be anything odd about the fact that a foreigner wants to have a go at *shu fa*. Well...my experience was a bit weird. My class consisted of me (a blissfully oblivious student) and three kids whose collective age didn't even add up to a half of mine. They had so much fun listening to me trying to communicate with the teacher who (even though he was perfectly capable of) refused to speak English. So, there I was, again. Learning the ropes in the fifth foreign language I was trying to command. Every class my classmates would use a pencil to copy characters written by the teacher, while I would use a brush and ink to basically copy the strokes for an hour and a half. I got frustrated after three months, where I still didn't write anything of value but instead had stacks of papers with single lines on them; most of which, by the way, were not perfect, according to the teacher.

I did, however, get a tattoo in Chinese. It reads *shi li*, which means inner strength. I did a survey among my Chinese friends before I got it, asking them to tell me one characteristic that came to their mind when they thought of me. That's what I got. The funny thing was that the guy at the tattoo parlour wasn't the best advert of his services for when I asked him whether he had any tats himself, he showed me a half of Tweety's head on his calf. He added it was too painful to finish it off☺.

Since it wasn't my first tattoo I still went for it.

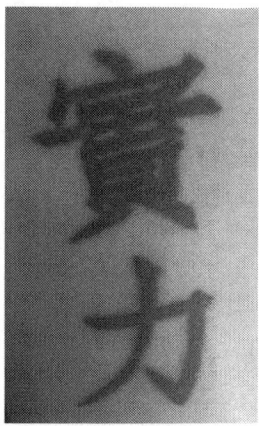

My proudly placed STRENGTH tattoo on my right leg, just above the ankle. I'm happy I didn't end up with the other half of Tweety's head☺.

Back to calligraphy. As an ancient art of Chinese handwriting, Chinese characters seem to cause headache not only to foreigners. It looks easy, but is the exact opposite. Basically, you are supposed to hold a brush and ink it on a rice paper. But there are so many rules and the order of your strokes matters, too.

Originally, in ancient times any form of writing was seen as a way of communicating with spirits so only a shaman was allowed to interpret the meaning of cracked shells (this was where the first written records were found). Later on, only scholars or officials could write and read; hence held authority over illiterate masses.

There are four main writing tools: a writing brush (笔 = *bi*), an inkstick (墨 = *mo*), a rice paper (纸 = *zhi*) and an inkslab (砚 = *yan*). Deep in Chinese beliefs lies the idea that if you read books you will become graceful (腹有诗书气自华 = *fu you shi shu qi zi hua*).

Using the brush is different from using a ballpoint pen. It requires perfect balance between one's mind and body, as it's aimed at revealing the calligrapher's heart to the potential readers. Every calligrapher has their own style and with time might even develop a unique font. Most of the time calligraphy is described as lively and vigorous (龙飞凤舞 = *long fei feng wu*), smooth and affluent (圆润流畅 = *yuan run liu chang*) or gentle and graceful (清和淡雅 = *qing he dan ya*). It is a sacred art to the Chinese. Even though I did not perfect it, it was extremely rewarding and spellbinding to learn the basics.

The rite of foot-binding.

If you had lived between the Tang Dynasty and 1949 in China, you would have known what *chan zu* (缠足) was. Foot-binding would have been your destiny if your feet hadn't grown as soft, straight, small, arched and sweet-smelling. If you were unlucky to have been born with "iron feet", your chances of tying the knot were very slim, too. All of this applied to women only, naturally. All in the name of beauty.

Today, this custom is seen as barbaric and inhuman, but for generations men adored calluses and gnarly bones. "Lotus feet" (三寸金莲 = *san cu jin lian*) in tiny "lotus shoes" were the most desirable fad, pretty much like double-eyelids in contemporary China. The bottom line is trends and fashions change, and thank God they do. Over 3 billion women got their feet tied as this ritual lasted.

There are multiple legends as to how it all started, but the most commonly heard one talks about Emperor Li Yu (李煜, who reigned during the Southern Tang Dynasty from 937 to 975 A.D.) who fell in love with a tiny-footed dancer, Yao Niang. She was performing on a lotus flower with her feet strapped by a piece of cloth. The ruler thought her feet were mesmerizing and much more stunning than the regular-looking ones. From feet looking like those of today's ballerinas', "lotus feet" stemmed. Pretty soon other ladies of the court (first the ones from the upper class and then everybody else) followed suit and then the practice spread to other regions of China.

Bound feet were considered sexy as they forced women to sway with their hips in an alluring manner, tucking their feet into minuscule shoes. It was also a common idea that this way of walking tightened their vaginal muscles. It added to a social status, as those whose feet were bound were publicly showing that their husbands were rich enough, so that they did not have to work themselves.

The whole thing was adopted by almost everyone with the exception of a Man zu (满族) minority group, who never warmed up to it. By the end of the 19ᵗʰ century, practically all women belonging to the higher social stratum were applying foot-binding, followed by over 50% of those from the lower class.

What did foot-binding look like in practice? Well, the first go at it usually happened when a girl was between 3 and 10 years old. Winter days were preferred as the cold was known for numbing the pain, and there was plenty of it. It wasn't the girl's mother who would do it, but a chosen female relative or a professional binder, who would be less empathetic in this long and excruciating procedure. The goal was to crush and tether the feet so that they could fit the petite three-inch lotus shoes. If this was unsuccessful and the feet were still too big, the girl would be considered doomed in finding a husband and a disappointment to the entire family.

First, the feet would be massaged with herbs and liquids, which varied from animal blood and ground monkey bones to urine and incense. Toenails had to be clipped to prevent their growth in the future and toes were twined towards the sole of the foot. This could either be a natural process or a forced one, where the toes would be broken, depending on the young lady's age. The big toe, however, was always left alone and continued growing straight. Then, the foot arch would be broken too, and after the application of a special powder called *alum*, bandaged with a ten-feet-long-strip. The fabric was tightly sewn at the end to stop the girl from any attempts at undoing the bundle.

The ideal lump, which was the result of the binding, would be able to hold several coins. The girls were not given any sick leave or extra time to rest, but had to carry on with business as usual until their feet framed into a desired shape. It is estimated that one tenth of them died, most of the time due to gangrene and other untreated infections. Some also lost their toes at last. The pain from this experience is reported as tormenting and intolerably intense. If a girl survived the agonizing rite, her lotus shoes would be shown to a prospective husband and his family before any further talks of a marriage.

As time went by, this practice began to picture China negatively in other country's eyes, so the government officially banned it in 1949. The remnant ladies with *chan zu* can still be spotted in *Liu yi cun* (六一村), which is a remote hamlet in Yunnan Province in China. Being a woman myself, what we are willing to do for the sake of beauty never stops to amaze me.

The Games of China.

<u>Mah-jong (麻将 = *ma jiang*) = old ladies' pastime?</u>

The only Chinese game I learnt during my stay. My students made it their mission to explain its intricacies to me and they were really excited to do so in English. I even got a bamboo mah-jong set nicely wrapped in a small suitcase as a gift from them.

To be good at this game, one needs as much luck as skill. It looks similar to 'rummy' at first glance, so if you've ever tried that one back home you should be able to learn the ins and outs of mah-jong in no time. The only noticeable difference is the fact that cards are replaced by tiles made of plastic, bamboo or ivory, with the latter being the most pricey one. So it looks like a game of domino but works like a game of cards, really.

Image by Karolina Achirri.

Mah-jong has a very long history in China. Some claim it was invented by Confucius around 500 BC, as three dragon tiles depict three virtues taught by the philosopher, namely benevolence, sincerity and filial piety. A lot of contemporaries use it to gamble, and quite often fall into huge debts due to their bad luck. It typically consists of 136 tiles (all based on Chinese characters or pictograms). Different regions have their own versions. I learnt how to play Hangzhou mah-jong, which means I would probably not be able to go against a Beijinger.

In a nutshell, each player gets 13 tiles. One by one players then draw and discard them until they are able to form a full hand (by using tile number 14 to create four melds and a head). If you know four main suits in an ordinary deck of cards (hearts, clubs, diamonds and spades), you will be able to categorize three main suits of mah-jong: *bing* (饼), bamboo (索 = *suo*) and *wan* (万). *Bing* resembles Moon Cakes (traditional snack eaten at Mid-Autumn Festival in China) a lot, *bamboo* is usually drawn as a sparrow (some critics claim it is to commemorate the alleged inventor – Confucius - who loved birds), *wan* is believed to stand for "character" which the Chinese see as one of the main foreigners' attributes. There are also four winds: north (北 = *bei*), south (南 = *nan*), east (东 = *dong*) and west (西 = *xi*). Apart from that we have three dragon tiles: one red *zhong* (中), one green *fa* (發) and one white rectangle (白板 = *bai ban*).

You must play this diversion at a square table, so four players can enjoy it. Whoever sits on the east side starts the game (a dice is usually rolled to decide who gets to begin). The tiles must be facing down the table and should be shuffled around with both hands. As I was told by my students (who were my actual teachers in this case), everyone needs to build a wall on their side of the table which will be joining their neighbours' walls to create a castle. Then, the madness begins. No matter how hard my students were trying to explain the rules to me, I kept losing every single game. Oh well, I was never a gambler anyways. All in all, the ultimate goal is to get 14 tiles (13 already possessed and 1 won over from the opponents). There are also some other commands one is supposed to shout out during playing, but I never knew when to shout which one so I ended up keeping quiet (probably losing my turn quite a few times☺). I did not worry about the points as much as I wanted to grasp the merriment itself. I did. I finally won, six months later. I am not sure my students didn't forfeit it, though.   My point is, even if you can't fully comprehend what's going on in the game, play it anyways and learn as you go. Most Chinese people would be more than happy to teach you a few tricks up their sleeves.

Chinese Chess (象棋 = *xiang qi*).

If you think you know how to play chess, think again. *Xiang qi* can puzzle anyone. The board is square and split in half by a river. Some pieces must always stay on one side, as to "defend" the home. There is also a palace on each side and the General, together with his Advisors, cannot under any circumstances leave the vicinity.

The way pieces are placed also differs from the Western version of the game as they move from one intersection to another. There are commonly 16 pieces in a set, all wooden and of a squat drum shape. On one side they have red characters while on the other black or green ones.

As far as the General is concerned, he can move one square forward but can never leave the castle. It holds 'commander' (帅 = *shuai*) in red on one side and 'king' (将 = *jiang*) on its reverse. His Advisors have a red 仕 (*shi*) and a green 士 (*shi*), which mean 'official' and 'scholar', respectively. Also worth mentioning are The Elephants and Ministers, The Horses as well as The Chariots.

Image by Karolina Achirri.

Since it is a Chinese game, the red army always begins the war. The aim is to attack the enemy and conquer their castle. The General, just like The King in the Western chess, has to be protected at all cost. It's a common view to spot men slouching over a board of chess, usually in parks and gardens. Even though only two players are allowed at a time, they manage to draw attention of passers-by who are eager to cheer them on.

Cards (纸牌 = *zhi pai*).

China loves a good game of cards. It might be related to a widespread vice of getting easily addicted to gambling, but more probably it's because it allows people to interact and simply spend quality time together.

The Chinese can play cards anytime and literally anywhere. I've seen groups organizing themselves on a train, in parks, on a long-distance coach, in hotel rooms during trips and even in queues at train stations (trying to kill time). There are so many varieties of card games in the Middle Kingdom that I got lost after the first few minutes someone tried to enlighten me. I only managed to master *Dou Di Zhu* (斗地主) which translates as "Fighting the Landlord", where three people try to rid themselves of all their cards in order to win. It starts with the gamers bidding for the spot of a Landlord, but the less fortunate ones continue to shuffle as Peasants. Needless to say, I've always ended up a bumpkin☺.

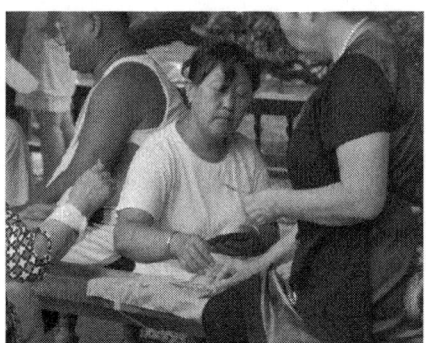

Image by Karolina Achirri.

What strikes me every time I either observe this recreational sport or play it myself, is the passion with which Chinese people play cards. I won twice, still not sure whether it was a legitimate win or the locals wanted me to feel better. But ehh, you know what they say: unlucky in cards, lucky in love!

Karaoke in China is not what you think.

Imagine a dim club with a scary-looking stage in the middle. Imagine crowds of slightly (or highly) tipsy people. Imagine yourself on that stage, behind the microphone trying to battle your fears and overcome your shyness. Imagine yourself sing. Wait! That's not what a karaoke club in China looks like at all.

Going out to sing songs with friends is one of the main social activities, seen as great fun and bonding time. No one needs to get humiliated trying to stay in tune. It's a completely different game.

I love singing, but I do not sing in public. The only few instances I made an exception happened in a church, singing psalms. I dread standing in front of an audience (how on Earth do I pull off teaching?) and lime lights blind me. When my Chinese friends invited me to a KTV for the first time, I was so relieved. 卡啦 OK (*ka la ok*), as the homonym of karaoke, offers private rooms, so you only get to sing with and in front of those who know you and can stand your voice. While Western karaoke is associated with heavy drinking, in China it is a respectable pastime. Everyone takes their singing very seriously, bending backwards to sing their hearts out. There are some light beers or soft drinks and definitely loads of snacks, but people tend to sing karaoke sober.

A typical room can accommodate between 5 and 20 people. There are also VIP lounges available which offer private servers and unlimited time and attention, including unrestricted access to the bar. In a typical club, rooms are charged per hour and afternoons have lower rates than evenings (yes, some team building activities take place in broad daylight in China). Inside an average room you will find sofas, a huge coffee table, an electronic console for choosing songs, microphones (both wireless and standing) and some games (mostly Chinese dice). The songs are arranged alphabetically and can be searched by artists, titles or both. You would be surprised how immense the selection of English songs is. You create a queue with songs chosen by each member of your crew and you are ready to rock. The thing that has always made me mad is the fact that famous and easy Chinese songs, which a foreigner learning Chinese would be able to belt out, always have traditional Chinese characters so one ends up with their phone and *pin yin* screening of lyrics. Videos are another story. Each song has a background video, but the trick is they are not the original videos from the artists. So, if enjoying a low-end establishment (an older KTV), you might have to sing *The Beatles'* song to the views of a sexy model on a Spanish beach.

A lot of foreigners I know strongly dislike KTV. But I think they are not giving it a chance it deserves. Even if you were not given the greatest vocal talent from God, singing with Chinese friends (especially simple Chinese songs) creates a special bond between you, bridging our cultures at odds. Fact is, the selection of songs in English is a bit bizarre, as it ranges from *Backstreet Boys* through *Westlife* to *The Rolling Stones*. The tunes are usually not the ones one might have got accustomed to when young and restless. Different foreign songs hit the Chinese charts from those well-known back home.

Why is karaoke such a popular venture in China? I would say it's because the Chinese tend to be quiet, modest and discreet in both private and professional lives. Singing (especially in a circle of trusted friends) gives them an opportunity to loosen up as well as show off. And who doesn't like some *extra face*. I cannot express the pride I saw on my Chinese friends' faces when I bravely sang a Chinese lullaby for the first time. Everyone was cheering me on like it was the Eurovision contest or I was about to be crowned as "the winner of the Voice of China". I am an avid fan of music and as much as it helped me in learning English many years back, I find it both enjoyable and challenging to sing in Chinese.

So, if you want to understand China and make real friends with the Chinese, tune up and embrace the mic.

What does your name mean? – The story behind Chinese names.

Have you ever thought why there are so many *Wangs* 王 (Kings) in China? In the 50s, lots of people were named *Wei guo* 卫国 (to protect a country), *Jian jun* 建军 (to establish an army) or *Jian guo* 建国 (to found a country). Having a patriotic name was a fad. Later in the 60s, every other baby was given *red* (红= *hong*) as a part of their name to celebrate China's colour of revolution. Before all that naming had been a lot simpler. If you were born with a mole on your arm, you'd simply be called "black arm". Today, on the other hand, everyone wants to be fashionable and unique when labelling their offspring. Westernized names have come to play as well as their homonyms in Chinese. Also, women in China don't normally take on their husbands' surnames, but those who do create a much longer option for their potential children. So, that's how Chinese names got prolonged.

Typically, Chinese names consist of three syllables: one syllable for a family name and two for a given name. Of course, all of them are then written in characters and carry a specific tone. Only some members of ethnic minorities would have four or more syllables to their names. I guess that's why I was given 李娜娜 (*Li Nana*), a new three-syllable name. I've been going by it ever since.

The idea behind a good name is all about prosperity and success. In Chinese eyes, one called 'luck', 'fortune' or 'gold' is bound to become a millionaire. That's a bit odd to a foreigner, who would think that success in life has more to do with determination and hard work than a name itself.

The order of names in China follows the Eastern tradition of starting with the family name preceding the given name. That's somewhat a problem for students planning to go abroad. We have to constantly remind students at my school to write their Chinese names in a Western style as their exam papers will be sent and marked overseas. Commonly, Chinese people also address one another by their full names, so I kept hearing Li Nana before a conversation is started.

Following the Five Elements philosophy (gold, wood, water, fire and earth), all of these must be balanced to provide a good life. When a child is born, it is assigned a particular element (based on the calculations of the birth's year, month, day and hour). It often happens that there will be a lack of one in favour of another. In such case, the name would need to include one of the missing elements to assure equilibrium, i.e. if you're lacking water you can be almost certain to receive water in your name. Some parents these days even schedule an emergency caesarean section to make sure their baby is born at the right (prosperous) time.

It goes without saying that fortune tellers have been making huge profits from naming children. Not only must the elements be provided, but also the number of strokes in a Chinese character representing a name needs to match a specific element.

Nowadays, the way Chinese people choose names is highly affected by the obsession with English. If you're called a butterfly, the *pin yin* version of it will be looking like the word 'die' in English. Other surnames like 'Lie' (列), meaning *a list*; 'He' (鹤) representing *a crane*, or 'Xing' (星) meaning *a star*; are just too hard for foreigners to say or comprehend.

I was given my Chinese name by a colleague at my first school. To her, 李娜 (*Li Nana*) sounded close enough to Karolina and I liked it because it's similar to a Chinese tennis star's name: 李娜 (*Li Na*), whose personality I appreciate. Also, I have made use of it for my Taobao account, causing shocks on every delivery man's face once I open the door to receive a package. They just don't believe that it is me☺. I also used it for my Chinese driver's license as my real name was too long to fit the system. Having a Chinese name is helpful. Not everyone speaks English and my name isn't English anyways. Expecting a Chinese person to pronounce a Slavic 'r' properly is a bit of a stretch, too.

When choosing a Chinese name, a foreigner should try a variety of tricks. Ask your trusted Chinese friends to help you out with that. Decide whether you want a real Chinese name or a 'foreigner' Chinese name (which would be a version of your English name written in Chinese characters based on the sound similarity). Make sure you choose characters that have a positive meaning. You don't want to be seen as 'death' (死 = *si*) or 'ghost' (鬼 = *gui*) in your Chinese friends' eyes. Make sure your Chinese name follows the appropriate gender as well. A name in China is something that defines you and to the Chinese it is supposed to reveal your personality. William Shakespeare doubted the significance of a name when he wrote: *"What's in a name? That which we call a rose; By any other name would smell as sweet"* (in *Romeo and Juliet*).

I wonder if we need names because we don't know who we are without them.

The infamous square dancing.

A few years ago nobody heard of *square dancing*. Now, if you've lived in China and not heard of it, you can consider yourself extremely lucky. Even my American friends told me some angered neighbours in the US tend to call the police reporting disturbances provided by 'the dancing grannies'. This rapidly spreading pastime even got its own Wikipedia entry now.

I think it is safe to say that *guang chang wu* (广场舞), or plaza dancing, has become China's new national sport. Many despise it, since it regularly disturbs peace and quiet, especially if one lives in a community with a square. Others hate the music in particular, as it's very loud and annoyingly repetitive. I've learnt to always have my earplugs at hand, regardless of where I was in China.

The main culprits of this pastime are middle-aged and retired ladies, who eagerly await evenings when they can jump into their tight dancing outfits to perform recently learnt routines. It is estimated that square dancing has over 100 million members, and these are only the officially registered ones. It is a good way to exercise and stay slim for the Chinese, hence I've seen kids and older gentlemen join them as well.

As for me, the layman observer, the routines are quite complicated. Once I got pulled into the troops and couldn't follow for long. It basically looked like a super long aerobics class with a mega baffling choreography. The most renowned dance, created for President Xi, got nationwide attention not only due to its convoluted moves but also because it incorporated patriotic elements. Check out the lyrics to the accompanying music:

Daddy Xi, Daddy Xi
On every street they sing his praises
He seeks happiness for all
He speaks the truth for the common
> *Daddy Xi, Daddy Xi*
> *Everyone loves him*
> *Full of energy and courage*
> *He attacks both tigers and flies*
Daddy Xi, Daddy Xi
All the Chinese support him
He's great at military strategies
And serves China with fierce devotion
> *Daddy Xi, Daddy Xi*
> *People of the whole world love and respect him*
> *All nations live peacefully together*
> *Striding to develop together!*

Who wouldn't want to dance to such a tune☺? I'm shaking a leg right now.

The problems start to crop up when the dancers don't take space or time into any consideration. Over twenty grannies once decided to perform on a night sleeper from Dalian to Shanghai. You can imagine that the other passengers weren't over the moon. On another occasion, a group of highly determined "damas" pushed the car out of their way to gain space on 'their' square to dance. One dance-off in Yunnan ended with dogs chasing after the running ladies (who had refused to stop despite the public's pleads) and poo being thrown at them. Desperate times call for desperate measures, I guess.

These days, with regard to public complaints, the government is trying to crack down the prancing shows. Xi'an Noise Pollution Police has already imposed a fine of RMB 500 (around $77) on anyone attempting to swing in public. Most people don't mind the ubiquitous phenomenon per se, they simply want some serenity. Those who view the unstoppable matrons as an embarrassment to the Chinese culture, should perhaps peek at the spitting elderly men or nose-picking relaxed passengers. Which one sounds more mortifying?

Would you like a cuppa? – Tea culture.

I am an avid coffee lover, but I did try most of Chinese tea types. I particularly liked those having medicinal attributes, such as releasing kidney stones or calming an upset stomach. Many times green tea also saved me from going bananas in the midst of stress and work pressure. Tea fields are so picturesque that one just wants to pitch a tent there and become a Nomad.

Longjing tea near West Lake, Hangzhou. Image by Karolina Achirri.

It was China that discovered that tea leaves can be used to make a drink as well in about 3000 BC. According to one legend, *Shen Nong* (神农) was boiling water one day when a few tea leaves dropped into his cup from the tree. A character for tea, 茶 (*cha*), seems to depict a person standing beneath grass but above a tree. There is a sophisticated tea culture in China, where the way tea is drunk and prepared matters. Tea brewing ceremony allows people to interact with each other. Tea houses are very popular spots for friends to chat away over a cup of freshly brewed tea as much as serve as great business talk venues. One can see Chinese people carrying their bottles with tea leaves floating inside on a daily basis. One serving can be brewed three to four times. A super renowned book by *Lu Yu* (陆羽) from Tang Dynasty, called *Canon of Tea* (茶经 = *cha jing*), can teach you about different tea types, how to grow tea, how to prepare it, which utensils to use and even how to analyse water. Actually, tea planting is not an indigenous process in China. It is believed to have been imported from India in 543 AD by a missionary named Bodhidharma, or *Da Mo* (达摩).

What is tea ceremony (茶道 = *cha dao*)? It is an artistic way of appreciating the drink. Not only does it function as a ritual but also as a form of relaxation. Literally, it is a way of savouring life (品味人生 = *pin wei ren sheng*). 泡茶 (*pao cha*), which means brewing tea, makes a gripping spectacle, too. I could observe it for hours.

Tea brewing in a tea house, Yunnan Province. Image by Karolina Achirri.

Westerners tend to brew bags of tea, while the Chinese use more tools for that. You'd need a tea pot (茶壶 = *cha hu*), tureen (盖碗杯 = *gai wan bei*), and a big bowl (大碗 = *da wan*), as presented in the photo above. Apparently, porcelain and purple clay (*zi she* = 紫砂) make the best pots. The table on which the tea master is serving the drink is called 茶几 (*cha ji*), or a tray of tree roots. Don't forget to warm both cups and tea pot before using them as it is supposed to evoke a stronger aroma. It is also very important to conduct a light conversation (闲谈 = *xian tan*) while waiting for tea to be ready. Since tea symbolizes nature, talking while drinking means one is reaching harmony between man and nature. There's even an idiomatic expression claiming that an ideally tranquil atmosphere of relaxation can be felt during tea drinking process (清和淡雅 = *qing he dan ya*). It's also crucial to be aware of different steps of tea appreciation. First, observe its colour (茶色 = *cha se*), then smell the aroma (闻香 = *wen xiang*) of freshly mown grass, and finally taste it (品茶 = *pin cha*). One cup of tea, therefore, can be perfect only if enjoyed in those three sips.

There are so many types of tea in China that one can easily lose count and get confused, especially if one is a foreigner. I would like to briefly introduce a few of them here, those that accompanied my daily life for six years in China; and hopefully will stay on the menu in my future endeavours.

White tea (白茶 = *bai cha*). Most of the leaves have white or greyish colour with some fuzzy hairs on it. Has the highest antioxidant content since it comprises of newest leaves. Actual tea turns out to be of a very pale green or yellow shade. It tastes delicate.

Green tea (绿茶 = *lv cha*). It requires a multi-stepped preparation process, which includes fixing, steaming, pan-firing, drying, rolling and curling. Since this type of tea is not fermented, it is full of a refreshingly raw flavour. Hangzhou's *Longjing tea* (also called Dragon Well tea = 龙井茶) is its most reputable representative. Locals told me the best-tasting green tea is produced from leaves gathered in early April. This batch can be even five times more expensive than the regular *Longjing* (gathered at different times). It is green or yellow in colour, with a variety of flavours ranging from sweet to grassy.

I love the smell of freshly made tea, even if it's not brewed yet. (Yunnan Province, October 2015)

Oolong tea (乌龙茶 = *wu long cha*). This one is notable for its lingering aftertaste (回味 = *hui wei*). Even after seven refills one can still taste its strong and rich zest. It can be coloured from green to almost black. It is mostly drunk in the Kung-fu style tea set, which means cups are tiny allowing for sipping, reminding me of a doll party. The best variety, called 铁观音 (tie guan yin) is often compared with a breath-taking musical performance, where the notes fill the air long after the audience is gone.

Black tea (红茶 = *hong cha*). I have always racked my brain over why they call it black if the name clearly states red. Often has the strongest flavour, which is why many Westerners like to add sugar, lemon or milk to it; which leaves Chinese people gobsmacked. My favourite black tea has a pinch of honey in its taste. It comes from Wu Yi Mountains, in Fujian Province. Remember to use boiling water for this one. It is also widely believed that black tea produces elements advantageous to the stomach.

Pu-Erh tea (普洱茶 = *pu er cha*). The process of making it is pretty similar to that of green tea, but *pu-erh tea* needs to be fermented for many years. The oldest one I have tried was over 60 years old. This tea is usually sold in a form of pressed cakes, such as the one in the photo below.

Pressed cake of Pu-Erh tea, Yunnan Province. Image by Karolina Achirri.

Since this tea type is famed for its dietary powers, my sister has been obsessed with it ever since she came to visit me in China. Its taste is very rich and earthy, but smooth at the same time. I only drink it to soothe my stomach. The tea I bought and photographed is believed to be able to reduce radiation in the body from mobiles or computers. Leaves should be washed a few times before brewing in boiling water. It is best to use a clay pot and this tea can be used from eight to fifteen times. After this tea is picked from the tree, it is sun dried, twisted and then compressed into bricks. It is its exposure to air that makes it aged enough. TCM believes *pu er cha* strengthens *yang* energy (阳气). That's why many people told me to drink Longjing in summer, but Pu 'er in winter.

Jujube tea (枣茶 = *zao cha*). I was given this tea by a Chinese colleague who was trying to convince me that it works miracles during menstruation periods. It balances female hormones and adds to your skin's softness. It's good to add ginseng to it, as they can improve your mood and energy levels when mixed.

There are also many flowery teas in China, which I personally do not fancy that much. They smell and taste like a dissolved perfume to me. Going to a teahouse is definitely a must. The host would be more than happy to introduce all sorts of teas to you for free and then suggest your best match. A commonly used metaphor: 人走茶凉 (*ren zou cha liang*), depicts the art of tea in China perfectly. It means once a guest leaves, their tea will cool; when an official is removed from his/her position, they will receive a cold shoulder from people since they won't be able to grant them any more favours.

The Chinese flag.

Like the Chinese anthem, the first time the country's official flag was displayed to the public was on October 1ˢᵗ, 1949, when the new China was created. The government had asked for suggestions from the public through an advert in a newspaper, which resulted in more than 4900 designs flooding the office.

The Chinese flag looks very simple to the untrained eye, consisting of only five yellow stars on a red background. It is often called "five-starred red flag" (五星红旗 = *wu xing hong qi*). It was Mao Zedong himself who waved it for the first time at Tiananmen Square back in 1949.

The flag's designer was Zeng Liansong, an artist and an economist, who had removed stripes placed at the bottom of the final version so as not to evoke the images of rivers Yangtze, Yellow and Pearl; since they would mean the nation is torn apart.

So what do these five stars on a China flag actually mean?

After some investigation I have learnt that the large star stands for the Communist Party of China, or the PRC leaders. According to Mao's division of the society, the four small starts were meant to signify the four social strata the Chairman recognized at societal pillars, namely the workers, the peasants, the petite bourgeoisie from the cities and the national bourgeoisie (mainly business people). However, when Mao's era ended, the stars' meaning changed. From then on they were supposed to represent the farmers, the workers, the teachers and finally the soldiers. Today, on the other hand, whomever I've asked said they see the workers, farmers, intellectuals and businesspeople in the stars. I guess it all depends on the times we live on.

Its red colour, of course, symbolizes the communist revolution and is considered the national colour of China. It transcends power and perseverance. It reminds people that China can be undefeatable and can rule the world one day. Michio Kaku, a Japanese professor, even said: "In 2015, don't be surprised if a Chinese flag is placed on the moon." Didn't happen, though.

By looking into the history of this flag's evolution one can grasp the political and social changes in the Middle Kingdom.

Traditional Chinese musical instruments.

I fell in love with traditional musical instruments in China since the minute I saw a street performer play *gu zheng*. He was actually playing Adele's hit *Rolling in the Deep* that day. I thought the combination of a classic sound and a contemporary melody was a brilliant tune. I have wanted to learn how to play at least one Chinese apparatus ever since. I did succeed two years ago, when I bought a *hu lu si* (葫芦丝) and signed up for actual classes with a Chinese teacher. It was fun but a challenging fun since the teacher could not speak a word of English and I couldn't engage in convoluted conversations about making music. So, I decoded what she was telling me and designed my own language of *hu lu si*. The moment I was able to play my first ancient song, I recorded it and felt like I had just played the most complicated sonata. Who would have thought I'd be able to play a

Chinese cucurbit flute one day. Nothing is impossible. This is my very own *hu lu si*:

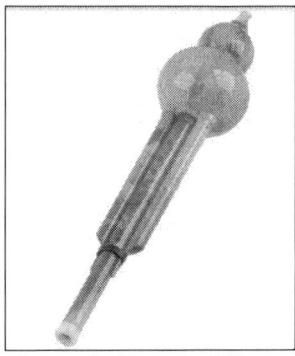

Image by Yunqing Xiang.

It was Confucius who brought music to its finest. He claimed music calms passions and lust, so its practical use was of his focus rather than its entertaining properties. The history of traditional Chinese music is long and complex, but I'd like to introduce a few of the most interesting instruments here.

There are eight basic materials (八音 = *ba yin*) which build musical instruments in China: silk (丝 = *si*), bamboo (竹 = *zhu*), wood (木 = *mu*), stone (石 = *shi*), metal (金 = *jin*), clay (土 = *tu*), gourd (匏 = *pao*) and hide (革 = *ge*).

From the stringed instruments (弦乐器 = *xian yue qi*), represented by silk, I really love *er hu* (二胡). It sounds extremely sad but has an amazing breath-taking tone. It simply lets one imagine the story behind the song. It's both subtle and decisive at the same time. Although it's most likely to be used at funerals, due to its melancholy, it clicks with my soul. In the ancient times actual silk was used to make the strings, but these days they are made out of metal or nylon. In English *er hu* would be called a spike fiddle or a Chinese two-stringed fiddle. It can be used as a solo instrument or a part of an orchestra. Liu Tianhua (刘天华) (1895-1932) was a pioneer of vibrato for *er hu*, which he learnt from observing skills needed to play Western musical instruments, actually.

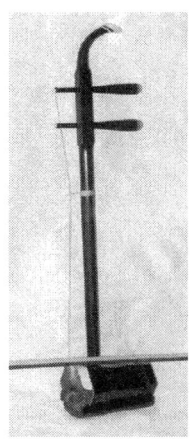

Image from https://commons.wikimedia.org/wiki/File:Erhu.png.

Another instrument that really captured my attention is *gu zheng* (古筝), commonly called a Chinese zither. This plucked instrument has over 2500 years of history and if that's not impressive enough, one needs to wear finger picks (preferably on both hands) to perform on it. It has a rectangular shape made of wood with resonating strings stretched. Every time I hear or see it, it's used solo. Thanks to being tuned to a variety of pitches, it produces a spellbinding sound. Some think of it as "an oriental piano". The only reason why I didn't choose to learn the ropes about *gu zheng* was the fact it was far too big for my flat. It practically requires as much space as an electrical piano. However, it also makes an amazing piece of decorative art, displaying a unique relationship between calligraphy and painting.

Then there is *pi pa* (琵琶), or the Chinese lute. It drew my attention for two reasons, first being the fact that its name (*pi pa*) in Polish stands for a derogatory version of a "lady part"☺ and secondly because I can already play the guitar. *Pi pa* does remind me of a guitar, only its more distinctive form. The name *pi pa* can be used with reference to other plucked instruments of a similar kind, such as *yue qin* (月琴), which literally means *moon guitar*. I found a few odes to *pi pa* in ancient Chinese poetry where its delicate tone is worshipped. The instrument has been changed by its players over generations. Today, it is held vertically, with the right hand strumming while left hand fretting the strings. It's the most expressive Chinese instrument, I reckon.

When I read a book about Mongolian culture, I discovered *ma tou qin* (马头琴), *Morin khuur*, or a *horse-head fiddle*. It is a string instrument indispensable for Mongolians. It reminds me of a violin, since it has a long wooden frame with two strings attached to it, but it has a trapezoidal sound-board. With its deep, mellow sound, it has a power to transport one to the valleys full of cattle and shepherds guarding them. Its name actually stems from a folk story of a shepherd boy who lost his pony. To commemorate his animal friend, he made it from horse's bones (for the neck) and hair (for the strings). At the top of the frame he placed a sculpture of a horse's head. That's how the first *Morin khuur* was created. The most famous Mongolian Long Song is usually gorgeously played expressing the freedom of the people of the endless grasslands, their emotions as well as mundane sounds accompanying them every day, such as shepherd's singing or the clip-clop of their horses' hooves.

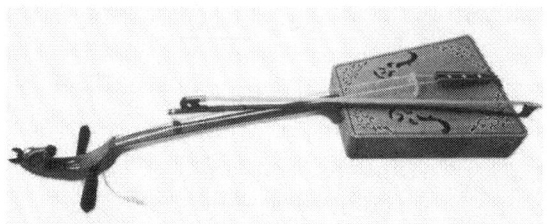

Image by Yunqing Xiang.

The last instrument I would like to mention is *suo na* (唢呐), or *la ba* (喇叭). It is a type of pipe with a loud and extremely high-pitched sound. Actually, it came to China from Persia and gained its popularity in 16th century. It looks pretty much like a Western trumpet, only thinner. When Luciano Pavarotti visited China in 1986, he tried it out, too. It is commonly used on special occasions, namely funerals or weddings. Some people can't stand it, due to the squeaky tone it gets at the top of the octave, but I like it because it evokes very colourful emotions in me. If I had better lungs, I might have picked it to learn.

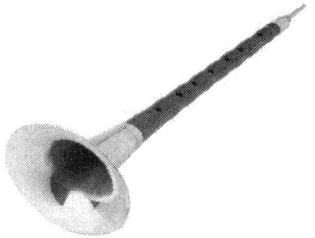

Image by Yunqing Xiang.

To conclude, Chinese musical instruments are surely fascinating, with their symbolic characters. The bells give out a clanging sound as a signal, the strings express melancholic purity, the bamboo instruments sound like a flow of water and the drums encourage one to move. I have to agree with Beethoven here, who smartly stated that "music in truth, is the mediator between intellectual and sensuous life". There's nothing more truthful than a sound of a traditional Chinese musical instrument.

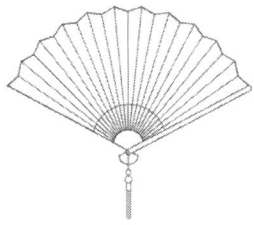

Why do so many people walk backwards? On Chinese martial arts.

If you've been to China already, you must have seen it. A few elderlies here or there walking backwards, usually at the exact same time (some ungodly hour like 5:30am), in the exact same place. If you've not seen it yet, embrace yourself for a puzzling view. It is a traditional belief that walking backwards balances one's *qi*, or life force within. According to science, walking backwards burns more calories than waking forward and has proven helpful with alleviating lower back pains and strengthening abdominal muscles. Also, shockingly, it is supposed to help your brain grow new neural connections as it helps you snap out of a boring routine. I have tried it once. Imagine the looks I got on one of the main streets of Hangzhou, when I briskly strolled backwards out of the subway station. An experience worth its weight in gold.

It is usually the elderly one can spot outside "working out". They don't lift weights or jog, but walk or stretch. Most parks have also been equipped with metal gym amenities, making such places centres of social lives for the old. Once I hiked one of the neighbouring hills by West Lake, in Hangzhou. An over-the-hill looking lady (might have been in her late 60s), raced to the top and stopped by almost every tree to apply some Kung fu-kind moves. We could not keep up with her. I did manage to snap a photo, though.

Image by Karolina Achirri.

China's street-life booms with the old people, who arrive first and leave last. Sword dance, *Tai Chi* or square dance (广场舞 = *guang chang wu*) are only a few of their favourite activities keeping them in the pink. There's a senior lady in my community, who, come hail or rain, every single morning plays some exotic music loudly in our square and practices *Tai Chi*. As a night owl, I admire her determination and the ability to wake up before dawn.

What I know about *Tai Chi* (太极拳 = *tai ji quan*) hangs on what I've observed and was told by those who practice it. Its holistic approach to health is currently winning over the hearts of many Americans, too. A perfect balance between the body and mind are of great importance. Such balance can only be gained through a series of slow and very elegant movements, which not only improve one's coordination but also burn calories. Many people I know praise its ability to significantly reduce stress. Some practice alone while others join groups. I was told half an hour a day of smooth *tai qi* movements through an extended period can really help one's inner serenity. Daily exercises would require lots of work on one's balance and body posture. It is still a mystery to me, though, why it needs to be done so early in the day.

Another form of staying fit is a breathing exercise technique called *qi gong* (气功 = *qi gong*). There seem to be over 3000 different forms of *qi gong* today. Beginners, like myself, are advised to start with "Eight pieces of silk brocade", or 八段锦 (*ba duan jin*). This method is a routine of eight simple gestures which take under 10 minutes to complete. It's not about moving vigorously at all; it's about letting one's *qi* flow. Allowing the energy pass unobstructed through one's body is the main focus here. The West has been obsessed with mindfulness for ages, but China has had this simple way to self-regulate one's thoughts through breathing. According to my traditional medicine doctor, dr. Joy, *qi gong* does have some rules to follow: stay natural and relaxed, combine the dynamic with the static, direct your *qi* with the mind, proceed step by step. It resembles "meditation in slow motion" as my Chinese friend likes to call. We should all try it; it is claimed to turn pessimists into hopeful ones.

Can't skip *zhan zhuang*. It looks ridiculous at first, as all one is doing is to stand like a pole, with knees slightly bent, and allow the body to relax. Can you imagine that? It doesn't sound like a comfortable position at all, does it? However, standing still might prove harder than you think. Our lives are so dynamic these days that we barely ever stand still, *so zhan zhuang* can activate muscles we forgot we had.

A real martial art I simply adore in *kung-fu* (功夫= *gong fu*). I have been a fan of Kung-fu panda for years and even before I came to China, as a little dumb kind, I had always dreamt of becoming one of the Shaolin (少林) boys (now I obviously realize this dream never stood a chance☺). According to an old kung-fu saying it is "better to sweat in practice than to bleed in battle". I have yet to try my luck at kung-fu, but my fascination with it never seized. What attracts me most is the morality code involved in it. There are morality of deed and morality of mind to be indisputably followed. When dealing with others, either the master or co-students, one needs to present politeness, humility, loyalty, sincerity and trust. Also, in order to obtain personal growth, one needs to stay courageous, perseverant and patient. All these traits must be in an ideal harmonic rapport. Since kung-fu is attack-oriented, one must know how to control themselves as to not hurt the innocent. For these reasons, many masters choose their disciples carefully, for they will become the most upright people upon training completion.

I must say that watching a show of martial arts gives me goose bumps. During my trip to Beijing, it was the highlight of my time in the capital, surpassing the climbing of the Great Wall.

Paper Cutting.

As the name suggests, it is cut by the use of very sharp scissors. Beautiful shapes and motifs create an atmosphere of mystery as well as folklore. When I was in a primary school, we learnt how to make a much simpler version of it, but nothing so spectacular as Chinese Paper Cutting (剪纸 = *jian zhi*). This little art is brought up to a whole new level in China. The designs are amazing, precise and very complex.

It is true that the most common themes are birds, flowers, bamboos or ancient gods. They are all supposed to bring luck and prosperity and rid of all evils at the same time. When Spring Festival approaches, one can notice them everywhere proudly decorating windows and doors. They fascinate me. Not only due to their extraordinary explicitness and attention to detail but also thanks to their stunning ideas. The most amazing ones, I reckon, are those which made lanterns back in Ming Dynasty. Their patterns would be so visibly stellar as lit by a candle light.

As commonly known, paper was invented by Cai Lun (蔡伦) in China's Eastern Han Dynasty (*dong han* = 东汉). Today, *jian zhi* cannot be missing from any Chinese wedding or a new flat. It is also a great choice of hobby for those who are agile around blades. The ones that depict Mother Nature, called 窗花 (*chuang hua*) or 'window flowers', beautify surfaces all around China. The designs are made mostly in red, since that's the national colour of China, and symbolize hope for prosperity and abundance of remarkable things. Some of them are also linked to The Chinese Zodiac animals. I guess the most prominent patterns I have seen would be characters for *fortune* (福 = *fu*) and double happiness (喜喜/ 双喜 = *shuang xi*). The first one is often hung upside down on people's door in China (*fu dao* = 福到) and means 'good luck and fortune are expected to arrive'.

Some more complicated outlines require the use of an engraving knife and a steady hand, but otherwise it is a comprehensible hobby for all. Bigger pieces are done in parts and have their elements sewn together in the end.

Image by Karolina Achirri. Knowing how much I love Chinese cultural elements, one of my students brought me this cool Paper Cutting before we entered a New Year of 2016, a Year of Monkey.

CHAPTER 3

FOOD AND RESTAURANT CULTURE

Anything that walks, swims, crawls, or flies with its back to heaven is edible.

(Cantonese saying)

The Four Major Cuisines & The Magical Chopsticks.

Food has always been a hot topic in China. People constantly think about it, talk about it and take pictures of it to later post them on social media. When I asked what the fuss was about, I was told it's because China is rich now and offers choices of food they could have only dreamt of in the past. People from different parts of China dispute over which regional cordon bleu is the best. They all vary in taste, form and preparation process, but 4 cooking styles (四大菜系 = *si da cai xi*) significantly stand out, namely *Lu, Chuan, Yue* and *Su Cuisines.*

Lu Cuisine (鲁菜 = *Lu cai*) *from Shandong Province.*

It is divided into two schools of cooking: the Jin An school and the Jiao Dong school. The first one is renowned for its milky white soup, while the second for its preparation of sea food. The ingredients must be fresh and salty, juices and sauces are also preferable. As Shandong is located on the eastern seaside, it naturally includes a broad range of seafood dishes. Qingdao and Yantai cities are homes to nationwide famous chefs, who serve *Sweet and Sour Yellow River Carp* or *Sea Cucumber with Scallions* as their signature dishes. Most dishes in China are remnants of "Confucius Family Dishes", whose descendants ate well and lived in luxury. Since Beijing was a country's capital during the Qing Dynasty, its cooking is massively impacted by Shandong's style. Many roast duck restaurants sell Shandong kind of food.

Chuan Cuisine (川菜 = *Chuan cai*) *from Sichuan Province.*

This food can satisfy any spicy food lovers. Located in the southwest of China, Sichuan prides itself in serving world's hottest and most picante dishes. This is related to the place's climate. Since most of the year the weather stays humid over there, the locals like to steer clear from the damp by eating strongly peppered food. Some of the dishes are tongue-numbing, if you ask me. What can be found in them are hot chilis, black peppers, garlic, *huajiao* peppers (花椒), and tons of ginger. Also, peanuts and sesame paste are almost always included. One Sichuan dish can be all sorts of flavours: sweet, hot, sharp and pungent. The most commonly used methods of cooking are steaming, simmering and smoking. There's a popular saying claiming that in *Chuan Cuisine* no two dishes ever have the same flavour as each one is too unique. Famous dishes are: *Pork Shreds with Fish Flavour* (my personal favourite) and *Chicken Cubes with Peanuts dipped in Hot Sauce*. And let's not forget about bean curd. 麻婆豆腐 (*ma po dou fu*) is a mouth-watering bean curd with minced meat in chilli sauce and often makes Sichuan a final destination for travellers from all around the world.

Yue Cuisine (粤菜 = Yue cai) from Guangdong Province.

The Western world knows this type of food as Cantonese cuisine. The number of cooking techniques and delicious ingredients it has been using since the Qing Dynasty is simply mind-boggling and could serve as a topic for a few separate books itself. Stirring, frying, stewing and braising are the four main ways of cooking in Guangdong. The temperature in a pot needs to stay very high throughout the entire cooking process, which is also quite a long one. The natural flavour is the main focus of chefs there, since tastes must be light but not bland (to fit the hot southern climate), tender but not raw, and oily but not greasy. The most popular dishes include: egg rolls, chow mein, pastries, dim sum and steamed fish. My friends from Guangdong joke that they are able to eat anything with four legs, except for a table☺; and anything with wings, except for a plane☺. They clearly have a great sense of humour as well.

Su Cuisine (苏菜 = Su cai) from the Jiangsu and Zhejiang Provinces.

The main ingredients here are fresh aquatic products, as well as tea leaves, bamboo shoots, mushrooms and pears. The flavour can be described as sweet, light and fresh. Basically four methods are used, namely braising, stewing, boiling and simmering. Dishes are often cooked in their own natural juices, making them tender and rich in zest. Since I lived in Zhejiang throughout my stay in China, I had a chance to savour the eminent *West Lake Vinegar Fish* (西湖醋鱼 = *xi hu cu yu*), *Beggar's Chicken* (叫化鸡 = *jiao hua ji*) and *Roasted Pork Cubes* (东坡肉 = *dong po rou*). They all suited my taste cubs perfectly.

One thing worth mentioning is the fact that Chinese food we (foreigners) know and like from back home (regardless of the country), is completely different from the real Chinese cuisine. Nobody gets 'fortune cookies' in a restaurant and it's really hard (if not impossible) to find any dishes one recognizes at first glance. Sadly, this means most of the Chinese restos in Western countries are not authentic and surely adjusted to the locals' relish.

However, experiencing all these wonderful delicacies can only be enjoyable if one has mastered the use of chopsticks (筷子 = *kuai zi*). It is definitely not as easy as it looks. It took me six months to be able to complete a meal without having to chase my food down the table. In the beginning, every time I'd go to a restaurant the waiting staff would bring me a fork straight away. I was also reluctant to try many Chinese dishes as they simply looked and smelt worlds apart from the Polish ones. As time went by, I warmed up to Chinese food and became braver about embarrassing myself in public with my poor chopsticks skills. The learning process was painful, and included my trying to catch a sleek aubergine in my bowl. I practised at home as much as I could because I wasn't willing to lose face any more I'd already had. I even bought a special version of plastic chopsticks linked together on the top, designed for clumsy foreigners, I'm sure. I didn't even have any forks at home back in China. I've won my chopsticks war. Might have lost a few battles and ended up famished too, but I'm the boss of my tools now.

My Chinese sister told me that chopsticks play a significant role in one's social status. We should never point at people with them, as it can bring them bad fortune. Never tap your chopsticks on the edge of you bowl either, as it reminds your co-eaters of beggars (specifically the sounds they make begging for money). In addition, forget about sticking them vertically into your rice bowl. This gesture apparently looks like incense burnt at graveyards. Generally speaking, chopsticks are to be held in the right hand, with the low one remaining stable and the other one placed between one's thumb, middle finger and index finger, to operate the movements. It is considered bad manners to hold your chopsticks throughout the entire meal. If you see a Chinese person holding their utensils in a wrong way, you can be sure he or she is judged by the onlookers for a complete lack of manners and their parents are judged for not having taught them better. My favourite rule links with digging. If you try to dig your food out, you are seen as digging your grave. What an image! Finally, to signal you're done, rest your chopsticks on the top of your bowl, not on the side of it. My little trick was to drill the chopsticks routine with peanuts. Worked like a charm.

Chinese food is eaten most conveniently with chopsticks. Everything is usually cut up into bite-sized pieces. Made of wood, bamboo, metal (the most slippery ones), bone or ivory, Chinese chopsticks are blunt and round on the eating end, which stands for the Heaven; and square on the other end, symbolizing the Earth. For centuries the Chinese had to be concerned with their food supply, so that's why an adequate food amount is of great importance. Some more traditional families still bury their family members with a set of chopsticks, to assure their food provisions in the afterlife.

Chopsticks were invented in 400 BC, but their creator is unknown to this very day. They were first mentioned in "The Book of Order", a Chinese classic. At first, they were used for cooking and stirring the fire, and became eating instruments later on, during the Han Dynasty. Traditionally, chopsticks had to be a part of a girl's dowry, due to their pronunciation. *Kuai zi*, with *kuai* sounding similar to 'quick' and *zi* similar to 'son', suggested a young lady gives birth to a son as quickly as possible. I guess that's why my husband and I got six sets of chopsticks as our wedding gifts in China☺.

Table Manners.

Barely any street in China is free of places to stop and eat. Any cuisine you wish for and any dish you can imagine can be easily found in China. I have never met a foreigner who would complain about not finding dishes to their taste in China, either. If you can't read Chinese characters well, most places come to your rescue displaying pictures of dishes on the wall. Sometimes even my Chinese friends struggle to decode the meaning behind names of food in their own language.

A meal in Sanya mountains. Image by Karolina Achirri.

I have learnt the art of Chinese eatery manners over the years. Of course, they differ from generation to generation as much as from city to city, but they are worth noting if you plan to stick around for a bit longer. First and foremost, be aware that whoever invites you is usually the one who pays. How many battles I've performed with my Chinese friends fighting over the bill, only God knows. It is not an unusual view to spot friends tussling over the Starbucks' counter either. Restaurants aren't used to having to split the bill between 10 people who are eating together. I was taught two handy phrases for the dining purposes. The first is 'to go Dutch', AA 制 (*AA zhi*), but only after I begged my friends to teach me that. They were always more than happy to cover my meals. Also, 请客 (*qing ke*), which means 'it's on me' helped me a few times, when I impressed my company with knowing it and using it before anyone else had a chance. 礼尚往来 (*li shang wang lai*), which means 'to exchange courtesy or courtesy requires a return' is expected from the other person next time. Chinese people are very skilled at quickly settling the bill, so a foreigner needs to practice their speed to match theirs.

Next, don't put your bones inside the bowl at the end of your meal. You are expected to spit them on a specially designated plate instead. It is, on the other hand, totally unacceptable to pick your teeth (with a toothpick) without covering your mouth. Unless you want to be labelled a slob. If your inborn instincts tell you not to eat the fish's head, make sure you know how to say that in Chinese (不要鱼头 = *bu yao yu tou*). This part, as well as feet, are considered delicacies and can reach exorbitant prices. Don't be surprised if in a smaller resto you'll be asked to follow the cook into the kitchen to actually handpick your vegetables. It's very customary in China. As shocking as it might sound, you need to specifically ask for rice if you want it with your other dishes. In China, it is considered a filler and isn't automatically served, definitely not at the beginning of your feast.

Make sure to carry your own tissues or wipes with you, as you might be given a roll of a toilet paper instead. Some places also charge extra for wet naps. When water is served, don't be dazed when it's lukewarm. The only way you can get a glass of really cold water is when you ask to have ice added to it. The Chinese believe warm water is good for one's health and even in scorching weather one should drink it boiled.

When the time to pay comes, make sure to say: *mai dan* (买单), which means *I'd like to pay now*. Do not try to leave any tips, it is not habitual in China. Even a small change of 1 yuan will be given back to you.

With a table being round, all dishes are shared. That is also why restaurants expect one person to do ordering and hence provide only one menu per table, to most foreigners' dismay. Also sitting locations hold special significance in China. The seating position reflects one's importance. Whoever sits the furthest from the door is considered 'a guest of honour', while the one in the chair by the door is expected to foot the bill. Everyone else is sitting according to their rank, too, with the most important being close to a big fish. Bigger tables, for 10 people commonly, are called "lazy Susan", as they are turn-tables. Food is first put in front of the eminent guest and only after he or she has started eating can the rest dig in.

Toasting is also a huge part of dining together in the Middle Kingdom. It normally happens in a certain order around the table, starting from the boss (or some other VIP). There are also other rules to follow so as not to offend your Chinese counterparts. Always raise your glass with both hands, with your right hand grasping and your left hand supporting the glass. Bear in mind that your glass should always be under the other person's glass. Try to follow the rule of *gan bei* (干杯), *bottoms-up*, but be careful not to get drunk first, which is really easy with Chinese *bai jiu*.

Another difference between the West and the East when it comes to dining etiquette is the napkin. Don't place it on your lap. You might notice that Chinese waitresses often slip one edge of a napkin under a plate and let the others naturally cover one's lap.

One thing that has been bothering me when invited to dinners is the amount of food being wasted. Due to ordering for everyone, there are always far too many dishes and not many people like to take a doggie bag home. Well, I do. Not only will I eat the remaining food the next day, but some courses taste better after a night in a fridge. Some more affluent people believe that having food left on the table proves their status, and deliberately order too much to *gain face*.

Most importantly, *when in Rome do as the Romans do* is my advice to everyone supping with the Chinese. It is through food that they show love and appreciation. If you're planning to visit China, remember to *live in Hangzhou, marry in Suzhou, dine in Guangzhou, and die in Luzhou*. These places are known for having the best views, the prettiest women, the best food, and the best wood for a coffin, respectively.

The bizarre Chinese dishes.

Frogs and tortoises obliviously waiting to be slayed.
Image by Karolina Achirri.

As much as I have always tried to stay open-minded in China, some of the dishes it offers bewildered me every time I saw them. What were they? See for yourself.

The thousand-year-old egg (皮蛋 = *pi dan*), also known as 'preserved egg' or 'century egg'.

I will never forget my sister's dumbfounded face when this dish arrived at our table when we were visiting the Yellow Mountain, Anhui Province.

No, no, the egg has not been kept for a thousand years. These are duck's eggs which for three and a half months are preserved in a mixture of salt and ash, hence their strong blackish colour and their distinct odour. The wrap of mud and straw basically cooks it so that it appears hard-boiled on your plate. Most Chinese friends of mine like to eat it for breakfast with congee or soy sauce to dip it in. To me, this serving tastes like vinegar with too much salt, and so I've only tried it once and parted ways with it forever.

Jelly fish and star fish (海蜇皮 = *hai zhe pi*) & (海星 = *hai xing*).

These two have nothing in common except for the fact they are both marine organisms. The first is known for lowering cholesterol and tasting like plastic; while star fish looks cool and tastes creamy when fried and skewered. Not a fan of either.

Sea cucumbers (海参 = *hai shen*).

Despite their ability to provide a lot of protein, it's the consistency that reminds me of slugs too much to favour them. They are typically sold either dried (at the pharmacy) or fresh (at the restaurant). You can't miss this course as it literally looks like a cucumber with feet and tentacles. The texture is extremely slippery and gummy, but it doesn't stop some people from using it as an aphrodisiac. Never tried it, not planning to, either☺.

Goose feet (鹅掌 = *e zhang*) or Chicken feet (凤爪 / 鸡 = *feng zhua/ ji zhua*).

Mostly offered in a form of a dry snack, available at almost every supermarket. They make it extremely difficult for a foreigner to choke them down, as they aren't like anything we might be used to. Many Chinese ladies believe eating goose feet can prevent them from getting wrinkles, as they are supposed to be rich in collagen. It's a common view to spot a person in the cinema munching on them like they were 'normal snacks'. As I always say *I'll try anything once*, well, I did and it was once too many☺.

Stinky tofu (臭豆腐 = *chou dou fu*).

I think it's safe to crown this dish the most infamous one among foreigners. Its smell is simply so off-putting that one needs to struggle to try and taste it. I know I never did. I've heard many times that once you've passed the pong, you might actually enjoy it. Blocks of tofu are soaked in a liquid made of meat, vegetables and fermented milk for months. It's supposed to be crispy on the outside and silky on the inside, I am told. My biggest problem with it are the street vendors who usually park their carts right in the middle of the busiest street, by the escalator at the overpass or near the subway exit. Even if one tries to shy away from its disgustingly reeking vibe, it proves impossible at times.

Pig brain (猪脑 = *zhu nao*)

If you like squishy parts of animal physique, go for it. I gave up the minute I heard the word *brain*. It is usually served in satay sauce in hot-pot restaurants in China. According to folk beliefs, tasting an animal brain will make one smarter. Not sure about that one, though. It is claimed to contain more iron and calcium than any other part of a pig's body.

Drunken shrimp (醉虾 = *zui xia*)

This is the cruellest dish I have ever seen. The shrimp is served alive and you have to bite its head off before gulping it down.

When I first saw them, I literally had tears in my eyes feeling sorry for the poor buggers who were jumping in the bowl and had no idea they were about to be butchered. Image by Karolina Achirri.

Yes, this dish is served while it's still breathing, dunked in a bowl of *bai jiu*. The alcohol is supposed to make them sluggish and tipsy, before the eater is to make his or her move. My friend enjoyed them all and tried to convince me that they were so drunk they couldn't feel anything, but I couldn't get past the 'killing part'.

Bee Pupae (蜂蛹 = *feng yong*).

Before you start imagining bees flying in your pot, you must know that only young bees (in between larvae and adult bees) are used to make this dish. They are first battered and next deep fried. As I'm told, as never craved for them, they taste rather simple and bland, and it's the water from the pot that adds some salty taste to it. I'm not willing to decapitate little adolescent bees to satisfy my curiosity yet.

There are also practices of eating dogs in China, Yunnan even holds its own annual Dog-eating Festival. This dish puzzles me as so many younger Chinese seem to consider their little miniature doggies their best friends, buying them brand clothes and taking them to a dog-hairdresser. I guess when it comes to hunger, anything will do.

A few people are reported to have eaten baby foetus as well. I know how it sounds: unbelievable. Well, better believe it, because it's true. Some time ago a photo of a man mouth-watering over a cooked human foetus went viral in the press. Millions criticized him by classifying his act as cannibalism, while others explained the medicinal pros of consuming it. I also read that a long long time ago the Chinese ancestors believed that having eaten a human embryo could make one live forever. Thankfully, we are way past that notion today. However, these days it often happens that a human baby soup is drunk for sexual power in China, mainly by ultra-rich older men with much younger wives. Aborted children are usually sold to restaurants which disguise the real thing by calling it 'rib soup' on the menu. Is nothing sacred in China?

On waiters, food safety and water in China.

The first time I went to a busy Chinese restaurant with a Chinese friend, I was puzzled at how loudly he shouted at the waiter to get the bill. Now, six years later, I am the one who always asks for the check, as my voice seems to be the most audible one. If you just raise your hand or try to call them quietly, you'll be deliberately ignored and can wait to pay for hours (during lunch or dinner time). It is a socially acceptable behaviour in China to draw staff's attention to your table through crying blue murder. So, I consider myself a pundit of yelling '*fu wu yuan*' (服务员), a 'service person', at the top of my lungs and my friends always designate me to call for attention.

I do not envy Chinese waiters. I used to work as a waitress myself, many years ago in London. But the dizziness of their profession is not something I'd like to experience. Every restaurant is busy, at least twice a day between 12 and 2 and then 4.30-7. They also usually have a job which I like to call 'a door opener', and that's something I've been meaning to try but surely nobody would hire me. These guys simply stand at the main door the whole day and when a potential customer is approaching they need to open it for them and say: 'Welcome' (欢迎光临 = *huan ying guang lin*). Then, when someone is done and leaving they need to repeat the movement of opening the door and say: 'Thank you. Come back again!'. Sounds like a dream job, right? I don't understand why no restaurant has come up with the idea of having an expat doing so, as they -just by being white- would bring the place crowds of new consumers.

Sadly, unlike in the West, waiters aren't tipped in China. When I served tables in England my tips would often exceed my daily wage. Waiters' salary is extremely low. I have also noticed different levels of waiting staff. There are those at the door mentioned above, then regular ones who normally take your order, the servers who bring the food to your table (usually a bit older) and then those who can only deliver the food to the main counter from where it is later distributed by the actual waiting staff. Oh well, there is pecking order to everything in China.

Linked with eating out are recent scares regarding food safety in China, noxious additives being one of them. I have witnessed scandals of the melamine-tainted milk that killed hundreds of infants, artificially pumped with hormones pork, etc. Such news spread as fast as your legs will carry you. Outraged netizens comment on and discuss it on social media platforms. CEOs are jailed and stocks plummet. It's public's daily bread. I found a few pieces of advice online, pointing to us, consumers, what signs we should look for in our quest to unmask food that has been tampered with.

1. If you spot kelp, also called alga, which seems too bright in colour to you, you are probably on the right track to discover it had been 'improved'. Normally, healthy kelp would be of greenish-brown colour.
2. If your mushrooms are too white, they might have been bleached. Also, if they feel smooth and glossy, rather than naturally sticky, you have been hoaxed.
3. Some stores use ammonia to give shrimps sticky texture and a fresh look.
4. Watermelons have hormones injected to speed up the ripening process. You can avoid being taken for a ride by paying attention to their stripes. If them look uneven, steer clear from this fruit.
5. Bean sprouts are soaked in fertilizers to make them lose roots. You can smell the odorous water when you crack one open.
6. Don't buy rice that looks too bright. Chances are it has been polished with an industrial wax or mineral oils.

7. If your dried chili peppers look too red, it's a signal they've been smoked in sulphur. You can also examine them by rubbing your hands in them. If you notice any yellow stains, someone has pulled your leg.

The list goes on and on. The biggest issue I have with food in China is the oil problem. Thousands of restos have been reported to having reused cooking oil, some for years! One has no way of sniffing it out before ordering anything, so exposure is extremely high. Smaller types of eateries have also been photographed and unmasked online for their atrocious lack of hygiene back in the kitchen. I almost puked when I saw smoky frying pans being simply rinsed with cold water every other week. Salmonella, anyone?

Last but not least comes water. Water offered in public canteens comes in room temperature, regardless of the season or weather outside. Chinese people believe water with ice cubes is too much of a shock for the stomach and internal organs and that warm fluids are wholesome for the body. China's Ministry of Environmental Protection revealed that only around 49% of the country's lakes and rivers water was safe to drink. Of course, I understand I'm in a developing country and do not expect to be able to drink water straight from the tap. However, water in China has elevated levels of chlorine which is used to remove the pollutants. Since sewage and industrial waste are not taken care of properly, most of that chlorine spills into natural reserves. Apparently, there is more chlorine in water than a swimming pool is allowed to have. I don't have to explain what drinking highly-chlorinated water can cause to one's body. The damage is quite obvious. Tap water also shows high traces of lead, which even in tiny amounts, frequently leads to anaemia, high blood pressure, colon cancer or kidney failures. So how do we cope with that?

First of all, at home everyone uses water from 50 litre-tanks, available in any convenience store. I previously didn't pay attention to the brand I was using until one day I woke up with an excruciating pain of a kidney stone. Since that day I boiled barrelled-water as well. The newest apartments tend to have in-built water filters at their sinks. I wasn't so lucky to be living in one of them, though.

Media regularly exposes water pollution, too. Oftentimes it is done days after the contamination happens, though. In 2013 the government officially admitted that 'cancer villages' in China really do exist. One year of my stay in China, 16,000 dead pigs were fished out of Huangpu

River.

The situation creates business opportunities for companies producing water filtration systems, from dispensers to ice makers. Yet, the future of clean water doesn't look so dark. Chinese citizens are starting to speak up and address the issue. Along with excessive air pollution (which is discussed in another chapter of this book), water contamination seems to be taken seriously by more and more people. The government is trying to make the rules to exploit underground water stricter as well as to develop new sources of drinkable water. Let's keep our fingers crossed that one day China will stop suffering from gross negligence of healthy measures.

Is China's lip-smacking street food any different from the actual fast food?

China reached a status of the world's junk food king in 2015. It's hard to believe by looking at the tiny Chinese bodies that people spent $12 billion on chocolate and sweets annually. Nutritionists are alarming that this gives a brisk rise to diabetes and obesity whose rates are on the increase.

Instant noodles, commonly seen in the hands of college students and night train riders, generate a market of RMB 54.6 billion (approximately $8.4bln), even though their main ingredients are salt, oil, flour and then some more salt. Can you imagine that 120 million packets of this convenient snack are gobbled in China every single day? That makes an average person consume 36 packets a year.

Macdonald's and KFC restaurants are springing like mushrooms after rain in every urban corner. They are also the only food providers in famous scenic spots, thus you can always count on hamburgers in most temples these days. Both companies have been competing with innovative menus, with KFC leading the race. It is obvious that KFC did its homework and conducted a thorough market research as it offers lots of seasonal dishes (typical for China) as well as regular rice bowls, mushroom soups and traditional Peking chicken rolls. It basically provides a standard Chinese meal in a compact version.

Why is American junk food so hip in China? While the Middle Kingdom suffered malnutrition on a massive scale decades ago, it is overeating today. The reason is pretty simple, China's economic situation improved overnight and so people started enjoying a higher standard of living. No more savings on food but eating out instead. Also, physical labour is becoming secondary to the growing number of white-collar jobs. Office workers realize the importance of time and their daily schedule often allows them for a quick lunch around the corner from their company or even more conveniently take-away delivered right to their door.

A typical hamburger served at one of the foreign bars near West Lake in Hangzhou. Image by Karolina Achirri.

Junk food's marketing strategies seem genius to me. By adapting to the local palates and creating new products specifically targeting the Chinese, international chains make them feel like a part of a family, like they belong. This emotional security is very important, especially to people who spent their lives in communally-oriented societies (such as communist China). The general idea ingrained in the minds of the young Chinese, that what comes from the West must be better than what is available in the East, brings more customers to fast food bistros as well.

Food in junk places isn't cheap compared with that offered in little corner shops. A bowl of noodles normally costs around RMB 5 (around 0.77) while a hamburger RMB 15 (around $2.30). But the price doesn't matter when one can get great service, clean facilities, calming music and well-trained staff.

Another factor pushing Chinese population to befriend a local Macdonald's is the fact that food safety in China is somewhat doubtful.

Multiple scandals with overused oil, failed health inspections and a complete lack of hygiene make it easy on the Western moguls to win over the local market. Plus, being able to post selfies from those 'foreign' places still seems smashing.

While doctors are ringing alarm bells that chronic diseases (such as heart disease and diabetes) are on the rise, the public says that eating junk food once a month is ok. I must admit I sometimes pop into a nearby KFC, especially when it's scorching hot and it's the only place with a working air-conditioning, to grab a quick bite. It's simply easier for me than queuing up in a Chinese restaurant for hours, only to discover that the menu has no word in English and no pictures of the dishes.

My favourite Chinese fast dish is *bao zi* (包子). I know many Chinese would disown me for saying they are junk food, but what else do you call steamed bums with varieties of fillings (meat, seaweed, seafood, vegetables)? And since I can get it anywhere and at any time, I classify it as food made fast. Whether I'm rushing off to work in the morning (7:00 am is my usual torture) or feeling famished after a day full of classes, *baozi* save my life. Two of them are very stuffing, so I can spend RMB 3 (around 0.46) to regain energy and keep going.

Street food in China, however, has its own long-lasting culture. There are even monthly food festivals, during which there's no time of day one can't get whatever the eyes want. The most sought-after snack is definitely *jian bing* (煎饼), which can be described as a huge pancake with all sorts of fillings. Usually it is fried on an iron griddle with an egg, sesame seeds and cilantro. Most options include a chili sauce as well, but you can opt out of it if your palate is too delicate. A wafer becomes crunchy and it is then folded and placed in a plastic bag. You can see many people with those bags on the buses during the usual morning commute hours. The average cost oscillates around 2-3 yuan (0.30-0.46).

Another commonly sold item on street stalls is *ma la tang* (麻辣烫). This can be compared to a spicy soup with sundry ingredients, from vegetables to assortment of meat. A potential customer gets to choose what will be put in their soup and whoever stands in the queue for the soup observes the cooking process. It's quite a communal experience, bonding, so to speak. Watch out for a runny nose from the amount of chili it contains, it is hot!

Have you ever tried a shashlik? If you have and enjoyed, you'd definitely become a fan of *yang rou chuan* (羊肉串). It is essentially a piece of lamb meat on a stick, just like kebab. Xinjiang Province prides itself on this dish which can be typically bought from Muslim men in circular white caps. It does remind me of a barbecue stick to some extent.

Image by Karolina Achirri.

My greatest discovery belongs to *you tiao* (油条), which can be translated as a *fried cruller* or *a deep-fried dough stick*. Once a friend of mine who is a doctor, Dr Yellow (it is his real name, translated into English☺) took me to a restaurant nearby his hospital. He bought this tasty thing and asked me to dip it in *dou jiang* (豆浆), a soybean milk. I've been obsessed with it ever since. It is said that its shape reminds one of a couple joined together. That is supposed to reflect the Song Dynasty official, Qin Hui, and his wife. He allegedly orchestrated a plot to frame the general Yue Fei and that's why these Chinese doughnuts are fried and eaten, as a form of punishment awaiting a couple of traitors. Some people claim it has too much aluminium inside, but I am fond of it nonetheless.

Now, a Chinese barbecue experience is also worth mentioning here. It's nothing like a Westerner would imagine. In Poland, we have occasional 'grill' sessions in people's gardens, where mainly different types of sausages are being burnt. Metal plates on a bucket full of stones do the trick.

Image by Karolina Achirri.

One of my schools organized once a barbecue outing for students and teachers. It was a relaxing time (we even had a water gun fight), especially that students got to see us in a less formal situation, dressed down and chilled out. We roasted chops of pumpkin, 'crazy mushrooms' (my personal name given to them because they literally look like they've just gone bananas☺) and potatoes.

CHAPTER 4

TRANSPORTATION FUN IN CHINA

The journey is the reward.

(Taoist Proverb)

Tips for travelling in China.

There are certain things anyone travelling in China should know before embarking on their adventure. Exploring the Middle Kingdom can be thrilling but equally frustrating, especially if you don't know the basics of Mandarin.

- ✓ Get information about your hotel restrictions. Many hotels have lists of countries whose citizens they're not allowed to accommodate. Some hotels make those lists up, too. Two of my friends told me their stories of trying to stay overnight in Shanghai. They didn't book a place beforehand so they were simply seeking one on foot. When they were finally able to hit the pillow, it was 2am and three rejections later. Those hotels in question were not some small shabby places, but typical two-star inns. The receptionists would look at my friends' passports and state that people from their country (in their case: one of the African countries) were not welcome there. One even said: 'Our customers will not accept black guests'. So, make sure you will be, actually, able to sleep in a room you booked, even if you'd booked it ahead of time.
- ✓ Avoid 'tour guides' at bus stops and train stations. Most of them are crooks simply looking to rip you off ☺ (There's a common belief in China that every foreigner is ultrarich and therefore will easily pay a lot of money for anything.).
- ✓ Don't ever go on a package tour! This is the most popular way to sightsee preferred by the Chinese, but trust me when I say it is no fun at all. I did experience it myself on one of my school's faculty trips. Instead go for *zi you xing* （自由行）, independent travel, and plan your itinerary according to your likes. Those tours organized by widely-spread travel agencies will only take you shopping, and to the most expensive and most touristy parts of town. Someone told me guides can gain benefits from bringing customers to certain shops. Also, you will be on the bus most of the time, trying to catch your breath after all the running you'd need to even glimpse at famous scenic spots. Even if you do manage to get off the bus and stand by a celebrated statue or building, there will be so many other people trying to do the same that most of your photos will contain their selfie sticks, not you.
- ✓ Don't get onto the taxi whose driver seems overly helpful or weirdly confused. They will tell you they know the place you

intend to get to only to call their friends on the way and ask for directions, telling them jokingly 'they just scored the best ride of the day with a dumb foreigner'.

✓ When taking a train, be aware of different classes. They vary from extremely slow to slow and from fast to supersonic fast. They are marked by different letters. Your best bet would be to find a G train (高铁 = *gao tie*), as these are relatively clean and quite conveniently placed on China's railway connection map. Be prepared to put up with wild stares and fingers pointing at you, in more severe instances also with having your photo taken (even if you fell asleep and you're drooling) and then being posted on somebody's *WeChat*.

✓ Always buy return tickets for anything right after you've arrived at the place. Otherwise, you'll find yourself stuck in a place for much longer than your heart desires and you might even end up sleeping at the station, if your passport happens to get rejected by the local hotels.

✓ Learn how to recognize and avoid the so called 'yellow tickets', 黄牛 (*huang niu*). They are fake 99% of the time and once you get on a train you won't have a seat. More serious cases involve not even being able to go past the security rails with such a ticket or being followed by the station's police and having to answer lots of questions you won't understand or have the answers to.

✓ Never travel in China during long national holidays. This is the Broken Bridge in Hangzhou, China, during *Qing Ming Jie* (清明节), which translates as *Tomb Sweeping Day*. It took me over three hours to get there (normally it takes about 30 mins), just to experience this. I was not even sure the Bridge was still there.

Broken Bridge, West Lake, Hangzhou. Image by Karolina Achirri.

This is what the Chinese call 'people mountain people sea', 人山人海 (*ren shan ren hai*). Under no circumstances should you take a train during the Chinese New Year, unless you're super-adventurous or suicidal. This is the time most people try to get home for the holidays, as for some of them it's the only time of the year they get to see their families (lots of migrant workers can't even take time off during the Spring Festival). People carry their entire life possessions (especially on slow D trains), standing tickets are oversold (so you might end up having six people over your head), travellers sit on filthy floors, sleep on their meticulously packed suitcases and squeeze by the toilet like sardines. Other days to avoid hitting the road include 国庆节 (*Guo qing jie*), National Holiday; 劳动节 (*Lao dong jie*), Labour Day; 端午节 (*Duan wu jie*), Dragon Boat Festival; 中秋节 (*Zhong qiu jie*), Moon Cake Festival.

✓ Always carry your passport along! These days to even enter a train station, every passenger needs to show their passport and the ticket. Be super cautious when it comes to pickpockets. I have friends who had their documents, phones, house keys, iPads, and even their books stolen from their bags when wending their way through. There are gangs of three or more people, oftentimes using kids, too, who have a smart routine practiced. One person follows the target and nobbles whatever there is to nip, while two others hide the scene from the passers-by. Then, your possession is handed off a few times just to make sure it is untraceable. Also, be aware that no one will probably intervene even if they've seen you getting mugged. It is not worth their trouble, especially knowing that organized groups of muggers can be too dangerous to deal with.

✓ Last but not least, have fun. Set specific aims for your trip and perhaps learn some useful phrases such as 太贵了 (*tai gui le*), 'It's too expensive'. Frankly, this was the first one I had mastered, even before I knew how to introduce myself in Chinese.

China's taxis or diabolical vehicles?

When my sister and my younger nephew came to visit China in

February 2014, things went wrong from the minute I picked them up from the airport.

Image by Karolina Achirri.

The driver had to stop in the middle of a highway because his wheel practically fell off. We were right at the toll gate when he said we should take our luggage and hail a new cab. The only problem was that we were in the middle of nowhere, at least not anywhere remotely close to a taxi rank or a road where taxis would pass through. After a lot of deliberation, many phone calls to his co-workers explaining he had a crazy foreigner there, we were told another taxi would come to pick us up. There we were, between the city and the airport, half an hour after my relatives landed, being welcomed by *this*. It took the next car over two hours to come and pick us up. Just my luck in China.

One cannot avoid taking taxis in China. There are times when where you want to go is further than the subway lines can reach, or you simply can't figure out what the Chinese characters say at the route's placard at the bus stop. In such case China comes to your rescue by offering phone applications to order a taxi. 滴滴打车 (*di di da che*) which translates as 'Beep, beep, catch a cab' and 快的打车 (*kuai di da che*) which translates as 'call you taxi quick' are two main competitors in this field now, after kicking many others out of business. The tool is extremely handy, but can be painful to register for a foreigner. Normally, it's better to use a Chinese name as taxi drivers can see the name of the passenger and many of them refuse to pick up your order, thinking that driving a foreigner is just too much of a 'ma fan' (hassle). Drivers receive subsidies for using taxi apps while passengers get to rank their services and pay electronically (via Alipay = 支付宝). It's a win-win.

Both companies: *di di da che* and *kuai di da che* race each other on various promotions such as giving a certain percent back to the clients, perhaps higher than the other one is offering. It's been quite a show to observe how those 2 companies' drivers compete with each other, as many people have both apps and use them simultaneously to have a better chance at getting a taxi (especially during peak time in big cities).

Last year (2015), Uber, *you bu* (优步) meaning 'a great step forward' in Chinese, came to Hangzhou. Everyone was so excited and so was I, until I realized I can't have an account because a credit card is required and foreigners aren't allowed to get one from Chinese banks. Bummer. I wasn't the only one upset. Local taxi drivers went on multiple strikes protesting against high cab rental fees. It is roughly estimated that rental contract fees for taxi drivers can go as high as RMB 9000 (approximately $1450) a month. While Uber drivers open the door for the customers, the regular cabbies smoke inside, shout at their customers, and hardly ever help with the luggage. No wonder they got ditched. Also, the cars Uber drivers provide range from the 5-class Mercedes to Audi and BMW 7 series. Who wouldn't choose comfort over misery?

As I said, I've been China taxis' regular customer for the past six years. I have reached a golden VIP level customer on my app. The sort of taxi experience my friends and I have gone through, though, could very easily drive one mad☺.

First off, the questions cabbies ask are hilariously bizarre. From standard "Where are you from?", through "How old are you?", "Are you married?", to my absolute favourite "How much do you make?". I used to get pretty ruffled but then I played along. In one taxi I was from Africa, in another from Switzerland. I told one guy I was married to three Chinese men and another one that I was single and not willing to ever get married. It was fun. As for the income question, I've developed a strategy to say: "It's a secret", followed by a long and appreciated silence. When a driver turned out to be quite nice and not nosy, I'd answer his questions accurately or explain to him why it is impolite in foreigners' eyes to be interrogated like that.

One night I was coming back from the emergency room in a hospital. I was with my Chinese friend, who was helping me with communication, and I was on crutches that day. I used my regular app to hail a taxi and when the guy came, we got in and gave him the address, which was only a few blocks away. It shouldn't have taken too much time or money to get back home. We had just spent over 3 hours in the hospital, so we were happy to be heading back. However, just before we were to set off, the driver told my friend he didn't want to use the meter and that we should pay him RMB 20. Without any hesitation, I took out my phone and snapped his placard, saying I'll contact his boss and give him trouble if we don't drive right away. Immediately, the taximeter was down and off we went, ended up paying legal RMB 12 instead. It was not the fact he was trying to overcharge us, as it wasn't a lot of money. It was the fact he was trying to take advantage of a person in need. Never mess with a foreigner in pain! My friend was giggling all the way back home. She said she was going to use that trick herself from then on.

I've also heard so many crazy stories from my friends. One had her thigh grabbed by a driver and needed to escape at the stop sign. Another one got a kick out of one cabbie who picked him up and immediately cranked up Eminem. My female foreign friend got serenaded by a driver, who turned on Kenny G and without knowing any English – in a very deep voice - started adlibbing syllables that sounded similar to the lyrics. She actually recorded him. Chinese taxi drivers can surely make one's day!

There are a few types of taxi drivers in China. There are 'the talkers'. These ones are garrulous and once you even say 'Ni hao' (Hello), they assume you are fluent in Mandarin and fire away. They speak fast and without paying attention to their accent, so if you're not into learning a few cool swear words or not in a mood for a conversation, you'd better pretend not to know a word of Chinese. Then, there are 'the silent ones'. With these, even if you want to practise your Mandarin, you won't get anything out of them. They are either taciturn or they simply patronise you. Also, there are those 'suspicious types', who would interview you through and through. My latest one went like this:

Driver: Are you Russian?
Me: No.
Driver: So where are you from?
Me: China.
Driver: Can't be! (a moment of silence) Oh, was your mother Chinese?
Me: No.
Driver: Your father?
Me: No.
Driver: You must be from Hong Kong. (a moment of silence) But your

eyes don't look Chinese and you're too fat!
Me: (silence)

He kept glancing at me for the remaining time of the journey, probably scrutinizing my appearance trying to see some Asian features in it. Then, we have 'the honkers'. Honking in China does not translate into the Western "get out of my way", but rather "I'm coming". It's a way of letting others know you are the king of the road. Drivers honk anywhere, anytime and at anything. Finally, there are those drivers whom I call 'patience testers'. They clearly want to see how far they can push a foreigner. You utter the name of the road you want to be taken to, he repeats it three times and then says he doesn't understand or that such a road does not exist. You are convinced you pronounced it correctly, just like you've done it many times before, but it takes a few minutes, many words angrily shouted from his mouth and a phone call to a friend to start driving. Still, this type isn't as wicked as the one who pretends to understand what you say only to take you to the wrong side of town (yes, it happened to me once).

On one occasion, the driver was pretty friendly so I carried on with the conversation. When I told him I was a teacher, he immediately got super excited and told me his son was learning English. Then, he called the son and made me speak to him on the phone for the rest of the ride. It was so awkward. When we finally arrived at the destination, he asked how the son's English was and I shortly said: "OK" and left. Did not look back.

A typical Shanghai taxi. Image by Karolina Achirri.

I hate 'the racers' most. Those are the worst as they are clearly fulfilling their childhood dreams of becoming a Formula 1 driver on shabby Chinese roads. I especially dislike driving on a highway, because they don't even care about the traffic cameras (in most cases their sophisticated road apps will tell them where CCTVs are). Don't get me wrong, I like to drive fast myself, but not at the speed of sound. They should not be stepping on the juice like that when they carry passengers. In my language, there's a phrase we would use to remind a driver to slow down, it could be translated into English as: "We are not a bag of potatoes". Go figure!

Last but not least goes my accident story from Christmas Eve 2015. I was on my way to the city to spend the evening with some friends. We had planned to prepare traditional dishes from our countries and celebrate the birth of Jesus in the Eastern European style. So, I had food with me on the taxi. When we were on the freeway, the rain started coming down in buckets. It was really difficult to see anything. Suddenly, I felt a strong push from the back and then my head bumped into the seat in front of me, the dishes started flying like a kite and our taxi came to a stop. The driver turned to me and asked if I was okay, then left the car. When I realised we were driven into by a car behind us, I already had a splitting headache. I could hear the two men shouting angrily and then my driver came back and started making phone calls. I thought he was calling the police. I could not exit the car, as we were blocking the middle lane of the highway. I started calling my friends to ask what to do. After about half an hour of sitting in the car, thinking I surely must have had a concussion, I heard a few heavy kicks to the boot, some more harsh words exchanged and off we went. The driver drove very slowly to my friends' house and I realized he had been calling for another taxi to come and pick me up. No one came, so he had no choice but to take the other driver's information and drive off. I really didn't want to die on a Chinese road, and definitely not on Christmas Eve.

The list of weird situations with China's drivers can go on and on. I think I felt most angry when a driver would just pass me by on the street. Some drivers still aren't accustomed to seeing foreigners, so they like to pretend you are not standing there in that torrential rain, waving your hand at them. One thing is sure, I will never forget my taxi rides in China.

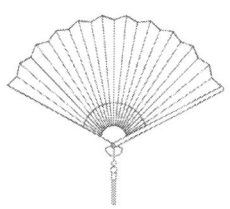

Driving in China - banging your head against the wall.

I got my Chinese driver's license for two reasons. My Polish one was about to expire and I wasn't planning to go back to renew it and I seemed to be needing it for my upcoming job in China. It was hell. I took the exam three times, and I'm a seasoned driver, which is considered not too bad as some foreigners I know attempted to pass the test 13 times and still haven't. Lucky me. It's one thing to get the license and a completely different thing to drive in China. The things you'll see on the road, the types of people you'll be forced to drive past, the policemen standing in front of the busiest intersection right during the rush hour are just a few things that can drive you bananas (pun intended☺).

My Chinese driver's license with my Chinese name. Image by Karolina Achirri.

But first things first. To pass the exam, don't think, just memorize. Don't even try to apply any version of logic into the questions, it's no use because there isn't any. It's the translation into English that lacks any cognitive features. At my second go, I thought it might have been easier had I chosen the test in Chinese. English is offered but the questions and answers make zero sense to an ordinary foreigner. They might have been translated on *Baidu* (Chinese equivalent of Google). My two favourite questions (which I jotted down during my exam) are:

1. The driver may drive a motorized vehicle...?
    a. After drinking alcohol
    b. When he suffers from a disease that impedes safe driving
    c. When he is exhausted

d. After drinking tea
2. If someone's intestines are protruding from an open abdominal wound, should you?
   a. Put them back in place
   b. Do nothing
   c. Cover them with some kind of container and fasten it around the body

Do you know the answers to these questions? Do they think we're stomach surgeons? They aren't as obvious as they seem. Luckily, when a foreigner already has a license from their home country, they only need to take the theoretical test. I've been told by my Chinese friends who also needed to pass the practical one that queues are horrendous and instructors spiteful and insulting. Apparently, they often make test-takers cry. It is also super costly to learn how to drive, but classes are compulsory. A common fee for the training in Hangzhou can even exceed RMB 10,000 (about $1538).

Another thing is that there is no book in English to prepare you for the test. I was given one in Chinese and told to ask my Chinese friends to translate it for me. How can those bizarrely formulated questions be accurately translated, I thought?

3. When other drivers correct you, you should:
   a. Learn modestly and accept the opinion seriously
   b. Not listen
   c. Accept but not try to improve

Instead, I found an app online and used someone else's translation of questions to study. Out of 100 questions, one must get 90 right to pass.

Secondly, people rarely make use of their mirrors, either the internal ones or the side ones. It is all about feeling comfortable in the car, so the Chinese often add cushions and pillows to their seats, which naturally limits their visibility. Also, since there is no concept of space in China, drivers tend to go wherever they want and whenever they want. This often results in them forcing their way through. I get agitated every time I'm on a pavement and a car honks at me, because he can't use the street but needs to use my lane. What's more, the cars never stop. That is why it is common to see pedestrians frantically crossing the zebra. They are used to running for their life. Public buses also do not follow the traffic laws. Although these days, as I am told, a new policy has been implemented on being able to call a hotline and report on a bus driver who did not stop for you at the crosswalk. The female drivers never stop. They are crazy. No rules or laws can hold them in check. Additionally, you should always smile when behind the wheel, as Big Brother never sleeps and most streets are monitored.

I love driving, I really do, but I loathe it in China. All it did for me was teach me a whole lot of new swear words. Yes, I'm proficient at effing in Chinese. One literally needs to have eyes around their head to be able to multitask at spotting other cars, pedestrians (crowds of them) and the bikers. One of the things that's significantly different from most Western countries is the right of way. Normally, in our countries, the car going straight has the right to go first, whereas in China cars will turn in front of you. They expect you to stop. Furthermore, cars entering the highway neglect to look if there's room to emerge. The way of thinking is that if I am to wait for the traffic to slow down, I'll never be able to get onto the road. It's playing offense not defence in China.

Also, I have witnessed road rages like they were taken straight from a thriller movie. Normally, when a crash happens and it's not serious, both drivers are supposed to take pictures with their phones, move the vehicles out of the way and call the police. But more commonly, you'll see two drivers blowing a fuse. They don't care that they're blocking a hundred other cars. Those fights often end up with the police intervention as nobody is willing to admit their fault. I once witnessed a fight between a middle-aged man and a very young beautiful woman. He was driving a Toyota while she was at the controls of a brand new BMW. She was putting on her make-up at the traffic lights (I saw her from the neighbouring lane). I was about to turn right and she was on a lane for going straight. When the lights changed, she didn't notice until got tooted at. Then, she abruptly moved but instead of going forward she turned left, driving right into that guy's car. I don't know how long the dispute took, but judging by the man's wrath, they must have stood there for a while.

If you think that your problems finished on the day you get to hold your driver's licence, you're highly mistaken. By the way, a foreigner needs to have a Chinese name on the license. I was told our real names are simply too long for their computer system. Your next step will probably be to look for a car. If you think cars can be cheap when second-hand, think again. Nobody wants to buy a used car in China (due to losing face or a lack of belief in anything used) hence the secondary market doesn't exist. It's also worth knowing that you can't drive with an International Driver's Permit (IDP) in China. You need the Chinese license. I have never tried to buy a car in China but my friends did. There is a law that forbids too many people from having a car, so the government makes one buy a number plate first (cost of about RMB 40,000 = $6155). For this, you need to wait in a queue, which these days in Zhejiang Province can take up to a year. My foreign friends weren't able to legally purchase a vehicle, so they needed to beg their Chinese friends to register it under their names. Not many people are willing to do so for you, as one of the penalties for traffic rules violations are points (given by the police). Once your count exceeds 12, you can't drive and you'll be fined. As with most rules in China, the Chinese have already figured out a way to outsmart them. I have been repeatedly asked to lend my license to someone who wanted to put some of these penalty points on my count, as they were scarily approaching 12.

What has puzzled me since I came to China are the number plates. I decided to unveil this mystery. Chinese license plate reveals a lot about the vehicle as well as its owner. They always begin with a character denoting the province in which the car is registered. Next stands a letter, which represents the city. The plates are blue with white lettering. What follows is the number and this is where the fun begins. Being a superstitious nation, every Chinese person wants to have a lucky number on their plate, preferably with an 8, 6 or 9. This opens door to auctions where people are willing to pay millions for the right number. One famous businesswoman was recently awarded a plate with a quadruple 8. She must have paid through the nose for it.

To recap, taking a test, buying a car or driving itself are far from being a pleasure in China. My levels of anxiety rocketed every time I was asked to drive to another city to teach. The fact that I was driving my boss' car only made it worse. If you're thinking of driving in China, get ready for quite a ride☺.

The longest gridlocks you will ever see are in fact in China.

Getting on any form of public transport in China can be a challenge. Be it a bus, a train, subway or even a taxi, one needs to present certain skills of how to handle being squeezed. Traffic has gone mad in the past few years, making it easier to get to one's destination on foot rather than by any means of transport. With almost everyone being able to afford a car, in some cases – cars, roads are packed not only during rush hours. As a matter of fact, any hour is a rush hour in Chinese metropolis.

The government has been going out of its way to solve the problem of escalating traffic jams by implementing what we call 'odd-even number plate policy' in a few big cities, Hangzhou included. Odd numbers aren't allowed to be driven in the city centre at peak times, i.e. on Mondays, Wednesdays and Fridays, while even numbers are banned on the road within the same hours on Tuesdays and Thursdays. Also, number plates not issued in Hangzhou are prohibited from driving inside the city during peak hours. Weekends are the only times when all numbers are free to drive. This causes a great deal of problems, especially to those who leave early for work in the suburbs and come back late. They sometimes need to wait somewhere out until they are permitted behind the wheel again. I also know a few people who own two plates, so they conveniently replace them according to the day of the week.

Surely, no one wants to spend most of their day in a car, surrounded by hundreds of other vehicles losing their cool and honking insanely.

Due to recent security threats – bus bombings, the Kunming knifing, Urumqi terrorist attacks – public transport drew more attention and its security has been visibly strengthened. There are more x-ray scanners at train stations and nobody can avoid one when entering the subway, either. There are thousands of non-uniformed security personnel riding public buses and one can spot a surveillance camera in nearly every corner.

Such an incredible number of people (current population of China: 1.4bln) links with a complete lack of personal space. This is when an mp3 or a Kindle come in handy. I've noticed that only listening to soothing music on my morning bus ride to work can tune out the fact that someone's bag is on my feet and someone else's elbow in my eye. At the same time, I envy Chinese passengers' composure. They don't seem to be either bother or annoyed by being sandwiched.

Perhaps encouraging car-pooling would be a good solution to this dilemma. Not everyone needs to drive their own car. If nothing else, we can always resort to tricking the mind into believing that being stuck in traffic can actually be fun, after all, a good traffic jam can allow some time for introspection, answering emails or even making friends with other passengers glued to your side.

On the bus or train – Oh dear!

I believe that living in China requires experiencing all walks of life, and bus and train rides are no exception. The public transportation system is amazing. One can basically get anywhere by bus (locally) or train (long distance).

City buses are the most crowded spaces I have ever tried to squeeze into in my life. Since the driver has to take every awaiting person, Draconian scenes such as people's backpacks hanging out of the harmonica door or simply one's arm half in and half out are a common view. I swear to God I once waited over 2 hours by letting my regular bus go to avoid being deprived of oxygen or any version of privacy. I waited and waited and waited until the next bus was ridable.

Most regulars would use bus passes (which are electronic cards) to settle the fare. Since one needs to keep moving deeper and deeper into the interior as new passengers hop on, sometimes the only way to pay is to pass your card from the back of the bus to the front. This might take about 20 minutes, as people are sliding it above their heads from one hand to another.

And the queues! Much to the rage of many Westerners, Chinese people do not respect the queuing system. People will jump in front of you without remorse, elbowing you on the way and even if they do attempt to create some sort of a line when the bus is approaching, there's no respect for personal space at all. I was pushed out of the way many times before I mastered the art of elbowing.

Also, a friend of mine (a foreigner) was attacked at the bus stop, right outside her apartment building. She was calmly waiting for her bus as a Chinese lady waltzed up to her and punched her in the face. Just like that. My friend was in such a shock that she jumped into the bus and recovered only as she reached her office. I guess that's "I'm curious about this foreigner" taken too far.

I rode a bus every day. One day, I'm coming back home from an acupuncture clinic downtown. A kid of 3 or 4 years old is running to and fro. The mum is cleaning the seat she just used. People are starting to move away from the front of the bus to the back, where I am sitting as well. I'm trying to figure out what's going on. Suddenly, it hits me. The kid had pooed on the seat. Of course, as it is often practiced, the kid is wearing crotch-split pants so everything ended up on that seat. The smell is now unbearable. The mum doesn't seem bothered at all. I'm praying: God, make this kid stay as far away from me as possible. Then, he notices me. With his finger pointed right at me, he goes: "Mum, a foreigner!" And he sits next to me. That's it. I've had it. I'm getting off at the next stop.

Don't get me wrong. I like Chinese buses. They run frequently, they are fairly clean and they usually have air-conditioning. What I loathe, though, are the secret (not-so-secret) stares I get. I have a habit of studying Chinese vocabulary when I'm on the bus. I use little flashcards (with English on one side and Chinese on the other). There's always someone willing to quiz me on the words, curious to see my handwriting or simply snapping a picture with their iPhone. I wonder how many times I have already appeared on the Chinese social media.

As for trains, do they run fast! China's high-speed trains can run up to 490 km/h. First time I had to go to Nanjing from Hangzhou, I prayed the entire time. I was convinced that train would take me straight up to heaven. They are very modern, air-conditioned, and have assigned seats, which is the best part.

Every time I need to take the train, though, I get a bit antsy. I can handle the ridiculous queues to the ticket windows (though, I usually ask a Chinese friend to purchase my ticket online ahead of time), but I have a real problem with the noise. Even if I listen to music, or attempt to, the loudness seems to be reaching dangerous levels of deafness. Chinese people are just so rambunctious on trains! There are people playing cards, watching Korean soap operas (without headphones), eating smelly snacks, slurping instant noodles; or spoilt kids either freely running or bawling boisterously. The world on a Chinese train is mad. Everything is noise. If one stops and observes the surroundings, it's complete chaos. Or maybe it's controlled chaos. Is it madness trying to be sane?

Nonetheless, the speed with which Chinese railway is developing can be daunting. One can get from Hangzhou to Beijing in 7 hours now (despite the distance between the two being over 1300km). New lines are being built, too, extending to the remote autonomous regions.

If you want to take the hyper fast train, make sure to buy a G-ticket (stands for 高铁 = *gao tie*). That's the code for trains that can take you on a race against time!

Fly me to the... - Delayed flights, airport security and the crazy.

When flying in China, one should always account for a few hours of delays. It's a given. No matter what airlines you pick, where to or from you're travelling, or how expensive your ticket was. You will be lucky if your long-awaited flight is only delayed and not cancelled.

Most of the time, it's "air traffic restrictions" that airlines blame the delays or cancellations on. One week, when I was flying to Beijing, the government decided to close the Shanghai Pudong International Airport due to the victory parade over defeating Japan. Lucky me. Coming back wasn't any easier, as we were all seated on the plane for over an hour but not taking off, without air conditioning. People were anxiously asking questions about the delay but since I was the only foreign passenger onboard, I guess the crew decided to blatantly ignore me and made all announcements in Chinese.

Scenes of despair and madness are also spotted at the airport when the board shows "Delayed/Cancelled" next to one's flight. I've seen passenger angrily throwing food at the airport staff, making videos with heated commentaries to post them on social media, and I even witnessed one lady's tantrum when she sat on the floor, started crying and refused to move. The airport security had to remove her with force.

Many delays are also caused by passengers' reckless behaviour once on board. Some people try to light a cigarette before take-off, others makes frantic phone calls (instead of switching off their mobiles) while others attempt to feed their children right when the plane is about to take off. Come on, people!

According to a popular online magazine, Chinese airports experience more delays than any other airports in the world. Even if a plane pulls away from the gate, chances are it will sit on tarmac for a few hours. 200 million hours were wasted by delays in 2012 (according to sohu.com). It is estimated that Chinese aviation industry loses almost RMB 5 billion annually because of delayed flights. I certainly don't want to be a frequent flyer.

When it comes to airport security, I can never understand why I'm being asked to show my passport so many times. By the time I reach the gate, I must have shown my ID more than 5 times. The airport security crew is, however, very respectful of foreigners. At least from my experience. I always feel safe and they never harass me (which does happen at times when I fly to the Western hemisphere).

Even though we all willingly take off our shoes, dump our razors and toothbrushes into the bin, and get rid of water bottles before going through check-in, I find it a wee bit paradoxical to have such a variety of shops and restaurants right across the line. If Chinese people manage to follow the regulations and bring the allowed number of suitcases (in allowed measurements), they still manage to come to the plane with many shopping bags and let's not forget: a KFC take-out.

Although crazy stuff on planes happens everywhere in the world, a few incidents in China really amused me. Once I was coming back from Yunnan (a trip I had planned for months). I was already on my way back, at the airport, waiting for my plane to be ready. I went to the loo and as I was washing my hands I used paper towels provided for drying. Since I couldn't find a rubbish bin (I really did look!) I left the paper on the sink, as I didn't want to litter on the floor (which could have been a bit cleaner to be honest). As I was exiting the toilet, a middle-aged Chinese lady followed me out, walked up to me, grabbed my arm and said in English with a heavy Chinese accent: "You foreigner, go back to dispose your tissue!" I was trying to explain to her that there was no place to throw it in, but she just got angrier and in a hopeless attempt to slap me in the face, she scratched my cheek. I was so gobsmacked, I ran out of there as fast as I could. I don't think she was mentally stable.

Another time, a friend of mine was flying from Hong Kong to Beijing and her flight was delayed for 6 six hours because (as she later learnt) someone filled the washroom sink with diarrhoea. When the stench filled the entire aircraft, passengers started to complain and that's how they were let out. I once heard that the American aircrafts (flying regularly between China and the US) need to replace their toilet seats after each flight. It is believed to be the result of Chinese passengers standing on top of them, instead sitting on them. Well, if they had squatting toilets the problem would vanish. When in China…

Rickshaw drivers or subway riders – Who's more annoying?

You can take a subway, but it's going to be crowded; you can take a bus, if you know how to read Chinese characters; you can take a taxi, but it's going to be pricey. You can also walk, but if you're in a huge city, it might take you a while. China offers a cheaper and faster alternative: a rickshaw (also called a *pedicab*).

The word itself comes from Japanese, *jinrikisha* (*jin* = human, *riki* = power, *sha* = vehicle), in Chinese 人力车 (*ren li che*). So, what we get is actually: human-powered vehicle. Makes sense!

Originally, rickshaws gained popularity in China in the 18th century, mostly because they were a symbol of royalty. They are now broadly present in other Asian countries, so one can hop on and be taken around let's say the Old Town for about RMB 10 ($1.5). They are economical and hyper-fast. Sometimes I don't know where the drivers get the strength in their legs to pedal like they do. Some of the pedicabs (the more recent editions) have a small motor that replaced human legs.

Why use them? Sometimes there's simply no taxi around or one needs to wait for them a long time (even with the help of a taxi app), especially in the suburbs or small city outskirts. The vehicles have green sign "VACANT" in front. Of course, as any business people in China, rickshaw drivers would actively try to rip you off, particularly when it's raining. The price then surges fast, so make sure to haggle hard. The vehicles are usually wrapped up in a protective plastic, which is attached to the buggy. So, no need to worry you'll get drenched.

Once on my way to work, I saw six people jam-packed into one rickshaw. I thought it was logistically impossible, but somehow physically doable. To make it even more bizarre, one of the passengers was holding two live ducks hanging out of the vehicle. What a view!

These days, big cities are swarming with new versions of rickshaws, though, named trici-car-axis. As opposed to rickshaws, these little inventions can go on major streets. They have three wheels and extra space in the back for two or more Chinese people (or one normally-sized Westerner😊).

If you decide to get around via subway (you must be in a big city), be prepared to meet all sorts of weird characters, hold on to your belongings like your life depends on it and be aware of possible nudges and punches as well as a full photo session conducted by bored Chinese passengers to whom you are a curiosity.

People on the subway in China can be categorized into a few groups. First, there are the *seat yankers*. A typical scenario: You are waiting for the train to come, you're knackered after work and all you really want is a seat to rest your tired feet. Finally, you see an empty seat in an approaching compartment. You are ready to grab it. But... The train stops, the doors open and you are being thrown aside and end up entering the train packed with people. Someone beat you to the curb. Face it, they are pros, you're just an amateur at the seat game. You can either suck it up and stand the whole ride home, or you can take a stand and be ready when the *seat yanker* gets off at the next stop.

Then, there are young people who are pretending they are asleep to avoid giving up their seats to the elderly. I call them *fakers*. We've all seen them. We can all recognize them by taking one look at their still posture even when the train rapidly stops and everyone else is being shoved all over. If someone just got on a stop ago, they are faking it for sure. No one can fall asleep in 2 minutes, sitting. The only thing you can do is to shun them! Once they open their eyes (pretending to have just woken up), it's your chance to show them how you feel😊. Be ready to give them "the look".

There are also Chinese men whose legs are so apart, they end up taking two or more seats. I named them the *stretchers*. They have this annoying tendency to always ride the subway during the rush hour. You want to take a seat and there's obviously space, but you don't want to sit on the man's lap, do you? In this case, I always ask them to scoop a little. I have learnt how to say it politely in Chinese and it has not failed yet.

Finally, the *ear-popping gamers*. These are my personal least favourite people on public transport. Why can't they use their earphones! If they can afford the latest iPhone, I'm sure headphones wouldn't ruin their budget. But no, they choose to draw attention to themselves. Everyone must listen to the sounds coming out of their annoying silly game. The gamers need to be approached head-on. Ask them to mute the sound or lend them your own headphones, if you have to. Silence is good. Silence is all one needs.

I'm sure there must be many other 'types' that one still has to nickname and observe. All I know is that I am blessed to be living at the end of a subway line. When I get on board, the entire car is usually empty. I am the queen of the subway!

CHAPTER 5

WEATHER

Wherever you go, no matter what the weather, always bring your own sunshine.
(Anthony J. D'Angelo)

Where's your mask? – The environmental rant about pollution.

Having trouble breathing? A monthly cold that never seems to fully heal? Terribly stuffed nostrils with something looking like tar? You have arrived in China. "Beijing cough" is one of the newest phrases amongst expat community in China's capital. It's real and seems incurable.

My dad used to smoke like a chimney. You would never see him without a ciggie. Honestly, I don't remember how many times my mum and I had to fight him on smoking outside instead of inside our tiny 30-square-metre-flat. Well, being in China reminds of those 'good old times'. In 2012, *The Economist* published its stirring article titled "Mapping the invisible scourge", in which spending a day in Beijing was compared to smoking 40 cigarettes. While I see it as a tad of a stretch, I can understand that-when in Beijing-one might feel as if they smoked such an exorbitant number of butts.

In a short span that Chai Jing's shocking documentary "Under the Dome" was accessible online, I managed to jot down its main concerns.

1. Half a million people die of air pollution in China every year (this whooping number was pulled from the former Minister's of Health, Chen Zhu, article in *The Lancet* – a medical journal)
2. Beijing's daily PM 2.5 levels are five times that of China's average (This, I am inclined to believe since my photos from visiting Beijing in August 2015 are all dull and dim, most scenic spots look like scenes from *Avatar*)
3. Shanghai burns more coal than any other metropolis in China
4. In 2013, Hangzhou had over 200 days of smog (Sadly, this is visible. When I came to Hangzhou in 2010, certain areas were very clear, green and smog-free. Now, when it's 2016, the same areas are visibly hazy.)
5. PM 2.5 levels are 25 times higher in winter than in summer
6. Only one percent of environmental disputes go to court

Apparently, the numbers of tourists annually visiting China also decrease each year, with main reasons being RMB appreciation and air pollution (according to echinacities.com). But China's wealthy are also fleeing the scene. I have heard many of my well-off Chinese friends say: *We plan to leave China soon because our son/daughter can't be raised in such environment.* I am always at awe with the Chinese who don't seem to be bothered by the dark cloud hanging above us. They say they are used to it.

Most of my students who had a chance to travel abroad flood their *WeChat* with posts of blue skies. One girl told me that she has never seen a blue sky in her life and that she's looking forward to moving to the U.S. That's a real bummer.

In the fall of 2016, Hangzhou hosted G20 and we could notice a slight difference six months prior to the event. Plants and factories were closed and one could actually see all that surrounds West Lake again.

At first, I was sceptical towards face masks. But later on, I became their biggest fan. Even though I had to dispose of them daily, I tried not to get horrified by the colour they turn by the end of the day.

When buying a face mask, one should follow certain directions to make sure the mask will in fact bring some benefits. First, check out the filter. There are two types: those that get rid of particulate matter and those that remove gases. There are European and American protection factors, which are marked as FFP2 and N95, etc. The higher numbered the mask, the greater the level of protection (against both solids and gases). Secondly, consider how often you are going to use your mask. Whether you plan to cycle, walk, or simply have it on all the time will determine if you should go for a reusable or a disposable one. Also, consider the cost. You can buy fairly-reliable masks produced by 3M on *Taobao* for about RMB 250 per box of 10. Other companies sell more expensive reusable masks with filters you can replace when need be.

While media point out Chinese government's hypocrisy, by announcing a war on pollution but refusing to build public awareness, it is somewhat understandable that the government has higher stakes in mind, i.e., strengthening the economy and becoming the global financial power.

Let it rain... Typhoon's dealings.

It was the first time I've got to experience a typhoon first hand, in Hangzhou. They do happen quite often in this part of China, but for some reason they had not reached my province before. Until last night.

It seems like the whole world is wrapped in a blanket of wind and the rain is so icy one could freeze into a sculpture. And this is May. We have had some heavy rain this year but the only thing the authorities seem to be doing about it is to minimize the casualties. Nobody is fixing the drainage system since it's so poorly designed no one dares to touch it. These are just a few pictures I snapped outside.

Image by Karolina Achirri.

Image by Karolina Achirri.

Image by Karolina Achirri.

This was the bus that brought me home from work today.
Image by Karolina Achirri.

I say Chinese people are so... patient. Had it been my car, half-soaked, I'd be raising hell. Even wellies do not help to go across huge puddles. And of course, bosses still expect one to get to work on time. Lol.

Coming from Poland, I am used to two adjectives for describing weather conditions: hot (in summer) and freezing (in winter). However, the weather in the south-east part of China, where Hangzhou is, has been radically unpredictable. There are practically only two seasons: summer and winter. A short period of spring lasts for about 3 weeks and autumn is almost impossible to notice. Summer is scorching hot and humid, while winter is cold and wet.

How can one prepare to survive such extreme weather conditions? There are a few tricks that have been helping me. First of all, dress for the part. When I see young Chinese girls wearing thin jackets barely covering their upper back, I foresee rheumatism in their future. Get yourself a thick parka or a long puff coat. And don't forget that this part of China does not have central heating so warm indoor wear is probably a good investment, too. Second of all, your electric bill will most likely eat all of your savings (if you have any☺) but run the AC in all rooms and buy an electric heater (preferably for each room). These aren't expensive but saved my feet from having frost bites while I was writing my previous books. Since we are in the south, chances are you won't see any snow, but good winter waterproof boots will prevent you from experiencing tons of cold-like symptoms. Also, China, as great as it is at inventing weird-looking but highly-useful gadgets, has already had you covered in terms of cold hands. Purchase a USB thermal pillow (they come in all shapes and colours), and in case you can't stand the frigid cold outside, adhesive patches for your pockets and your clothes, which heat up on contact.

Now, I find the heat a much bigger problem than the cold. When the temperatures reach 40 degrees Celsius, there is simply nowhere to hide. Everyone is saying: 热死了 (re si le), which literally means: Hot to die! I saw people buried in the sand on the side of the road, just like on the beach, to keep cool; playing mah-jong in water; and fearlessly buying ice porridge. Even if you get lucky to have your AC working throughout summer, the heat will find you inside your flat. Unless you like to spend your days in your birthday suit, get equipped with a bamboo pad (凉席 = *liang xi*), a mini electric fan (迷你电风扇 = *mi ni dian feng shan),* most often USB-charged, and a cooling spray (防晒喷雾 = *fang shai pen wu).*

When summer is coming, brace yourself! Stock up on ice cube containers, other cooling accessories and lots of ice-cream to face this sweltering time! If you want to follow fashionable Chinese girls, a nice umbrella is a must, too!

CHAPTER 6

CHINESE SCHOOLING

Education breeds confidence. Confidence breeds hope.
Hope breeds peace.
(Confucius)

Can you survive Chinese schooling?

The Chinese characters for 'to study', i.e., 学习 (*xue xi*), literally stand for 'to learn' and 'to practice'. In my opinion, they encompass schooling in China quite well. Confucius claimed that everyone around you can teach you something (*san ren xing bi you wo shi yan* = 三人行必有我师焉), "If three men are walking together, one of them is bound to be good enough to be my teacher". It is because of Confucianism that teachers are glorified in China. It is expected that teachers never get tired of teaching and stay open to learning from their students. As for students, getting into a university opens a lot of doors for them. It is considered an achievement to get in but an easy thing to finish. But, before they become college learners, they must cram day and night to pass the infamous *gaokao* (more on this exam in another piece), the National College Entrance Exam. However, due to over-recruitment of college students, changing job market and the high unemployment rate among college graduate, it is estimated that China will be in demand of blue-collar workers (aka skilled workers) pretty soon.

Since I have not taught in all types of schools in China, all my experiences in this section will be based on an international division of a public high school in Hangzhou. Students I taught got up at ungodly 5.30am. Many of them started their days with reciting what they'd memorized the night before, just to get ahead of their classmates. They'd have self-study from 7 to 7:45, when the classes start. For them, education is a serious deal, a key to the West. All my former students are currently in the UK or the US, since that's the main purpose of attending an international high school, namely to enrol at the top university abroad. Also, completing an international programme allows them to skip *gaokao*. All they have to do is maintain a decent GPA and get an IELTS score of over 7 or TOEFL over 100. This will guarantee them a smooth entry into one of their dream schools overseas, given that their parents can afford to pay full tuition anywhere in the world.

However, testing methods in China appear to be very nerve-racking. The general mentality is 'if you don't do well, you'll be publicly shamed'. I know it sounds awful to a Westerner but that's every Chinese student's daily bread. Teachers will rebuke you in front of everyone, your parents will feel disappointed with you and even your classmates will not want to befriend you. Many subjects focus gravely on testing skills, which leads to a situation of well-trained 'robotical' young people who lack any ability to think critically and analyse things.

Innovation and creativity aren't emphasized. The endless rote memorization, learning stress and anxiety levels skyrocketing as well as the constant fierce competition create overworked, underestimated and uninspired students. Even the educational reforms after the year 2000 do not seem to be defying the old-fashioned methods of learning and teaching. At least not yet.

Every Monday morning our school had a flag ceremony. Designated students would guard the flag pulled on a pole to oversee the upcoming week's events on campus. Also, one teacher was chosen each week to give an inspirational speech, either in Chinese or in English. This is when I learnt the words of the Chinese anthem, too, by singing it chorally every Monday at 7 am. A student would also give a speech, which normally looked like reading an essay (probably because that's what it actually was). The idea of the ceremony was noble: to encourage students for the next week of study, to cultivate patriotism and to exchange experiences between faculty and students. Whether it was successful or not is hard to tell. Many foreign teachers would get rebuked for talking during the anthem singing or keeping their hands in the pockets. I thought the ceremony was outdated as students themselves did not seem to either enjoy it or benefit from it. Plus, oftentimes these flag ceremonies would happen on a freezing morning, always outside, sometimes in the rain.

So why are Chinese students so brilliant at Maths and Science? Well, from my observations, they learn in 3rd grade what Americans study in college. It's true. They learn so much and at such an advanced level that it's hard for anyone not to become a Maths genius. Many students hate Maths, but even so they might choose it as their college major simply because they feel it's a safe option. Also, Maths classes fit perfectly into the mode of teaching testing skills. Repetitively solving long formulas by following teacher's method is the best way to learn by memorization.

Another thing is the number of students in one class, which ranges from 25 (if you're lucky to be at an international school) to 60 (in a typical high school). Students are therefore expected to sit quietly and attentively, which is honestly what makes teaching Chinese students so easy, no misbehaviour. I remember I had to forcibly pick on students to answer my questions during our first class, because no one was brave enough to speak. Also, when I asked one student: 'What do you think?', he was so shocked he almost fainted. He later told me no teacher till then had ever asked of his opinion. I understood how to deal with Chinese students right then.

Our school was already very westernized. It didn't look like a military boot camp, which is what most high schools in China reminded me of. The morning roll call and compulsory running at 10.20 were still there, but no crazy headmaster would scream propaganda slogans through the loudspeakers. In fact, the only people to egg on students to do better were their class supervisors, whose role was more like classroom police (e.g., they had to make sure everyone was present and ready, if not, they had to deliver a valid explanation to a given teacher).

As for teachers, they would teach from 10 to 18 classes, on average. The contract stipulated 20 teaching hours and 20 office hours per week. Each period lasted 40 minutes and we had to be at school from 7 am to 4 pm every day (one of my previous schools had a card-swiping device installed at the gate to monitor teachers' tardiness and then to punish us with RMB 50 fine for each 10 minutes). Some Chinese teachers were also required to supervise night study sessions (which typically lasted till 10pm). If you didn't teach, you'd be in your office preparing classes or (more often!) shopping on *Taobao*. There were meetings for everything. I felt like if a day didn't have a meeting, it was a holiday. Some of those meetings were in Chinese, so we would need our colleagues help to interpret or we would just pretend we were following but, in reality, secretly sending messages on *WeChat*. I didn't feel overworked but I felt very sorry for my Chinese colleagues, because a lot was expected from them, far more than simply teaching.

In my school, students were divided according to their destination, so UK or US groups, respectively. Still, many schools (some of my previous employers, too) divide students according to their overall test scores. So, students with good English would end up in the lowest level class, which for us meant teaching multiple levels of English in a single class. Man, did I learn to multitask!

Chinese students are generally overworked and exhausted. When their school week is over, many of them still attend weekend classes in training schools (often taking place from 8am to 9pm!) to beat the competition. Since the only method they practise is memorization, I saw students role learning SAT dictionaries. They knew the words but they had no idea how to use them. Suffice it to say, English textbooks used in many public schools are simply English translations of Chinese sentences, making students remember what to say in which tense but never why it is said that way or how it could be said another way. Besides, the 'why' question is often not allowed, as it undermines teacher's authority. The saddest part was the fact that neither students or their parents nor teachers had enough power to change the status quo, so everyone was just trapped in this vicious circle of educational madness.

Finally, the rote learning culprit. I get it. The only way to become proficient in reading and writing Chinese is to copy lists of characters for hours on end until they are permanently imprinted in one's mind. Perhaps that's why I could never master the characters. The problem is, English can't be learnt well solely this way. It can get you a 5 on IELTS, for sure. But it can't help you survive abroad or communicate with foreigners. I'd get so angry at my students reciting speeches in a monotonous voice. Memorization and rigidly copying information without creating new sources of knowledge comes at a high price for Chinese students when their college essays are flagged for plagiarism and their CVs rejected due to 70% copied language. When I had to teach my students about plagiarism and copyright in our Academic English class, it took them a while to grasp the concept of intellectual property. I learnt the hard way (after my first week) never to assign essays as homework, unless I wanted to read 50 *Wikipedia* entries.

However, not everything is bad in Chinese education. Many contemporary Chinese students are breaking out of the traditional styles of learning and teaching. Some of my students are truly brilliant, creative and imaginative young men and women. They proved it when I gave them their last semester assignment to write a children's book. What they came up with exceeded my highest expectations. They were witty, original and (to their own surprise, which came after their primary hatred towards me and the assignment!) enjoyed transferring their deepest and unheard ideas on paper. I intend to publish those stories one day. I think more emphasis should be placed on one's individual strengths and weaknesses, but I understand that it might take time in a collectivist culture (集体主义者 = *ji ti zhu yi zhe*) with over 1.3 billion population.

On being sooooo indecisive.

I have been wondering why Chinese students are so indecisive. Was I like that when I was their age? Anybody who knew me then would fiercely disagree.

Most of my students were about to graduate from high school to continue their studies abroad. However, if you ask most of them why they have chosen that particular university, you'll hear: I don't know. God only knows how I dislike this answer. If you go deeper and try to figure out why they have decided on that specific major, sadly the majority of them wouldn't even know what their major is actually about. Not to mention those who still, after almost a year, cannot properly pronounce 'Economics':).

I can see two reasons here. The first one is definitely a lack of interests. If they had hobbies and even just things they fancied doing in their spare time (no: sleeping doesn't count), it would be so much clearer to know what they want to do in the future. An average Chinese student is so study-oriented that they do nothing for fun which I could classify as 'smart pastime'.

Then, due to the fact they have had other people making decisions for them their entire lives, they seem to be simply incapable of selecting for themselves. Many of them would go and study Business because their parents want them to take over family business one day. Others would go for Accounting (I know, sounds like the most dreadful major on the planet) because it's a hot job in China, easily bringing quick profits.

The funny thing is, they pay all those bags of money to be exposed to foreign culture and get some contact with foreign teachers. But actually they do not want to be vulnerable to it. How can one ever fit in a new type of environment without the willingness to adapt and tweak bits and pieces of one's mind?

I look at it all and I sigh... Their priority is to get into top 10 universities abroad but their English is very often far lower than the actual 'survival abroad' level. I barely meet students who want to read English books. Also, all English-speaking TV shows in China are broadcast with Chinese subtitles anyway.

When I go back memory lane and think of myself setting off for

London years ago, I see a sea of differences. Maybe my English was not there yet, perhaps I was silly in the way I thought of the world and people, but I definitely knew what I wanted and why I wanted it. It's time to be fearless, China!

The infamous 'gaokao' exam.

Everyone awaits the end of high school. It marks the beginning of adulthood, hence freedom and independence. In China, not so much.

Every year from June 7 to June 8 or 9, around 10 million Chinese school seniors undergo the biggest trauma of their lives, namely The National University Entrance Examination, or *gaokao* (高考 = literally 'high test'). Since it's the lone criterion for university admission, for these young people everything rides on it.

Students sit three compulsory subjects: Chinese, Maths and English, which usually takes up to 6.5 hours. Additionally, there is a comprehensive exam for Humanities, which includes Politics, History and Geography, or Science, comprising Physics, Chemistry and Biology. I jotted down these exemplary questions from a newspaper one day. (Correct answers are at the end of this section.)

Politics:

Last October, President Xi Jinping said that while art is based on imagination, it should still be down-to-earth. There may be hundreds of ways to create art; the best way, however, is to trace it back to the people's daily lives and create something based off of that. From a materialistic point of view, this is because:

1. Art originates from the daily lives of people
2. Art depends on innovation
3. The way art reflects on society and its style is unified
4. Art is a form of ideology that reflects people's lives while at the same time serves them

A) 1 and 2   B) 1 and 4   C) 2 and 3   D) 3 and 4

History:

What happened in Soviet Russia in the 1920s?

A) Private enterprises began to emerge
B) State-run businesses had more autonomy
C) The government prohibited the sale of food
D) Peasants were active in collective farming

Mathematics:

Given $f(x) = sinx - (2sqrt(3))(sin^2(pi/s))$:

A) Find f(x)'s smallest positive revolution
B) Find f(x)'s smallest value, given that the period is [0,2pi/3]

Chinese language (essay questions):

1. Because her father always uses his cell phone while driving on the highway, no matter how many times other family members have told him not to, college student Xiao Chen was fed up. Concerned for her father's safety, Xiao Chen contacted the police through a private social media channel. After the police investigated, her father was sentenced to education and punishment. Later, the whole matter was published on the police's social media outlets and netizens debated the issue from different perspectives.

What is your view on this? In no less than 800 words, write a letter to the daughter or her father expressing your thoughts and opinions on the issue.

2. In 说起梅花 (*Speaking of Plum Blossoms*), the author expresses his 'passion that comes from the soul' for plum blossoms. In your life, what kind of things have caused you to have such a similar passion? And why has this kind of passion touched your soul? In no less than 800 words, write an essay based on the topic of 'passion that comes from the soul'.

Please pick an item (plant, animal, electronic device, but not plum blossoms). Feel free to describe, narrate, or write lyrics – you are not stylistically limited.

-Can you tell us your _____ for happiness and a long life?
-Living every day to the full, definitely.
A. recipe
B. record
C. range
D. receipt

Elaborate preparations for the test are taken not only by students, who need to decide on colleges they want to get into in advance, but also their parents. Some parents take time off work to accompany their offsprings to the school's campus. Then, they nervously wait for them outside the gate. Wealthier families can even fork out an auspicious RMB 888 (around $130) for a stay at a fancy hotel, which includes a night's accommodation, spa treatments and a discounted limo service to the venue, apparently to intimidate the competition. Also, more religious parents camp out outside, burning incense and praying to Buddha for their children's success. It is really 'Make It or Break It' moment!

Due to the psychological and physical pressure high schoolers experience prior to the test as well as tons of money spent on private tutors and weekend training schools, cheating is no rare case. If caught, one faces from one to three years of being banned from *gaokao*. Might sound more like a blessing than a punishment to many! Types of activities considered cheating include passing on questions after the exam, transmitting questions during the exam, forging IDs or even paying someone to take the test for you. The unlucky students' test scores might be cancelled, too. Since there is no age limit, there are news circulating about a few over 40s who have been taking *gaokao* more than 14 times. Kudos for perseverance!

Police has a lot on their plate during the test as well. Test questions are transported between schools in armoured vehicles, cameras monitor the classrooms and recently even drones were flown to oversee smooth procedures. The police also set up network towers that are supposed to block mobile phones' signal. The more creative students, however, somehow manage to hide cameras in their pens, glasses or even underwear. Some faint too, so medical services are on stand-by. In my last school, all other years had holidays during *gaokao*, school bells were switched off and guards were checking everyone's ID at the gate, even ours, who had to come to school nonetheless, to sit in the office, obviously, not to teach.

There have been vivacious debates regarding the fairness of the test. All provinces take the same test (but versions may vary according to a particular province's educational bureau) to and some claim it's unfair to those who are educated in underdeveloped areas, such as small rural schools. These students also don't have access to private classes or the means to hire tutors. Despite the screams of the opponents, the government is still working on thoroughly reforming the test, mostly on deleting its English part, though, as a part of maintaining Chinese patriotism and purity of a native language. One thing for sure, any time I mention *gaokao* in the presence of a Chinese person, a cold shudder runs through their spine.

ANSWERS to the QUESTIONS:
Politics: B
History: C
Mathematics: A 2pi   B -sqrt(3)
English: A

Chinese students and their drive to flock abroad.

The trend of more and more Chinese students preparing to study overseas is clearly visible in the contemporary society. Even more so is their age, lowering year after year. Why is the Chinese youth escaping their home country's education?

Firstly, a snapshot of history. When I was doing research for my PhD paper on Chinese students adapting to American academia, I learnt that the first Chinese student to ever study abroad was a businessman Yung Wing, who started his education at Yale University in 1847. He then graduated, returned to China and made it his mission to encourage more young people to go abroad. The number of Chinese students in foreign countries were steadily rising since then, but the Cultural Revolution in 1969 put a stop to all study abroad programs. It wasn't until 1978 and Deng Xiaoping's speech to open the China doors to the Western educational influences. Today, over 350,000 students from China study in the United States alone[2]. What a surge! Other top destinations include Australia, Canada, the UK, Western European countries, Singapore and New Zealand.

Before 1995, mostly poor students (or those who could not succeed in Chinese schools) would decide to go abroad because they were failing in Chinese schools, but nowadays more and more excellent students abandon their national education and continue being honours students overseas. It is no longer the case of political elite who can afford foreign education for their offsprings, but middle-class families invest their life savings into their child's future. Formerly, Chinese students were leaving for grad school, whereas now some of them even leave to become middle school pupils.

What drives them to leave? A variety of reasons. For starters, a degree from any foreign university (not necessarily highly ranked) carries more prestige than one from a top university in China. Everyone wants to be ahead in the Chinese job market, which becomes more competitive every year. Secondly, many students would do anything to avoid taking the horrid *gaokao* exam. Also, some hope to somehow stay long enough to have a shot at earning citizenship. Last but not least, of course the many shortcomings of Chinese education system do not help to keep these students at home. Ivy League and Oxbridge schools continually make headway with luring the Chinese youth. However, as I was told, lately, China has been looking down on those returning from education abroad. Apparently, they are not familiar with domestic job market, demand high salaries, aren't willing to work hard, or simply want a comfortable position.

So, what needs to be done to have one's dream of studying abroad come true? Parents will leave no stone unturned to make sure their precious son or daughter gets all the best help. Students applying to study abroad need to take language tests, such as IELTS or TOEFL, plus SAT if one plans to study in America. Parents often want only one-on-

---

[2] According to Open Doors. (2016). *Open Doors Report Highlights: Social Media Toolkit*. Retrieved from https://eca.state.gov/files/bureau/iew_opendoors_socialmedia_toolkit_interactive.pdf.

one tutoring, no matter the cost. They are willing to pay top dollar to so-called experts, who advertise their magical abilities of predicting questions to those high-stake exams. Quite a few of my students took individual classes with one Chinese SAT teacher in Hangzhou, who charged them RMB 10000 (around $1500) per hour just to go over SAT past papers and explain the correct answers (one could easily find at the back of the book). I asked them why they paid so much and if the classes really helped them, but most of them said it was their parents' idea because the guy is famous. I found it utterly atrocious to be charging people such exorbitant and unreasonable sums of money. But, at the end of the day, no one forced these parents to pay. It was their own idea.

Also, foreign study agencies are making a fortune by charging students for filing their applications online and proofreading their statements and resumes. One of my American colleagues figured out how the system works and started charging RMB 3000 (around $450) to simply read and correct potential students' essays. What a business mind! Additionally, the fee one has to pay the agency depends on the rank of the school the kid finally gets into. Only a few Chinese students realize that if they take all required exams and send in their applications, there is no way any university abroad is going to refuse them. After all, they are the only nationality able to pay tuition fees in full. Even though my students were very smart and advanced when it comes to their English proficiency, I saw none of them apply for a scholarship or a fellowship programme.

Do these students come back? According to statistics, yes, they do (over 72% percent came back from the US in 2013[3]). With their fancy Western diplomas and the ability to speak English, they have it easier to compete at the job market. There is a pun in Chinese: sea turtles (海龟 = hai gui), which describes Chinese students who return home after graduating from Western schools. However, the domestic job market welcomes them with a starting salary of RMB 3000 (around $500) a month. Interns get around RMB 1200 (around $200). These returnees quickly realize that their high school friends moved on, started families and succeeded at work, while all that's waiting for them is a minimum wage job and starting from scratch.

---

[3] Wall Street Journal published an article in March 2013 with this number.

Since my last school in China was an international high school, all my former students are currently abroad (hopefully done with their freshman year). Before I left, I interviewed my six favourite ones (I know, a teacher isn't supposed to have most likeable students, but I did☺). They allowed me to publish the interview along with their photo.

Interview conducted on January 19, 2016. They are Lydia, Si Yu Yuan, Jrong, Ricardo Fu, Lucas and Victor.

Me: How did you choose or get your English names?
Ricardo Fu: I got my first English name in my elementary school. My English teacher chose it for me. It was Bill, so different from what I have now. I didn't really like that name because it was too short, so when I fell in love with Economics in Grade 6, I renamed myself as Ricardo, after a scholar named David Ricardo. I really liked his theory supporting classic Economics, so that's why I chose his name as my name.
Me: Do you think that Ricardo suits you better?
Ricardo Fu: Yeah. And I got used to being called that.
Lucy: I got this name in my kindergarten. My teacher said: *You look so happy. I'd like to give you a name, your name is Lucy.* I guess she named lots of students Lucy. I also really like the movie "The Chronicles of Narnia". There was a little girl called Lucy and I think she's pretty and smart.
Victor: I got it because it means "victory". My parents want me to live a successful life so my older cousin named me Victor.
Lucas: A few years ago, my favourite actress gave birth to a son and his name is Lucas. I think this name sounds cute, so I chose it for myself. Before that, in my middle school, my English teacher called me Phillip,

without "s". When I travelled to the UK, some people mistook it for Phillips. So, then I changed my name.

Lydia: Actually, I've had three English names. The first one was Susan, which my primary school English teacher gave me. There are many people called Susan, I even met three Susans in my primary school. So, when I got to high school I decided to change my name. I picked Lolita, because it sounds nice. But later I found out that it has a strange meaning which refers to an "early mature girl". So, I switched into Lydia.

Me: Which one do you like most?

Lydia: The current one and I'll stick with it.

Jrong: I got my name (Belle) in my kindergarten. My parents bought me a Disney DVD called "The Beauty and the Beast". The girl's name is Belle. I really liked her 'cause she was wearing a yellow dress which made her look extremely beautiful. So that's how I got this name.

Me: If Chinese teachers give their students English names, how do they decide on them?

Lucas: Randomly. Perhaps because the teacher just watched a movie and that's how they end up calling 10 girls Tracy.

Me: When I taught in a kids' school in China, students would always come up to me and ask me to give them an English name. I was confused and kept asking them: Why? You already have a name. But they insisted on having an English name. And then at the university, I'd hear: "So, what's my English name? I'd say: I don't know. You tell me".

I tried to match their names with the way they looked or the way their Chinese name sounded. My Chinese name 李娜娜 (Li Na Na) and my real name sound similar. So, I thought that when you guys get your English names the pronunciation of your Chinese names is taken into consideration.

When did you start learning English? How many years have you studied English altogether?

Ricardo Fu: I started speaking English in my kindergarten (when I was four), because it was a bilingual school. But formally, I started to learn it in Grade 3, so that's 9 years now.

Lucy: Also in my kindergarten. It was not a compulsory course but the parents asked the school to organize the classes for us. Actually, the teachers' pronunciation was so bad that I acquired some bad habits back then. It's hard to get rid of them now.

Victor: I didn't touch English before my Third Grade. It has been nine years. And I think 3rd Grade is the right time to begin, as we are ten then and so we can write, too. I think it would be inefficient to learn English earlier as we spent most of our time playing, not studying in a formal way.

Lucas: I started learning English at the same age as Victor, in my primary school. I could not spell the word "milk". [laughter]

Lydia: My parents, originally, wanted me to start in my kindergarten but back then I was still learning the Chinese pinyin, and even though the English alphabet looked similar to pinyin, the pronunciation was completely different. So, I was struggling really hard to differentiate between the two. So, I dropped English and went back to it in my third Grade of elementary school.

Jrong: In my primary school, we were forced to study English in Grade 1, but we didn't have to take any tests yet. So, the classes were like a rest to us, always very active. But my parents asked me to watch some English videos when I was in the kindergarten.

Me: Do any of your parents speak English?

All but Lucy: No.

Lucy: My mum speaks poor English. (laughter) She has to do business with foreigners. In the past, she worked in the petrol industry and always met foreigners there.

Lydia: My mother always hires professional translators.

Me: Have you ever asked your parents why they would force you to learn English if they didn't speak it?

Lucy: They want a better future for us.

Victor: They don't need English.

Ricardo Fu: They think they aren't able to learn it, because they are too old to learn.

Me: I see.

Lydia: My mother is learning English now.

Jrong: My dad is also learning.

Me: Oh, that's pretty cool. So, normally students in China start learning English in 3rd Grade, yes? Some students can start in kindergarten, if there's such an opportunity? OK.

What other foreign languages do Chinese students tend to study? Why?

All: Japanese, French, Spanish.

Me: But you can't choose these languages in school, right? You can only learn them privately?

Jrong: Yes, but 10 years ago many places offered Russian as a foreign language. My dad could choose between English and Russian.

Lydia: I heard that if we attend a Chinese university, the choice of foreign languages is bigger.

Lucas: Students on the main campus of our school can choose Japanese, but as an elective course, not a part of the curriculum.

Lucy: Because it is not tested on *gaokao* (the national university entrance exam).

Me: Oh, I see. That makes sense. Did you think English was easy or difficult when you began learning it? Why?

Ricardo Fu: In kindergarten, when I only had to speak it, it seemed easy. It was integrated into games.

Lucas: It was easy in the beginning but not after that.

Lydia: Because at the beginning teachers taught us easy things, such as the ABC song.

Lucy: Also, kids don't care about losing face. They are brave to speak and don't care if they make mistakes.

Ricardo Fu: That's why some parents think that kindergarten is the best time to learn English, not only physically but also mentally.

Me: So, what do you think now?

All: Difficult. [laughter]

Me: Why?

Victor: Because when I was in primary school, I could easily improve by memorizing a few words, like cat, dog, pencil, etc. But now the requirements are higher and the vocabulary is not the only standard.

Lucas: Now, there's a lot of pressure to learn English. Every chance you'd have to escape this pressure, you would.

Lucy: I think our previous purpose was to get good grades, and now our purpose is to use it, so we have to speak and know the foreign logic.

Me: What common methods or techniques do teachers use in a traditional Chinese school to teach English?

Lucy: Dictation. For words. Every day. They ask you in Chinese and you have to write down English.

Lydia: Also, to memorize a lot of essays from textbooks. They believe that if you are able to memorize the whole essay, you'll be able to use some structures from it as your own.

Victor: It can also improve your grammar level for tests, especially multiple-choice questions. This way you can choose the right answer just by scanning the question.

Ricardo Fu: Students also have to read out loud the entire essays and their vocabulary each morning.

Me: How do you find Chinese English teachers' level of English?

Ricardo Fu: They are literate in English. They can write and know a great deal about grammar, but they can't speak. Only a few of them can speak.

Jrong: I think they are very good at the textbook material, but there would be a problem for them outside of textbooks.

Lucy: They are obedient and they don't allow students to express their own opinions in their essays. I always wanted to express some unique ideas but they never allowed that.

Me: Do you have more female or male English teachers?

<u>All</u>: Female.

<u>Lydia</u>: Mostly for English, Chinese and Literature.

Me: What's the hardest part of learning English in your opinion?

<u>Jrong</u>: I think it's to sound more native. We have to change our behavioural pattern and try to behave like the foreigners do. This is different from the techniques we know.

<u>Lydia</u>: For me it's still grammar. I know all the grammar rules, I know how a sentence should be made, but if I need to speak it right away I won't notice grammar problems.

<u>Lucas:</u> It's the same for me, grammar. I don't know how to see my grammar mistakes to be able to correct them.

<u>Victor:</u> I think the hardest part is to speak like foreigners, including their accent or their way of thinking. Also, when I have limited time, I can't use the right words.

<u>Lucy:</u> I think the most difficult thing is to follow the foreigners' logic. When I entered this school, I was always curious what foreign teachers were thinking about.

<u>Ricardo Fu:</u> Speaking fluently. Before going to high school, I was always translating (from Chinese to English) in my head. I always want to create my own usage of the language.

Me: What was the biggest challenge in your leaning process that you overcame? And how did you do that?

<u>Ricardo Fu:</u> To increase the vocabulary a lot. I overcame it two years ago. I started to do some IELTS readings, although it was really hard for me. Only a few sentences could be understood.

<u>Lucy:</u> I think it must be writing. It's hard for me to develop my opinion in the essay, because I'm thinking in the Chinese way and I don't know how to express my ideas, in the native way. I'm still working on it. I read a lot of good essays and ask other students how they develop their ideas.

<u>Victor:</u> I also found out that memorizing words from reading is better than reciting words from a vocabulary list. It helped me understand how to use these words.

<u>Lucas:</u> How to remember vocabulary was a challenge to me, because repeating these words would help. I used to be afraid of speaking in public, too. I think making friends who are talkative could help.

<u>Lydia</u>: For me is to scan the essay, because I really like to understand every word in a sentence. That really slows my speed down. So, I tried to read an essay in a specific time period. Now, I'm reading *the Guardian* essay every day and I push myself to finish one essay in one

minute.

Jrong: I think reciting academic articles is very hard. That was the most terrible thing for me in the past.

Me: Sounds like hell.

Jrong: I couldn't remember anything but my parents wanted to help me so they asked me to recite those essays to them before going to school.

Me: So, why did you decide to study in an international high school?

Ricardo Fu: Ridiculously, I came here by accident. In middle school, I did really bad in Mathematics. My English teacher recommended I took an entrance exam to this school. I tried and I got into. The previous leader of the school told me I can't quit once I'm in. So, I just came here. After the first year, I realized that international education can bring me a better mindset.

Me: You must admit it's not as strict as a typical Chinese high school.

Ricardo Fu: My parents wanted me to continue studying at a traditional Chinese school.

Me: Since your plan is to study abroad, another question is: why did you decide on the UK and not the US, for instance? And what's your dream school?

Ricardo Fu: Previously, I wanted to go to the US but it's recommended to take SAT, which is really miserable. I think the UK is much easier to get in. At that time, my dream school was Cambridge, I really wanted to study Medicine there, but the competition was really strong. So, I gave up. Now, my dream is UCL and studying Biochemical Engineering.

Lucy: In my middle school, I was not an obedient student. I was too creative. I always wanted to try lots of things but teachers never allowed me to do so, because exams were more important. My Maths was not really good. Someone told me that international education has easier Maths classes. And then I found it's not really true. I used to want to go to another high school (also international), but I changed my mind. I think some people came here just to avoid these stressful Chinese exams (like zhongkao: at the end of middle school or gaokao: at the end of high school). My dream school is KCL (King's College of London) and majoring in Digital Culture.

Victor: Basically, I made this decision by myself, because I was good at English in my middle school. My English was better than other subjects, such as Maths or Science. My dream school is UCL and I just got an offer from them today.

Me: Wow! Congratulations! And you want to major in?

Victor: Urban planning and real estate.

Lucas: I didn't know about this school's programme until the registration day. My Science teacher told my mother it's a good opportunity to get into those higher quality universities later. I wasn't sure at first because my English score was extremely low. I think Hong Kong University is a good choice for me in the future, but some of their requirements are too high. I would like to major in Quantitative Finance and it only takes 25 people. I think a Maths related major will be easy to complete. If this university doesn't work, I'll go to UCL. Then, I'll study Statistics and Finance.

Lydia: Actually, I was really anxious about *zhongkao* and my dad said: You can treat this opportunity at international high school as a mock. Surprisingly, I got in. So, I thought I'd stay in this high school. My dream school has always been Cambridge but I was rejected. So, now I plan to go to Hong Kong University. I chose Clinical Medicine and Surgery there. But I haven't got an offer yet. My major requires Cantonese rather than English. It's too difficult to go to Europe. For example, Cambridge only offers 22 spots for international students each year.

Irong: My father told me about this programme. He thought an international school might be a better choice for me. I had nothing else but to take *zhongkao*, but this school came just like light in the dark. I want to go to LSE (London School of Economics) for Mathematics and Economics. But an IELTS requirement is 7. So, I've got another plan, which is Toronto University. I'd like to study International Relations there.

Me: Did all of your parents support your choice to come to this school?

Lydia: Not my parents because they've lately found a new school, where my younger brother is. It's more traditional Chinese school. They believe I should read more Chinese classics, and books about Traditional Chinese Medicine.

Lucy: Before I came here, my parents thought it was a really good idea. But, after one year, they think the management is such a mess.

Me: Throughout your two and a half years here, did you ever want to give up?

All but Ricardo Fu: No.

Ricardo Fu: Because sometimes I couldn't face the facts and I tried to give up, but I didn't. In my spirit, I didn't want to lose hope, but it was difficult to stay.

Me: How would you compare a traditional Chinese style of teaching with the Western way? What are the biggest differences?

Lucas: The interaction between teachers and students. In a traditional Chinese school, the teaching style is more like a lecture. They both have ups and downs.

Me: You still have Chinese teachers here, who co-teach with foreign teachers. Is their style also different?

All: Yes.

Ricardo Fu: They can always explain things to you in Chinese if you can't understand English.

Victor: Chinese teachers are good at explaining things and achieving the target in a short period of time. They have a way to stick knowledge into students' brains but it's not always effective.

Lucy: There are also differences in writing. In a Chinese class, teachers tell you what to memorize to get full marks. But in the Western style, you have to express your own idea and evaluate critically.

Me: So, what's your favourite English word? Why do you like it?

Jrong: *Brilliant.* I heard it in a song. It's also a good adjective. It's optimistic.

Lucas: *Lucas.* I think it sounds cute.

Victor: *Heck.* It's not a bad word and I can show my emotions through it.

Lucy: *Independence,* because studying abroad is expensive and I don't want my parents to pay a lot for me. It's also hard for Chinese students to ask for financial support. So, I want to be more independent and try to release the pressure from my parents. Also, I like the word persistence.

Ricardo Fu: *Phenomenal,* just because I want to be phenomenal. I will be like that.

Lydia: *Interesting,* because it's like the first long word I've learnt. The pronunciation is funny.

Me: Before we wrap up, can you tell me why you agreed to do this interview?

Ricardo Fu: Firstly, it's a precious chance to practise English and speak naturally. It's not like a test or a conversation in class. We are all very close so there will be no shame if we make any mistakes. Secondly, just because I want to help you, since you helped me a lot.

Lucy: Because I like you and I like your courses.

Victor: Same with Ricardo.

Lucas: Just because I like you and I think it's worthwhile to give my ideas which could be helpful to others.

Lydia: It's interesting to think that I'll appear in your book. Also, I believed this conversation would be really fun.

Me: A lot of people are interested in what you have to say. People always ask me questions about living in China.

Ricardo Fu: I also want to give people a fair view. Some foreigners spread bad news about China.

Jrong: Because I was curious about the content of your book. And many books about China are misleading so I wanted to express my own opinion.

Me: Last question: what advice would you give to other English learners?

Ricardo Fu: No matter if you have the talent or not in English, you must be hard-working. Chinese teaching is enough to bring you to the survival English level but foreign style will bring you to an advanced level.

Lucy: Practice makes perfect. The most vital component is thinking. Also, you should learn culture of foreigners because you don't want to be impolite.

Victor: Do not be embarrassed by speaking English. Even if you speak poorly, just keep practising and you'll improve.

Lucas: Speak out.

Lydia: Keep calm and move on. As non-native speakers of English, we will always struggle with a lot of problems, but we need to find something in English that interests us to keep learning it.

Jrong: Be brave and be patient, because learning a language is a time-consuming process.

Lucy: I think English is like a woman. You already know lots of things about it, but you still have to discover some.

Me: Very deep, philosophical answer. Thanks a lot, guys!

"Chinese School: Are Our Kids Tough Enough?"
– A BBC documentary.

One day my colleague knocked at my office door and asked me if I had already seen the new controversial BBC documentary. Since I hadn't, I asked her to share the link on it with me. People were already discussing it on *WeChat*.

5 Chinese teachers from Beijing headed to the Bohunt School in Hampshire, southern England, for a month a typical Chinese instruction. The students were from 13 to 15 years old British kids who were formed as a group of 50 'chosen' ones to attend the experiment. While their schoolmates continued to study with their regular English teachers, the viewers were anxiously waiting to see the comparison of the two groups' test results. Indeed, such was the purpose of this

programme, to establish which educational practices bring better results. Lately, Britain has been openly acknowledging their students' lagging behind their Chinese counterparts.

The documentary has three parts and the results are revealed at the very end of the series. To much pride and elation on the Chinese side, students who underwent the trial showed on average 10% higher test results than those who stuck with home-style schooling.

However, the whole endeavour looked like a chaotic clash of cultures. Even though Chinese teachers seem to have succeeded in preparing their students for the tests, they certainly appear to have failed on the emotional level. The complete lack of classroom discipline and their inability to handle it made their days in Hampshire a living hell.

The chosen 50, experienced a very authentic Chinese school regime. The day started at 7 am, they had to wear a ridiculously looking tracksuit, clean their classrooms every day, do group eye exercises, salute the Chinese flag and last but not least bow in unison to their teacher at the beginning of each class. Many of the students commented that a month of army-like schooling made them feel like robots, who were expected to obediently listen to lectures and memorize rigid information. God forbid they dared to ask questions!

Netizens in China shared their views on the show online, with some of my favourite being: "British classroom discipline is rubbish!"; "Ha, ha, ha. Finally, those foreigners can suffer."; "Foreigners' physique seems several times better than Chinese. They must be living good lives."; and "Female British students all wear tights.".

I personally enjoyed watching the programme a lot. Not only because it was a classic example of an unwelcome and unpredictable encounter of two cultures poles apart, but also because it stayed objective, depicting pros and cons of both education systems. I must admit my respect for Chinese teachers notably boosted, as they persevered the (at times) unbearable treatment when they could have just packed and left. I guess my Chinese sister was right always saying: "Chinese people suffer a lot!".

So, which education model is better? I'm sure everyone holds a different opinion. To my mind, creating a school with a truly intercultural curriculum, inclusive of both cultures of learning and open to experience the Eastern and Western academia seems to be the best fit.

The weird side of Chinese schools.

First come the eye exercises (眼保健操 = *yan bao jian cao*). I was sceptical at first when I saw kids do their daily regime of eye drills, until I tried it with them, and I must say: They do work, at least for a while. In some primary schools, every two classes or so, a loud recording from loudspeakers directs children to follow the instructions. It provides soothing music and counts for them, too. Each class would have a designated kid, who gets the privilege of walking around with a stick and cracking down on those who don't participate. One primary school in Hangzhou, near my house, implemented new eye exercises last fall. The kids are to stand up and roll their eyes back and forth following their own fingers (this method is based on acupuncture and those eyes movements are supposed to press on specific points called 穴位 (*xue wei*). These forms of relaxation are believed to instantly relieve stress and strain on the eyes, stimulate eye muscles and enhance the conductive functions of brain neurons to improve eyesight. If it works for a billion people in China, why wouldn't it work for you?

Another day, Hunan Foreign Vocational College became egregious all over the Internet for its unusual punishment. Students were being forced to wrap themselves in blankets and lie on the ground under the sun as well as run with plastic buckets on their heads. Apparently, they had to face this torture due to unclean dormitory. One school's administrator commented that it was unfair to impose such discipline on girls and suggested psychological counselling instead. And this was happening in September, when summer wasn't over yet.

Additionally, the vice-principal of one of the Wuzhou's (Guangxi Province) schools, *Huang*, stirred netizens' discussions on one October afternoon when a video of him publicly cutting several of his students' hair went viral. Supposedly, it was retribution for their tardiness. As if this wasn't humiliating enough, he made the whole school watch, too. When interviewed, he claimed that he was looking out for those students, making sure they don't imitate Japanese and Korean pop cultures. That's taking a 'bad-hair day' to the new level!

This next one really shocked me. Huizhou Comprehensive Middle School (Guangdong Province) purchased knives for all female students and provided them with compulsory stabbing classes. There were 8 different movements and each time the girls performed one of them, they had to scream: Kill! This idea was one of the responses to recent stabbings in hospitals in China. It seems that the only thing that can stop a guy with a knife is a girl with a knife...

Talking about exam security, a Baoji College (Shanxi Province) conducts two sessions of a big exam for over 1200 students each year. Every session is equipped with 80 invigilators, telescopes, ladders, high-def cameras and loudspeakers. Their reason for such advanced security measures is to make students realize the severity of the exam and of course to prevent cheating. I wonder who would dare to cheat in that Fort Knox!

Now, I cannot omit the Chinese school uniforms. According to *China Youth Daily*, over 50% of students deem their uniforms to be "ugly". Typically, in autumn and winter pupils would wear sport uniforms, very loose and large. One skinny student of mine managed to squeeze both of her legs into one pantleg. In summer, girls are allowed to switch to skirts with built-in shorts, but they rarely do so, since the uniforms are so hideous. Most students continue wearing their tracksuit-like uniforms all year round. Chinese educational institutions see those uniforms as a symbol of fair education, with no chance to show off one's wealth at school. A recent survey[4] proves that the most important factors in a school uniform are: nice looks (62.9%), practicality (60.8%), cultural connotations (58.3%), unified looks (50.6%), simplicity (50%), distinctiveness for each sex (47%), and affordable price (44.6%). Only 24.9% of respondents opted for a customized option. Prices of school uniforms vary and can even reach as high as RMB 2500 (around $360). They can also consist of up to 18 pieces. I hope they come with some instructions.

A lot can be said about Chinese schools, but one thing is certain: they are interesting places to study. I have observed and analysed various school practices during my stay in China and I was never bored, always learning something new and exciting.

---

[4] www.echinacities.com/china-media/Survey-Chinese-School-Uniforms-Deemed-Ugly-by-512-of-Participants

CHAPTER 7

THE ENGLISH FAD

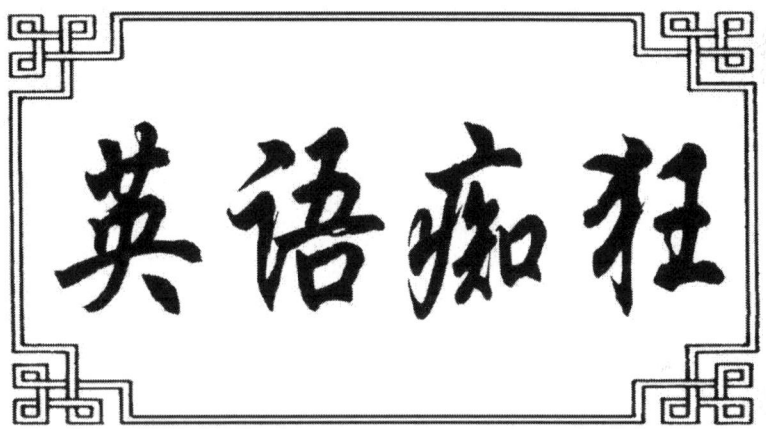

Language is the dress of thought.

(Samuel Johnson)

Teaching English in China.

Let me start with generally circulating perceptions of foreigners teaching English in China. *LBH, Loser Back Home*, is a term that sadly describes many (but not all) foreign teachers in China. They are unemployable back home and while teaching in China often come to classes late, unprepared and drunk (or hangovered). People teach English in China for many different reasons, of course, but those who do it for the right reasons face hateful snubs such as: You're smart, for an English teacher; You're an English teacher, I'll try not to hold it against you; You couldn't find a job in McDonald's?, to list just a few. I don't know why there is this prevalent belief that teaching English in China is a super easy job, involving jumping around like a monkey, singing songs and watching Western movies.

When it comes to Chinese employer's perceptions, the situation isn't any better. Many schools try to hire foreigners for the 'face' factor, preferably blond skinny white girls. Qualifications are often overlooked at job interviews if only one fits the image of a perfect foreign teacher. A Westerner in the classroom, even if he or she has no idea how to teach, justifies high tuition fees Chinese parents are not afraid to pay. Even though a typical contract stipulates medical insurance and all sort of luring benefits, nobody tells you that you need to pay the insurance company first to get paid, if that happens at all.

The on-going obsession with a native-speaker has made it impossible for many talented and well-educated individuals to land good, stable, well-paid teaching jobs. I was lucky because I was an IELTS examiner, which raised my status to being an English god. Many guys I met from countries like The Philippines, Germany, or South Africa (a black skinned person) were sent off from school's HR, because they did not meet the obsolete native-speaker requirement. Needless to say, they had Master's in TESOL or even a PhD in Linguistics. So, if you want to find a lucrative teaching gig in China, make sure to be white, handsome or pretty, skinny, and be holding a US, UK, Canadian or Australian passport.

I came to China originally to teach for one year, at a language institute for adults in Hangzhou. My salary was RMB 4000 (around

$580) back then, and that was because (as I was told) my Master's degree was from a non-English speaking country and so was I. After a year, I found a better job in another training school and filled my weekends with part-time kids' school classes. I was making more money but still nothing spectacular. When I came to China, I already had had 6 years of teaching English experience and that did help me negotiate for a raise and fewer classroom hours. Or it might have been my natural charm and bubbly personality, who knows! I never applied to schools that required teaching according to rigidly set lesson plans, although novice teachers might prefer this system. I started developing new curricula for my schools and enjoyed creating my own elective courses. After four years of bouncing from one training school to another, I finally got a job at an international high school. That was a game changer for me. Not only was my salary now decent (RMB 24000 = around $3500), but also students' English and motivation to learn were on a completely different scale. They wanted to improve their English, they understood how important it was for their future abroad. It was a sheer pleasure to teach them during my last two years in China. Throughout the 6-year period, I was also actively testing IELTS in various parts of Eastern China. That brought me prestige and tons of private clients.

As far as qualifications, TEFL certificate is one of the government-required papers, so make sure to get one (you can do it online) beforehand. CELTA and DELTA lay among more advanced certificates but also welcomed ones. BAs and MAs from non-English speaking countries, or not in English, won't give you much, but nowadays one must have at least a Bachelor's Degree to obtain a work visa, anyway.

If you happen to be a well-educated individual with a certificate and a valid teaching experience and if your goal when entering China is to teach English (because you want to, not because you have to), you will have chances for climbing up a career ladder. I was offered managerial positions 4 times, but never took any because I wanted to teach, not manage. Plus, I would make a terrible boss.

There are different types of English teachers in China. Some want power more than money, so they let their Chinese supervisors push them around, while hoping to be recognized for their loyalty and hard work one day. One thing that is universal in Chinese ESL schools is the complete lack of respect for loyalty. Don't stay in the same school for 10 years because you want to get promoted in your 40s. With such a turnover of foreign teachers, schools and students are used to having new teachers on a daily basis. Another type is 'the rebel'. This kind of a person basically awaits any weird or outside-of-contract request from their Chinese manager simply to fire back immediately and stir trouble. A lot of such individuals are visibly miserable where they are, and since they can't find any other reasonable jobs in China, they make it their life's mission to make everyone else as miserable as themselves. Then, there is 'the quitter'. I have worked with guys who wouldn't show up for work on their second day. Nobody knew what happened to them, but they apparently knew that once a work visa was in their passport, the only way to have it revoked was for the employer to physically have it removed/cancelled. Some schools kept foreign teachers' passports for that very fear of having them run away. Finally, 'the real teacher', those who come to teach, know how to teach and enjoy teaching. Even though still in the minority, those ones enjoy getting to know China, oftentimes learn Mandarin as well, love their students and work with passion, not a hangover. However, these are usually the quiet types, not wanting to be used as marketing faces of the school, so management barely ever notices their hard work and devotion.

If you are thinking of going to teach in China, before you make that move there are a few tips I'd like to give you.

- Research the school. Make sure they have legal right to arrange a work visa (that's the only visa type that allows you to teach). Request to see the contract before deciding anything. Although contracts don't hold much legal power in China, it is a good tool for your own protection in case of trouble.
- Ask for a detailed contract. Make sure your contract clearly states the number of hours you'll have to work, national holidays and number of days-off you can take. Don't sign a generic contract without this information.
- Learn Mandarin. You don't have to know it before going (I didn't), but you should definitely make use of local resources and learn it once in China. It will help you read bus signs, names of products in shops and it will make your life much easier once you can communicate with taxi drivers, shop keepers, etc.
- Research the city, not just the job. You might enjoy living in a metropolis or you might be a nature lover. Check the place's population and possible things to see.

- Prepare yourself for pollution. I know it's easier said than done, but I've seen guys getting ill with unknown diseases so you want to avoid that. You can also purchase your disposable masks beforehand (because it might take a while before you master *Taobao*).
- Be open to new experiences. Don't compare China to your home country. It's pointless. Instead, stay open to new adventures, people, tastes, and views. Embrace the new and different! Don't waste your time and energy on judging!
- Check your resilience in large crowds. No matter where you end up, places are crowded everywhere in China (unless you decide to become a monk and join the Buddhist monastery on a top of a mountain).
- Say goodbye to *Facebook*, *Youtube* and *Google*. You heard me right! They are blocked in China. There are a number of VPNs available to break through the Great Firewall of China, but they are expensive and the free ones aren't reliable.
- Save-up. Before you start making any money, you'll be spending money on things you never knew you'd once need, such as bamboo mats, USB fans, heated mittens, etc. Usually schools will pay you after your first month of work is completed and opening a bank account can prove to be a long and tiring hassle as well.
- Don't go for the wrong reasons! First and foremost, make sure your reasons for choosing to teach in China are the right ones. You don't want to be stuck in the middle of Asia feeling unhappy, unfulfilled or unemployed (never quit your teaching job before landing another one).

Once you've decided to go, you got your visa, bought your ticket, landed and started teaching, there are a few things to expect at work.

- Regardless of your school's level (university, high school, primary school, kindergarten, etc.), all students love to play games in class. Make sure you have enough ideas to last you a few months.
- Don't expect good teaching materials to be provided by the school. There rarely are any materials and if there are some, one needs to practically re-write them for each class' needs.
- Develop your own reward system. Stickers worked best for me. One thing all Chinese students love to do it compete against

each other. Make sure you have something to give them as prizes.

- Get ready for a scheduling rollercoaster. I don't know why but all schools I worked in had a complete inability to handle scheduling classes. They'd give you a tentative timetable for the first week, which then might change up to 10 times.
- If classes are cancelled because of holidays, in public schools you'll have to work those off at the weekend.
- Chaos. It's everywhere. No one knows anything and everyone pretends to know everything. China is a hierarchical society and this is highly visible in its management style. If you have a question, prepare yourself to be sent from pillar to post.
- You'll work overtime and without being paid. It's very common. There are always activities to attend, meetings to sleep in, I mean attend😊, and other miscellaneous duties. You're expected to show your face there, but don't expect to be paid for that.
- You'll be monitored in classrooms. Public schools have installed monitoring systems on premises, including classrooms.
- You might need to teach classes of 50-60 students. Grow patience and establish a good routine from the very beginning. Also, having students work in permanent groups saved me many times from pulling my hair out.
- Enjoy your job. Students are psychically skilled at recognizing those who are there with forced and negative attitudes. Chinese students are lovely and very well-behaved. As long as you're doing your job, they'll do theirs.

How does it feel to be a 'non-native' English teacher in China? It feels great.

Ever since I came to China, this issue of *native-speakerism* has been popping up like mushrooms after rain. When teaching in China, one needs to either go with the flow and turn into a conformist or drown. I chose neither. I chose to be my own person, not ashamed of being Polish, not having any chips on my shoulders due to the fact that my mother tongue is one of those 'underdeveloped' ones. To all those haters I met so frequently, I say: Sod off!!! From my experience, Chinese people automatically assume that every expat grew up using English. They can't be more wrong.

Among foreigners I've met in the Middle Kingdom, especially Americans, none has held a recognizable and reputable teaching qualification yet. I'm not counting in those online courses that anyone can buy for about $500. These teachers' grammar begs for repair and their general academic knowledge could also use a boost. Still, it's hard to believe that wealthy Chinese are willing to pay even $100 for an hour with such teachers.

I'm not trying to be judgmental here. I did meet some decent teachers, too. I did meet people who were interested in something more than clubbing or dating Chinese girls. Sadly, they are still in the minority.

Now, what can a person like me, who belongs to 'the others', do in order to avoid the constant need to prove herself? I'd say: Do your job the best you can and never let others bring you down. Because they will try, believe me. Stay confident about your teaching skills and don't lie. Contrary to the advice you might get from many, truth has a way of always resurfacing. Lying and pretending to be a fake American, British or Canadian will get you nowhere, only into deeper water.

I have studied hard in my life. Those who have known me for many years still remember what I needed to give up in order to become an English teacher. Having had 5 part-time jobs in London at the same time (including *Starbucks*, babysitting and cleaning offices at night), working for 3 different schools full-time later in Poland, and paying for it all with my own money (tuition fees) were all made of blood and sweat. I have sacrificed health and spare time just to always learn more and become knowledgeable enough to answer my students' questions.

I do feel accomplished today. I have got into a prestigious PhD programme at an American university, in a field that not many natives can thrive. I was never in China for the wrong reasons, or just to fill the gaps in my personal life. That would have made my life there miserable. That's not the way to tackle China. Staying open-minded is, though.

So, to all those who worked with me or will work with me in the future, start judging from yourselves. Let's take out our diplomas and talk about what qualifications all of us obtained, first. Then, we can start throwing stones.

Since this is not supposed to be an attacking piece, I'll end it on a lighter note. Life is great if one does what they love. It's surely true in my case. Stay faithful to your choices and learn to take it easy at times. Nobody is just their job. After all, we can't take any of our earthly treasures to wherever we're going next. Quoting my sister: Coffins don't have pockets.

Wishing every struggling non-native teacher of English a waterfall of self-esteem. We rock!

Teaching stories: The sad, the funny and the scary.

#1   The first class after the holidays I asked my high school students: "What did you do on your holidays?" One young, innocent-looking girl answered: "I was alone because my friends were travelling and my parents had to work, so I just stayed at home and *played with myself.*" Given that all the students in that class were supposed to go to a foreign university in less than 6 months, I thought it was about time to nib that answer in the bud. Trust me, they will never make such a mistake again☺.

#2   I was observing my foreign friend teach kindergarten the other day. In international kindergartens, there is usually a foreign English teacher with a Chinese teaching assistant in each classroom. The assistant said to a 3-year-old-girl: "Say, thank you, teacher." She followed: "F*ck you, teacher". We were all in stitches for hours, except for that teaching assistant who took it very seriously and continued to reprimand the poor girl.

#3   One of the training schools I worked at had a nasty habit of splitting our salaries into three portions. Of course, nobody explained to us what this division was based on (Honestly, I don't think the accountants knew, either), so we would receive three bank deposits at the end of each month. One had to wait till the 5th of the next month to finally have enough cash to pay rent. The second part of the salary included (as we figured) all the classes and activities we were teaching beyond our contractual hours. One British colleague of mine had been frantically borrowing money from everyone around so I asked him what was going on. He said: "I hadn't been paid in three months." I was gobsmacked because he was teaching almost every day. I asked if it was possible that the company had made a mistake with his bank account, but he'd been trying to talk to the HR/accountant person for weeks now, to no avail. The lady had been successfully avoiding him. Finally, I found him sulking on his desk. He said they had actually fired him but didn't bother to mention it to him. That was three months back. Apparently, they had hoped he'd take a hint to clear out his desk when not paid. Poor mate!

#4   For a brief period of time (thank God!) I was teaching in a kids' training school. It was a kind of school parents would send their children to after school and at the weekends, simply to have someone else take care of them. The school was located near a primary school, in quite an affluent neighbourhood. One day we were doing riddles with my middle group (5-year-olds). One boy dropped his pencil. I waited a few moments for him to pick it up, but he wasn't going to. When I prompted him to do so, he said completely seriously to me: "No, teacher, you pick it up! I no pick up, you pick up!". This was the moment I realized those kids had people to do everything for them, as the other day I saw the same boy's grandma doing his shoelaces and holding his cup to help him sip some juice. Figures!

#5   Normally, training schools I worked for would stipulate 40 contractual teaching hours a week. This one school had a weird policy of letting students pick their favourite teacher's classes. To my misfortune, I was the most popular teacher there so I'd have 8 classes booked every day while other teachers would sit in the office shopping on *Taobao* or watching soap operas. The school was supposed to pay me extra if the number of hours in a month exceeded 160. One month I'd worked 225 hours and they had to pay me overtime. They got smarter from then on and every time my hours would cross 150, they'd give me fewer classes and distribute them to those teachers lazing around. So, they never had to pay me overtime anymore. They explained it to me by saying they wanted me to have more rest. So, since then, I'd be teaching full load for about three weeks and nothing during the last week of the month.

#6   I was teaching a Grammar English corner, which basically is an open class for all levels of students and potentially new ones as well.

We were studying the "what if" structure. I asked the students to come up with hypothetical scenarios to complete the sentence. I asked: "What if there was no electricity?" After those predicable answers, such as: "there would be chaos on the streets" or "we couldn't cook"; one guy said: "there would be a dramatic increase in population". It cracked everyone up.

#7 I asked my college students to prepare a 2-minute-talk about their lives outside of school. As they were presenting, one student stood up and could not stop laughing hysterically. Nervous laughter – I thought. She started talking about her trip to England a few years back and told us she met a 'very enthusiastic foreigner', who turned out to be from Turkey. In their conversation, she was so puzzled and so she asked him: "How is that possible? You're such a big man and you come from a small bird?" He explained to her that Turkey was, indeed, a country, after having called her an idiot. She recalled this experience as one of the most embarrassing in her life. No wonder.

#8 I was testing IELTS the other weekend. I asked one of the examinees: "Have you done a lot of travelling?" And he went: "Yes, I went to South America. I saw the jungle." So, I kept going and asked: "Did you see any exotic animals?" His answer killed me: "Yes, I saw a pigeon!" I couldn't burst out laughing because the exam was recorded, but I decided to do a bit of research on the matter. As it seems, voices are divergent. Some people claim the Chinese government doesn't allow pigeons on the streets as they are not...clean. Others would say the weather doesn't suit them. However, my favourite answer was: "Yes, you can get them in China, almost on every menu. They taste a bit more gummy than chicken." I rest my case!

#9 Once, in my IELTS Writing preparation class, one of my students came back after a long period of absence. He was excited to tell us that he had attended some special (top secret) type of IELTS training programme in Beijing. It was his parents' idea. He was supposed to go to the UK the following year. The topic they were writing on that day was *Reasons for and effects of overpopulation*. From his essay: "Secondly, the roads are crowded. No thinking. No moving. If your wife do hot rice waiting for you go home. The results your blocked one hours. She will sad, if she will angry. She will kill you!" Hard to decipher what it all meant? His concluding sentence was: "Thank you for watching!" No comment!

Chinglish is my favourite English!

One day, my university students welcomed me in class by handing me these photos:

One of the students came up to me and said: "I washed them for you". Having seen my confusion, she quickly explained that 'to wash photos' is a direct and literal translation from Chinese (洗照片= *xi zhao pian*, which means 'to develop photos'). Great stuff! I love Chinglish!

What is Chinglish (中式英语 = *zhong shi ying yu*)? It's basically a Chinese version of English, which means English with occasional Chinese vocabulary and some structures copied directly from Chinese. The best way to explain the beauty of Chinglish is surely through its examples.

A few years ago, *Weibo* (the Chinese equivalent of *Facebook or Tumblr*) went crazy over this picture:

Image from www.weibo.com/u/1908763543.

Obviously, there are many ways to tell the gents how to use the urinal, but this one ignited a long-going debate among netizens. Apparently, the actual translation of the Chinese characters here is: "One small step closer to the urinal is one giant leap closer to civilization." I don't know which one is worse!

Some other photos I managed to snap while out and about:

Outside my living complex. Still not sure what it was asking of me.
Image by Karolina Achirri.

Shanghai subway. Image by Karolina Achirri.

When trying to get on the escalator, saw this. Image by Karolina Achirri.

*When you decide to go to a restaurant without your Chinese friends.
On the menu. Image by Karolina Achirri.*

*In case you need to have a smart conversation. Randomly spotted during a walk.
Image by Karolina Achirri.*

How does one master Chinglish? First, through a complete mistranslation. Just write what you see word-by-word and you'll achieve a desired effect. The street signs are the worst. The directional words are always hanging in different places in the names of Chinese streets, so you can have North Zhong Shan Road, Zhong Shan North Road or even Zhong Shan Road North. Oftentimes the officials responsible for English translations (be it on the subway or street signs), instead of hiring a professional, try to cut corners and either do the translation job themselves or turn to *Baidu Translate* (the equivalent to *Google Translate*).

As a linguist, I completely agree with my Chinese colleague, Wang Rongpei, who in 1991 already knew that Chinese English is 'an objective reality'. He believed in the uniqueness of Chinglish as a social product, and so do I. Some more influential Chinglish phrases have already permeated Standard English, such as "paper tiger" or "long time no see". I see a certain charm to this English variety.

During my stay in China, I would always jot down those Chinglish phrases that impressed me the most. A list of them is below.

Chinglish phrase	Correct phrase
Good good study, day day up.	Learn something new each day.
You have seed. I will give you some colours to see see.	You've got balls. I'm going to teach you a lesson.
We two who and who?	We are best friends.
Horse horse, tiger tiger.	Fair to middling.
People mountain people sea.	There's a huge crowd of people.
Sorry, could you pardon?	Pardon?
No door!	No way!
You give me stop!	Don't move!
Add oil!	Go! Go! Go! Cheer up!
Where where!	Thank you. It's so nice of you to say so.
Watch sister	Cousin
Face try	An interview
My sky!	My God! Dear me!

Mind your crotch!	Mind your head!

Finally, it is my duty as a linguist to mention *jia za ti* (夹杂体), which has been appearing online lately. It differs from Chinglish in that one is speaking Chinese in general but throws in a few English words. This is what my field calls 'code-switching' or 'translanguaging'. Examples are: OK 了 (*OK le*), 你 out 了 (*Ni out le* = You are out of date), 有没有 feel? (*you mei you feel*? = Do you have any feelings for something?), or (你能不能 follow 这个 case? (*ni neng bu neng follow zhege case?* = Could you follow this case?), etc. Since language is an important part of a given culture, the advocates of Chinese language purity have been trying to convince the contemporary Chinese youth to stop using *jia za ti*. Naturally, with no success, since the young in China are obsessed with the Western world and its languages. Personally, I use it all the time, especially when I can't remember a piece of Chinese vocabulary😊.

CHAPTER 8

HEALTH STORIES

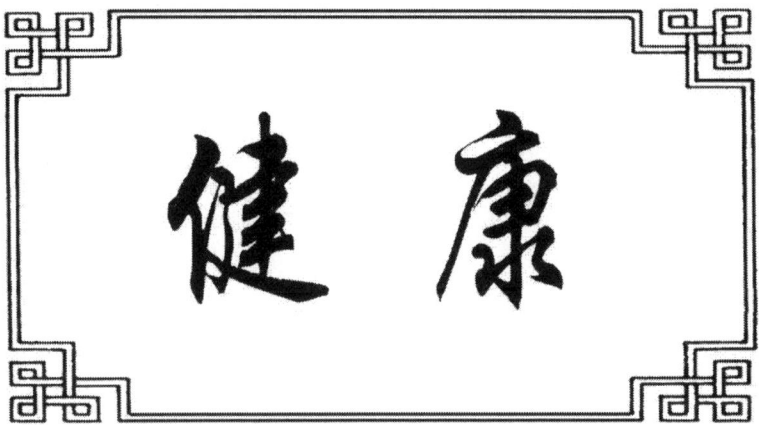

Going to a hospital in China feels like visiting a zoo.
(Karolina Achirri)

Traditional Chinese Medicine really works. At least on me.

Traditional Chinese Medicine (TCM), or 中医 (*zhong yi*) in Chinese, is rooted in wisdom from books such as *The Yellow Emperor's Inner Canon* (黄帝内经 = *huang di nei jing*) and *The Treatise on Cold Damage (*伤寒论 = *shang han lun)*, as well as in cosmological ideas of *yin-yang* (阴阳）and five phases (五行= *wu xing*). It sees Western medicine as 治标不治本 (*zhi biao bu zhi ben*), which means curing the symptoms without eliminating the causes. Also, Chinese people are concerned about its side effects (副作用 = *fu zuo yong*). Both types of medicine define an illness differently. In TCM, if a person has too much heat inside (内火太旺 = *nei huo tai wang*), they have a *yin-yang* imbalance. Anecdotally, it is culturally inappropriate to mention sickness in greetings, but Chinese people always wish patients to "get well soon" (早日康复 = *zao ri kang fu*), to "have a good rest" (好好休息 = *hao hao xiu xi*) or "to regain one's health and energy" (好好养病 = *hao hao yang bing*). Chinese medication is believed to have less harmful effects on one's body, too.

I had been struggling with spinal discs protrusion for over a month. Western medicine and Westernized doctors were of no help. All they wanted to do was to ease my pain or cut me open. All I wanted was to get rid of the cause, hopefully for good. So, after a myriad of pointless visits to the hospital, countless IV drips with painkillers and a ton of pills, I decided to give acupuncture a try. A former student of mine was experiencing the same issues and so she hooked me up with her acupuncturist. At that point, I was willing to try anything, as I had to struggle with stubborn sciatica and extreme back spasms constantly.

A small local TCM clinic had a grave smell of burning incense, making me feel like I was about to enter an ancient temple, not a hospital. I met Dr. Joy there. She was an older lady, who, to my great surprise, was able to speak some basic English. The rest was history. In my 8th week of recovery, I could put on my shoes, get dressed and function again, including an 8-hour-teaching shift. So, what did she do? I'm no expert, but there is some mystery hidden in those wooden walls curved with dragons and snakes. First, we tried the needle acupuncture.

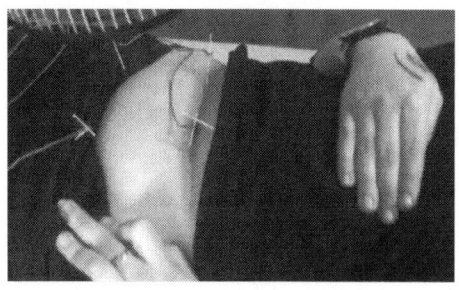

This is me during my first treatment. Image by Karolina Achirri.

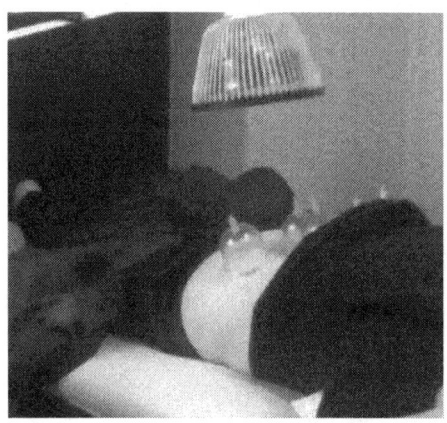

My back is getting some cupping. Image by Karolina Achirri.

For those who think it hurts, sorry to disappoint you, it doesn't, even a bit. It cannot even be compared to a pinch experienced during blood drawing. Besides, the needles are entirely different, too. They are longer, but much thinner and very flexible. Once the needles are placed in carefully chosen points, meridians (according to acupressure, different meridians on our body are responsible for different internal organs), the doctor attaches wires in the form of tiny electrodes and turns on a device responsible for sending electrical signals to one's nerves. As odd as this sounds, the process itself is highly relaxing and makes one super sleepy. Secondly, Dr. Joy applied hot wooden and glass cups on my back (cupping, in Chinese 拔罐法 = *ba guan fa* or *ba huo guan* = 拔火罐). Actually, we use those in Poland in severe cold or pneumonia cases. They create suction on one's skin caused by heat (fire). This is a bit of an awkward feeling, cause your skin feels like it's being pulled into some sort of dark pit of pain. However, one feels like new afterwards. Step three of my treatment was moxibustion (艾灸 or 艾灼 = *ai jiu* or *ai zhuo*). This one, as Dr. Joy explained to me, was an ancient Japanese method, which basically means mugwort leaves herb, in Chinese *ai ye* (艾叶) (in its grinded form) is being burnt on one's skin like a frankincense.

This whole experience, to which I became so accustomed I chose to undergo anytime I could after that, made me dig more about TCM. Following the philosophy behind it, a person has all they need to heal themselves. There's no need for external interventions. But healers and TCM doctors play a role of important facilitators. Here comes the concept of *qi*, which is very hard to define, actually. The most appropriate words in English to describe it are *energy*, *life flow*, *substance*. It's a vital force sustaining all life. It surrounds us. It's like a vast container of water filling each molecule of our being. I had learnt that we obtain our *qi* from the world, by interacting with it. There are three channels that can provide us with this indescribable but highly desirable element: food, air and natural catalysts. Thus, the quality of the environment we choose matters a lot. Where you direct your attention, influences where your *qi* flows. That is why it is advisable to generate some internal *qi* towards those areas of our bodies that need healing. It's a combination of body and mind. Once we let life predicaments block our *qi* flow, we get fatigued and stressed. This notion makes a lot of sense to me. It reminds me of my 'positivity theory'. If I set my eyes on the better, the amazing, the extraordinary to come, it will. I'm sure of it.

I know TCM has a lot of sceptics. I used to be one of them. But after a series of treatments with Dr. Joy I was so much better. She knew was she was doing. After all, she's been a traditional doctor her entire life. The pain went away and I was able to return to my regular activities. She also taught me which points on my body to press in case of flare-ups.

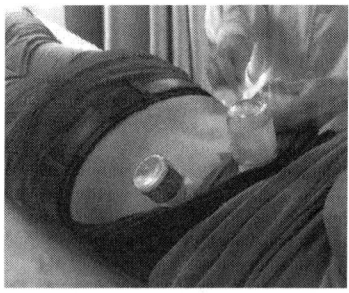

Dr. Joy's healing hands and my broken back. Image by Karolina Achirri.

Another famous and popular Chinese treatment is *tui na* (推拿),

which looks like a massage with some bone setting. This technique involves pressing, kneading and pampering those acupressure points we all have. You don't have to take off your clothes, though, which is what distinguishes it from a Western massage. Since it's done dry, no oil is used. However, some practitioners do place heated bean bags all over one's body. I was surprised how rough it was, though. Having my predispositions of a typical massage, I expected to end up relaxed and refreshed. Instead, I felt as if a truck had run me over. The purpose of *tui na* is to get one's *qi* flow through the muscles again. Its price was also shocking, compared to similar treatments in Western countries, only RMB 60 (around $9) for an-hour-long session.

Furthermore, I became a big fan of *gua sha* (刮痧), or back scrapping. Yes, your eyes did not deceive you. I wrote: back scrapping. One's back is being scrapped with a ceramic spoon, an old coin, worn animal horns or a smoothened piece of jade. Marks after that look amazing, especially in summer when one wears tank tops. The literal meaning is 'to scrape away' the fever, so I must admit I felt entirely purged of all toxins after that. This treatment cost me as little as RMB 20 (around $3).

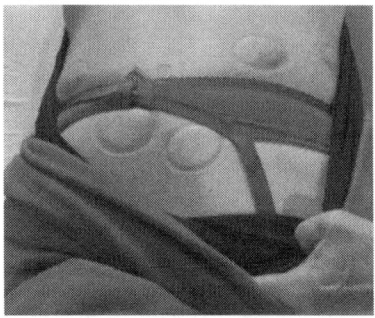

Just a light version of my marks. Image by Karolina Achirri.

The only downside to the Traditional Chinese Medicine I see is the fact one needs to patiently wait for the results. It does not work as quickly as a pill would, but it's definitely worth the wait. These days a lot of Chinese ladies use acupuncture as post-pregnancy weight loss remedy. It does work well, I've seen it.

Reflexology, or foot massage, is also a very popular therapeutic activity. It's the cheapest form of a massage, but possibly the most painful one. When my sister visited me in China, I took her to get her feet massaged but she couldn't stand the pain and left the building literally crying (Photos below).

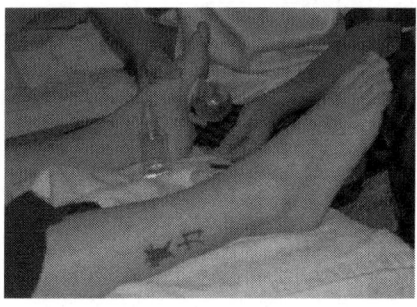

I lasted till the end of it, but it was not pleasurable at all.
Image by Karolina Achirri.

Last but not least, the blind massage, (*mang ren an mo* = 盲人按摩). The parlours are available anywhere in both big cities and small rural areas. The masseurs are indeed visually-impaired but they provide the highest quality full-body massage. Fact is I couldn't move the next day, but it did relax my stress-caused knots. Still, be aware of brothels that look like massage places. If the windows are dimmed and the staff are all young girls wearing pink, steer clear. Because of those places, the government in China created a rule which stipulates that no professional parlour is allowed to have secluded private rooms for one person. Private rooms begin from 2 people. This is to make sure that a place is legitimate and isn't used as a front for prostitution. Apparently, the genuine Chinese massage can improve one's circulation, strengthen the brain, improve eyesight, keep us young, maintain healthy stomach, give your spine a healthy boost, strengthen arms, relax stressed heels, protect our hearing and our teeth. So, why not give it a go?

On a lighter note, the other day, I met with my Chinese sister and my Polish friend in Starbucks to chat. My friend got prescribed some Chinese meds for her discomfort. She was showing them to my Chinese sister, who recognized them right away as famous TCM herbal pills. When we asked her how they worked she said: 'They cheer you up!' All of us burst out laughing as we imagined my friend levitating after drinking a magical tea from some crazy mushrooms. That's how it is in China. They have stuff to cheer you up😊.

The bizarre Chinese health practices.

Every morning around 6am I'd see a few people slowly walking backwards around our living complex square. It has been puzzling many expats, including me. I asked my Chinese friends to explain the logic behind it and they all said it balances one's *qi*. Walking backwards has proven to assist in preventing lumbago and strengthening the abdominal muscles. This came as a shock to me, but apparently walking the other way burns more calories than walking forwards. It may also improve one's balance and coordination. Interestingly, it is considered a neurobic activity, which helps one's brain grow new neural connectors. If this doesn't convince you to take up backwards walking, imagine the expression on a Chinese person's face when they catch a glimpse of you walking backwards down the road.

I stopped fighting the waiters on serving me hot water a month into my stay in China. Let's face it. The Chinese just love their water warm, anytime, anywhere. Now, one might assume that this is to fight all possible bacteria in tap water in China, but actually Chinese people believe in numerous health benefits of drinking hot water. Drinking it before breakfast smooths your digestion, while drinking cold water after a meal solidifies the oils, which can eventually lead to cancer. Sadly, many other drinks would come lukewarm in restaurants, too, including you dreamed ice cold beer.

Another thing that caught my attention was that my Chinese colleagues would always shut down our office's air-conditioning and open the windows instead. Even on scorching hot days. They kept telling me: 'cold things are not good for your health'. Scientific explanations I had been given include opposite temperatures messing up one's immune system and chilled air can make one fatter. There's some truth to it, especially that most ACs are located right above beds in most Chinese flats. I would wake up with runny nose and unbeatable colds in the middle of the summer. Also, interestingly many people in China would rather stack on layers of coats in winter than turn up the heat. Plus, it saves electricity, too.

Further, some fashion accessories women wear when on their e-bikes are intriguing, to say the least. If you ever see huge reflective visor hats, don't point your fingers and laugh (even if you really want to). They offer double protection to both your eyes from sunrays and your face from the dust. In the similar vein, shiny arm sleeves are to safeguard the overexposed areas of one's arms. Same goes for the hilarious umbrellas in the air. We can laugh now, but we'll see who we'll laugh last.

Oftentimes I saw babies swaddled in really warm clothes when it was over 30 degrees outside. According to a traditional folk belief, if the infant's toes and feet are exposed, he or she might get sick easily. If the child begins to sweat, instead of removing layers of clothing, their parents will simply wipe its neck with a cold cloth. Feeling hot yet?

In addition, none of my female Chinese colleagues would eat anything cold or chocolate during their menstruation. They would basically sleep with their heads on their desks the whole day. This precaution is practiced in order to keep one's *qi* flowing. Spicy dishes and any liquids other than water are also a no-no.

Finally, I learnt about many interesting weight loss methods. One of them is the 'tape worm diet'. For a bargain price from RMB 200 to RMB 600 ($30-$90), a lucky lady can buy a pack of pills containing parasitic worm eggs. These, once swallowed, will actually hatch in your belly and start... eating your insides. Medically speaking, they can grow to 25 meters in length and might cause constant diarrhoeas, itchiness and even vomiting. I can't imagine who would be desperate enough to try this. Lighter versions of dieting miracles include cleansing green teas and herbal patches. The latter are currently also sold in the U.S. Supposedly, the patch is to make fat leak out of the body in the place where it's stuck. Realistically, it may turn out to be the oil that was built into the patch. Lastly, the fat burning soap. If only losing weight was as easy as taking a bath! *Taobao* claims it's made of homeopathic elements, whatever that means. The soap is to penetrate one's skin by osmosis and flush the fat out. As I was told, most crazy dieting strategies are adopted from Japan or Korea, though.

You gotta love China. When I think of all those practices circulating in today's society, luring people to their magical powers, I smile. And so should you.

Better not get sick in China.

My least favourite part of Chinese hospitals was always getting 'the number', or as the Chinese like to call it: *gua hao* (挂号). You basically need to get to the hospital as early as possible to get the number which later will make you queue for hours to be seen by a doctor. My record is actually waiting over 6 hours to have my blood drawn (on an empty stomach). This is the ticket I got at 10 am in one of the best and biggest hospitals in Hangzhou.

Image by Karolina Achirri.

Even though it states there were "only" 413 people in front of me (yes, you read that right), my blood was drawn as late as at around 4pm. Given that almost every patient in China brings their entire family to keep them company at the hospital, when I got to the window I was determined to have the nurse change her gloves. The response I got when I asked her to do so (in Chinese) was: "These foreigners. Such trouble. I changed them a hundred patients ago". I kid you not. This was the moment I knew if I were not to die in China due to inexplicable illnesses or lung cancer, I could certainly as well die in a hospital waiting to be helped.

In China, hospitals serve as what's known to Westerners as health centres or clinics. There are small clinics in the vicinity of every bigger residential area, but they offer mostly Traditional Chinese Medicine. The big hospitals reminded me of a zoo, and a busy one for that matter. Everyone was pushing and shoving to get the number first and then to win the race to the doctor's office. Now, if you think once you got to the office your problems are solved, you are very wrong. You are never alone with the doctor. I witnessed men having had their rectum checked, women having had their breasts examined and really sick people vomiting on the doctor's shoes. The door to the office is another jungle struggle. If you're skilled enough to elbow your way inside, the doctor will likely ask you all sorts of uncomfortable and confidential questions in front of twenty other people, who will be super curious about that foreigner and what can be wrong with him/her.

After a few experiences like that, I was lucky to have found Dr. Huang (Dr. Yellow, in English). He helped me when I was in excruciating pain with my kidney stone. He was educated in the US and could speak English. We've been great friends ever since. If it hadn't been for him and his help, I would have surely died of misery trying to solve all of my health troubles in China. I'd just call him from then on and see him without getting the number or queuing up. He would also close the door to listen to me describing my symptoms. He saved me from being cut open by incompetent doctors who were not even interested enough to run more tests and actually locate my kidney stone. But hey, nothing can beat my Polish friend's experience who went to see a doctor with a kidney stone pain as well. The lady looked at her x-ray and said: "The baby is developing fine". My friend bought her ticket to Poland the next day.

I could probably write a separate book on my health issues in China. I was unlucky enough to have gone through the abovementioned kidney stone, plantar fasciitis, lower back disc protrusion, neck pain, etc., etc. I don't know why all these ailments found me so "attractive", but I know I went through hell seeking medical help. I heard doctors say: "There's something wrong with your heart, but don't worry another million people here also have it". When my Chinese friend went to the doctor for her falling out hair, he said: "It's because you use your brain too much. You must stop it." I don't know which was more ridiculous, his advice or her believing his words. I heard: "You foreigners have different bodies, we don't know how to help you". One doctor refused to see me when I entered the room with a Chinese friend (for translation purposes) claiming he didn't treat foreigners. He said: "This is China, you know. You must speak Chinese, you know". I did use all the swear words I knew in Chinese that day, you know☺.

However, the day I looked death in the eye was May 15, 2015. My left foot was hurting me a lot. After weeks of pain and having been unsuccessful with ointments and pain relievers, I finally managed to convince a doctor to give me an x-ray. I'd been on crutches for a while then and the pain didn't want to give in. After the test, I went back to see the doctor and heard his diagnosis. He did confirm plantar fasciitis and while prescribing some tablets I specifically told him I was allergic to aspirin and penicillin (in Chinese, as I'd learnt it pretty early). He said: *Mei guanxi* (没关系), which basically means that the meds he was prescribing wouldn't interfere with these allergies. My Chinese friend was with me and she confirmed with him that the meds were safe and so we went our way. Relieved in finally knowing what was wrong, I returned home and took the tablets. It didn't take long for my whole body to start feeling funny. My legs and tongue got swollen, hands started shaking and heart was racing. I went online to learn that patients allergic to aspirin are not to take those meds. Scared and bloated like a balloon by then, I called my friend and we headed to the emergency room. By the time we arrived, my skin was already itchy, legs were double in size and my throat was beginning to clot. After getting the number (of course!), and sitting in a waiting room, they gave me some antihistamines and a shot of steroids. Couple of minutes later the swelling went down. As we were waiting for the doctor to see us, a frantically looking man ran into the ER shouting: "My wife, help my wife". The nurse gave him a trolley and, I swear to God, told him to bring his wife from the car by himself. The lady was very pregnant and visibly in distress. My point is: don't trust doctors and always double check the meds you're given. I could have died. When we complained to the hospital the next day, they said they could make the doctor publicly apologise to me. I wanted him fired but as I was told for this to happen: "He'd need to kill someone, preferably more than 10 people". I rested my case.

My first week in China ended in a hospital bed, too. I went out to dinner with some Chinese colleagues and they were enthusiastically introducing exotic Chinese dishes to me. The next morning, I woke up with my throat swollen and unable to speak. I had no idea I was allergic to soy sauce. I had to be hospitalized for over three weeks. In China, you need to pay up front to be admitted. Since it was my first week in China I didn't have a lot of money (most of what I had brought with me was spent on my rent), so I had to borrow from my church friends. When I was being released, I saw that the most expensive item on my bill was... oxygen. Fresh air can cost you an arm and a leg in China.

I'm not saying China doesn't have good doctors. I'm saying even the good ones would crack under pressure of seeing hundreds of patients a day. Some of them really come with simple problems, like a common cold. Also, beware that test results show different 'normal levels' from the Western ones. I was almost always within 'normal' but felt like I was dying.

I had my ears un-waxed one day as I had been struggling with a recurring ear infection. The tool they used was so scary-looking I almost ran away from the chair. It basically looked like a huge needle with an ultrasonic tip. It was painful to undergo this test, but not as painful as having had an endoscopy done without anaesthesia. I had been complaining of an abdominal pain for a while and of course no one could tell what it was. Finally, Dr. Huang arranged an endoscopy for me. I had no idea I would be awake and non-numb the entire time. The room was full of patients and some of them were taking photos as I was lying on my side having my stomach pumped and trying not to cry. Whenever I tell this story to people here in the US, they can't believe me.

Basically, no matter what problem you come with, the medical advice is almost always: "Drink lots of warm water and go to sleep". IV boosters are the most commonly prescribed healing processes. There are even special IV rooms in hospitals, usually full of girls with menstrual cramps.

News are also full of stories that can make one's hair stand. Blood banks officially promised to adopt stricter testing methods after a 5-year-old girl in Fujian Province was contracted with HIV. In the hospital! Women with scalpels still hanging in their bellies after C-sections are practically a common encounter. Nobody even gets upset anymore. But when a man was told he was 3 months pregnant, only after taking the story to the local news was the doctor penalized and fined. Surgeons taking selfies in the operating room (with a patient on the table) raised citizens' anger for a while but this piece of news died very quickly.

I am grateful to dr. Huang for saving me from going insane so many times. I am sure there are many more great doctors like him, but I wasn't lucky enough to have met them. China surely needs a health system reform, and it needs it quick!

A note from Sherie C., the cultural consultant:

The doctor - patient conflicts have remained unresolved in China. Both evil and innocent doctors have been beaten up or even beaten to death in extreme cases. Due to the medical resources shortage, a huge population and high medical costs (if one does not have medical insurance), getting professional and correct treatment is really a tough experience to go through. I always suggest visiting big public hospitals located in the city; those newly built branches in the suburbs are not as good as the flagship ones in a city. Of course, the staff resources and their service are poor and out of practice compared to those experienced ones who have been working in the city hospitals.

A dentist or a butcher?

One of the best stories regarding Chinese dentists I tell people in the US is of when I had my 4 wisdom teeth pulled out in China, in one week, with no anaesthesia. Well, I got a shot when I nearly fainted in the chair. As I was told, Chinese people are used to having their teeth pulled out without any numbing agents since they are little kids. Well, I was not. I think I would classify the pain on the scale from 1 to 10 as a hundred. I was so scared to see dentists after this experience that my American doctor made it his mission to change my mind of dentists. So far, so good.

It took me a while to find a nice dentist, who for one could speak English and also understood my need to be jabbed before working on me. I heard cities like Shanghai have more modernized dental practices with even Nitrous Oxide being available for *only* RMB 6000 (around $900). Nowadays, there are coupons available online to go and see a dentist, so you can become a client just like in a beauty parlour.

I once went to a dental hospital in Hangzhou. Ibuprofen wasn't helping at all anymore so in my desperation I went to seek help. I regretted it the minute I had to take a number and wait in pain for hours to be seen, only to be told that all they could do is to give me an injection for the pain. No tests or x-rays were even mentioned. I left faster than I entered.

Prices of dental services in China are surely much lower than in the US, but the quality of service suffers, naturally. Just before I left China, I had an *Onlay* done (for about RMB 6000), and that was the first thing my dentist in the US had to take out because even after weeks of having been moulded by a computer, there was still a hole that could only be fixed with a new crown.

I think the worst part of my dental adventures in China was not having been able to communicate fluently about the pain and what I wanted to have done. I had to trust the dentist, which was difficult given that my wisdom teeth were the focal point of my nightmares for weeks. So, fix your teeth at home. Or better still, have a ticket on stand-by whenever you feel the slightest pain. I have friends who go to their home countries regularly just to have their teeth checked out.

CHAPTER 9

FAMILY IS EVERYTHING

Family is the most important thing in the world.

(Princess Diana)

Filial piety, respect for elders and family money dealings.

Generally speaking, filial piety (孝顺 = *xiao shun*) stands for treating one's parents well, taking good care of them, and engaging in good conduct outside the home in order to bring a good name to the whole family. It is considered the first virtue in Chinese culture. According to Confucius: "In serving his parents, a filial son reveres them in daily life; he makes them happy while he nourishes them; he takes anxious care of them in sickness; he shows great sorrow over their death; and he sacrifices to them with solemnity".

There is a law stating that Chinese children must visit or at least send greetings to their parents often. If this responsibility is neglected, parents have the right to sue their children who then will be likely fined by the government. Among many other things, one needs to be courteous to one's parents, shouldn't be a wild child, ensure male heirs and, most importantly, according to filial piety rule, support parents in their old age. This way, we see mature adults either still living with their parents (by their own choice), or supporting them financially on a regular basis. It is a dream of many to graduate from a good university and land a well-paid job, not for one's own comfort, but rather to be able to support the wellsprings. However, the current generation, especially if educated abroad, seems to be much more rebellious, hence ancient Confucian ideals frequently cause frictions in families.

In times of crisis, *Taobao* comes to rescue. For only about RMB 100 ($15), there are people willing to visit your parents for birthdays, Spring Festival, etc. trying to fill the gap in the elderly's heart, made by an estranged offspring. Since China's social security system isn't working as it should, many retired parents wouldn't be able to simply get by without their children's financial backing. No wonder young people in China are considered one of the most stressed group on the globe.

On January 28, 2015, *That's China* magazine published a story about a "Daughter Wanted" ad spotted at the Zhengzhou recruitment market (Henan Province). It read:

I am a doctor, female, age 68. I own several properties around the city as well as a medical clinic. However, my husband and I have no children. As we grow older, we would like to find a kind-hearted girl who's obedient and caring to the elderly to be our dependent. If we get along well and are satisfied with each other, she will inherit our family properties. The girl we're looking for has to be under 40 years old. Please call if interested.

According to the Ministry of Civil Affairs, China's senior population accounts for almost 1/8 of the country's total population. Currently, the retirement age in China is 60 for men and 55 for women (blue collar workers retire at 55-male and 50-female). Seems like the consequences of the One Child Policy were slightly overlooked. I've heard a phrase "4-2-1 problem" many times in conversations with my Chinese friends. It basically means that a young couple would have to care for 4 parents and their child, while it used to be the ratio of 10 young people caring for one elderly person.

Unlike their Western counterparts, a young Chinese person is almost never independent financially from his or her family. Also, parents are responsible for their child's wedding or wedding gifts. For a son, they are expected to buy an apartment and a car in case of marrying off a daughter. That's exactly why many parents prefer to have daughters, because their financial burden is much lighter than that of sons (although, many rural areas still strongly prefer sons). Even when Chinese couples move abroad, their parents would often buy them their first house. In return, parents have the right to visit their children whenever they want and even stay for months at a time. This practice has been causing a lot of conflicts in multicultural marriages, where one spouse doesn't appreciate having their in-laws live with them most of the year. If a young couple has a baby and lives abroad, the child is likely to be sent to China for the grandparents to raise him or her, or the grandparents are asked to come abroad to take care of the baby. I have currently 3 Chinese families as neighbours here in the US and they all have little kids that are being taken care of by one of the grandparents who came here from China specifically for that reason.

Another thing is expressing love through food. You know your mother loves you in China when she spends days in the kitchen before your arrival, preparing your favourite dishes. You plate will be refilled many times until you have utterly pigged out. In fact, a lot of my students (during class discussions) said that they had never heard "I love you" from their parents, but when asked how love was expressed in their homes, they all said their parents always made a feast when they went back home for the weekend.

The ancient Chinese ideal portrayed five generations under one roof (五代同堂 = *wu dai tong tang* or *si shi tong tang* = 四世同堂). As opposed to the West, a newly married man holds the responsibility to buy a house, sometimes as a prerequisite. If a young man can't afford it, his parents need to chip in and support his future family bliss. I heard it from a few Chinese friends that Western parents are seen as egoistical when watching their children struggle to make a living. I remember once I had to borrow money from my colleagues, as I was changing flats and needed a three-month-rent along with the deposit and didn't have enough saved. They asked me whether my parents couldn't help me out. It took me a while to explain to them that I'd been on my own since I was 17 and there was no way I could ask my parents for money. In China, many parents are willing to support their children after college, even when they are already getting paid. They would rather have them at home, nearby, than have to face never seeing their children working too hard. I also think Chinese parents are very patient as many of them calmly wait for their offsprings to find stable jobs and continue giving them money until that day comes.

When it comes to parenting in China, well... it's another interesting phenomenon. Normally, parents would drive their kids to school every morning and wait for them at the school gate in the afternoon. The roads adjacent to schools look like a miniature space swarming with giants. It's almost impossible to get through the crowds of mums and dads anxiously awaiting their children.

I must say that the majority of Chinese children I came across were visibly spoiled. Parents and grandparents do every little thing for them, including carrying their backpack on the way home from school (they believe a heavy backpack can affect the child's height). Surely, many parents are strict, which in turn results in having no actual emotional bond with their kids. But, there are also those who seem to have forgotten they had kids the minute those kids were born. I have seen parents berating their kids in public as well as listened to mums explaining their 17-year-olds truancy with "she's only a child, she doesn't know any better". From one pendulum end to the other. Everyone has heard about tiger mothers and their brilliant children. The question, however, still stands, are you trying to raise a child or mould them into a genius? The countless piano lessons, calligraphy classes and extra English trainings from a very young age might not be the best recipe to breed a confident, independent individual.

One tiger mother became infamous on the Internet for having told her 13-year-old daughter her real mother had died and that she had been adopted. Her logic behind the lie was that the girl was supposed to study harder and not to feel entitled to anything in life. She revealed the truth to the girl when she was already a married woman. Indeed, her school grades had improved and she had reportedly become more independent. A white lie taken too far?

On the 'a yis' of the 'little emperors'.

Childcare in any country is a dilemma. One needs to be particularly careful about whom they let into their child's life. In China, the search for a perfect nanny, called *a yi* (阿姨), is a troublesome one.

References for any kind of position can be easily fabricated in China. I met foreigners with fake degrees from universities that don't even offer the imagined programmes. In terms of *a yis*, as I was told, it often happens that their previous employer isn't available or simply can't be reached to provide endorsement. This is a red flag for already anxious parents. Even using an agency doesn't put one at rest. The agency can just as easily falsify any references if they want their caretakers to be given employment.

Age is also something that needs to be considered. You can choose between a young (and hence seen as inexperienced) person or an older lady who has raised her own children (risking generation differences in your child's upbringing). The latter wouldn't (most likely) spend their days glued to their mobiles, though. So, there's a chance they'd actually pay attention to your kid.

Potty training is another factor to be taken into account. If you are a foreigner, you'd likely want your baby to wear diapers until he/she is ready to hit the thunder mug. However, many traditional Chinese parents execute so called "elimination communication", which means they watch for their children's cues and then find a place for them to use a bathroom. Many of them don't even bother reaching a WC, instead, they let their kids pee on the side of the road, on a subway platform, or (as mentioned elsewhere in this book) on the bus. No place is off limits. When the little one has to go, he/she has to go. Funnily enough, this habit is also quite present among taxi drivers, who have no problem stopping in the middle of a highway and releasing themselves.

I have witnessed a few of my friends going through a childbirth in China (both Chinese and foreigners) and they all seem to have a deeply rooted mistrust for Chinese products in common. One friend of mine started stocking up on Japanese formula milk and American diapers in her first trimester. They had to devote their spare bedroom to store all the products they had bought awaiting their baby boy. Granted, Chinese products in general are not safe. Yet, some people would say parents should invest in the local economy and make their children get used to the Chinese quality of things from the very beginning.

So, is it possible to find a perfect *a yi*? It all depends on one's requirements. Worth considering certainly are their previous childcare experience, trust, level of education, and frequency of their going through cleaning supplies (I heard dreadful stories of nannies using one cloth to clean everything in the house, from the toilet seat, through dishes, to the child's mouth). I wouldn't count on finding Marry Poppins, but decent *a yis* do exist, even though they might need to be hunted for a bit longer.

Also, *a yis* in China do not only handle the kid. In fact, the richer families hire two ladies, one for house maintenance and another one to be with the baby. But the majority of families go for 2-in-1 and require the nanny not only to care for the child but also to clean, do the laundry and oftentimes cook for the entire family. It can be a very demanding job.

You might think an *a yi* is looked down on in the society. Nothing further from the truth. Some *a yis* are richer than their employees. Many have their own children studying abroad at prestigious universities. Auntie Zhang became the Internet hit in January 2015, when she went to the bank to withdraw RMB 500 ($74) and she queued up to see the bank teller. He got frustrated with her low amount and told her to use an ATM. Then, to teach him a lesson, she demanded all of her money, in the amount of RMB 200 million ($30mln). Next, she was told it wasn't possible due to the bank's policies stating that such fortune would need to be pre-arranged. What she could do, however, was to get RMB 300 thousand ($44.000). So, she politely accepted this amount, took RMB 500 from the stack that was handed in to her and said: "Can you deposit RMB 299,500 for me?" Way to go, Auntie Zhang!

As everywhere else, Chinese nanny stories are not free from a certain level of horror. One *a yi* was discovered to had been medicating the child with a sedative similar to Valium, another one was a kleptomaniac, while others sought vengeance in court after getting fired. So, how about grandparents? Should they be hired to look after their grandchild and if so, should they be paid for babysitting? Opinions vary, I guess depending on the closeness of the family. After all, looking after a toddler is a full-time job.

This is where the *little emperors*, 小皇帝 (*xiao huangdi*), come into play. Since the one-child policy took place in China, not only the parents, but also grandparents and uncles and aunties on both sides started focusing all their attention, efforts and finances on the only kid in the family. Kids who grew up like that have psychological features that place them directly amongst the *little emperors*. These children must have grown up alone, surrounded by adults but not many children to play with. A certain self-importance is visible in their behaviour as well as their treatment of others. As I like to call it: "the me-me-me-generation". Often addicted to gaming, swimming in money and attention, these young people grow up to be the future of China. I don't know what such future will look like, if no one cares about anyone else but oneself. As an educator, I was often conflicted as whether or not I should tell my students off when they said or did something inappropriate in class. I felt like I should have reacted in some way but couldn't quite figure out what way would be best. After all, I was a guest in their culture.

Having a baby in China.

Just so we're clear: I did not have a baby while in China. Nor did I even think about it. But, a few of my friends, both Chinese and foreign, did so. They are my heroes.

Since the one-child policy implementation in the late 70s, Chinese women have been enjoying the luxury of going through child birth only once, mostly through a C-section. However, on December 23rd, 2013, the government passed a bill to allow couples to have two children on condition that either parent was an only child. That was a major shift not only for Chinese economy and family planning but also for people's thinking. Many couples are facing a dilemma whether to decide on the second baby. On the one hand, bringing another kid to this world could help the first-born avoid growing up in loneliness. It is seen 'sad' and 'lonely' to grow up an only child in China. On the other hand, costs of raising two children are often seen as 'the best natural contraceptive'. The economic pressures in today's China stop many from having a second child. Interestingly, when I raised this topic in one of my English corners with adult learners, they all said they'd only decide to have a second child if they were ultrarich. Similarly, when asked if they wanted to have a sibling, my high school students all said: "No way", justifying it by the unwelcome need to share things. Some of them already had a younger brother or sister but such students complained that their parents forgot about them the minute their sibling was born. I will never forget a piece of news in *China Daily*, which covered a story of a 44-year-old woman in Wuhan (Hubei Province), who was forced to abort her second baby as her teenage daughter threatened to kill herself. After 13 weeks of pregnancy, the woman underwent abortion as her daughter's temper grew worse and suicide threats escalated. Another couple posted a letter to their daughter, titled "Guarantee of Love" on *Weibo*. In order to get her permission to have a second baby, the parents vowed endless love and never-ending prioritizing to their 8-year-old. It was the girl's idea. She demanded a pledge if her parents wanted her to sign the agreement letter. Crazy?

Giving birth in China has always seemed like a daunting task to me. I will never forget when my goddaughter was born in a public hospital in Hangzhou. Since she's African, her parents had more visitors, mostly onlookers, than West Lake. People would just stop to snap a peek at her when passing in the hall. My friend had to battle the doctors to let her give birth naturally. Till the very last moment, they were trying to convince her she needed a C-section. Generally, the cost of natural birth in a Chinese hospital runs at around RMB 3000 ($550), with a C-section doubling it. This covers only basic labour and delivery, any medication administered are charged separately. Many hospitals these days start to open VIP wings for foreigners and Chinese women married to foreigners. The costs over there match a private hospital's expenses and start at about RMB 40000 ($6000). One thing is certain, one should start saving up years before even planning the pregnancy, not to mention additional costs like post-delivery services, vaccinations and post-natal care.

Once the baby is born, it is all about the mother's comfort for the next month. Chinese culture sees a new mother restoring to health as upmost priority. There's an entire regimen called *zuo yue zi* (坐月子) or "sitting for a month". This practice dates back to as far as 2500 years ago. Basically, it is a thirty-day bed rest. The mother is to spend the entire month indoors, preferably in bed, not to bathe, wash her hair or brush her teeth. She'd have a caretaker during that period, originally a mother-in-law, contemporary more often a nurse or an *a yi*, who would do everything for her. She'd feed her, help her nurse the baby and take care of all household duties. Also, the new mother is expected to eat hot food and avoid any cold dishes, since after the birth her *qi* is unbalanced and needs to be restored. The diet regimen includes eating lots of chicken or fish soup without any salt, to boost the production of breast milk. In order to protect her eyesight, the lady should not watch TV or read. To avoid getting cold, she is to wear long-sleeved shirts, long pants and socks, as they protect joints from getting inflamed.

Many of the rules one needs to follow during *zuo yue zi* have logical backings. However, there are also quite a few superstitions. For instance, the new mother is not to be eating any lamb (羊 = *yang*), as the same character can be found in the word for epilepsy (羊癫疯 = *yang dian feng*). Traditionally, the baby is not supposed to be named during the first month either or given too much attention for that matter, as an evil spirit might come and take the child away. Many parents would give their baby a temporary name for the first month and give the proper name afterwards.

Today, many Chinese women pick and choose how they go about this custom. Many of them shorten the one-month post pregnancy period, some stay at home but take showers while others only stick to the nutrition restrictions. To help a woman slim down her middle section, some midwives still practice wrapping a 10-meter-long cotton cloth around the new mother's belly. One older generation lady told me that her heels hurt now because she did not wear socks after giving birth to her child. The Chinese believe that with birth, a woman's body has the power to heal itself. One friend of mine swore to me that her chronic shoulder and back pain disappeared after *zuo yue zi*. Yet, I find it odd that most women opt for a C-section if a natural birth is proven to be healthier and easier to recover from.

One custom in the new baby's life is common for both China and Poland. The Chinese call it *zhua zhou* (抓周), or a baby test. On a child's first birthday, a table is set up in the middle of the room. Then, meaningful objects, such as books, scissors, fabrics, seals (a glass of vodka, the Bible, a book, car keys – in the Polish edition) are placed on the table. Following Chinese traditions, books would mean a life of scholarship, seals would signify a future official, scissors a tailor, fabrics a loafer. In my country's beliefs, a glass of vodka would mean a kid has is prone to becoming an alcoholic, the Bible would mean a priest, a book would equal a teacher and car keys a mechanic. In China, these days parents also add stethoscopes (for potential doctors), computers (for IT geeks) and even microphones (for a singer), to keep up to date with modern careers. Next, everybody anxiously awaits to see what the baby picks. It is a very symbolic ceremony and I'm glad my country shares it with China.

CHAPTER 10

LOVE IN CHINA

If you love someone, set them free. If they come back they're yours; if they don't they never were.

(Richard Bach)

The gay China.

Being gay in China is no fun. My very good friend came out to a group of us (his foreign friends) one day in a restaurant, by telling us his friend (whom we all knew) is actually his boyfriend with whom he lives. We were not shocked as we suspected as much, but it was a big deal for him. He still hasn't come out to his family or Chinese friends.

I was surprised to hear that his boyfriend was getting married, not to him, but... to a woman, and a lesbian for that matter. To make matters more bizarre, my friend was his boyfriend's best man ☺. As he explained to me, there are online portals for gay people in China, where lesbian women can find gay men (and vice versa) whom they would have an agreement over marriage with. Basically, two gay people of opposite sex get married for the family, in order to avoid parents' nagging and to be seen as 'normal' in society. Oftentimes the couple lives in a big city but the parents stay in the rural area, so they won't know what's actually going on in their children's lives. In my friend's case, him and his boyfriend were actually sharing and apartment with his boyfriend's new wife and her girlfriend. They also took a honeymoon trip together to the US, as two gay couples.

The homosexual culture is slowly emerging in China, as young people get exposed to the Western ways of expressing their sexuality, but nevertheless it is still suppressed by mainstream heterosexual beliefs. Prejudices exist everywhere but in China they stop gay people to come out of the closet, even to their closest friends. One problem lies in the inability to provide grandchildren to elderly parents. Many older people live to take care of their grandkids and if their son or daughter strips them of this privilege, they take high offense. Actually, in Daoism, there are several gods who seem to be of homosexual preference. The mountain spirit *shan shen* (山神) and local god *tu di gong* (土地公) are believed to live together as a gay couple. So, homosexuality is by no means new to China. It is, however, new to some Chinese people's mentality, especially those who belong to the older generation.

Although the public believes that both heterosexual and homosexual are equal individuals, the government begs to differ. Chinese authorities have been refusing to permit gay marriage over and over again. Given the reluctance towards solving this matter, it's hard to specify how many gay people there are in China. Some studies claim

30000 while other go as high as 30 million. In case you ever need them, the Chinese survival gay words are: a gay man, *tongzhi* (同志); a lesbian, *lala* (拉拉); and a bisexual, *shuang xing lian* (双性恋).

I asked my friend what is going to happen when his boyfriend's parents demand a grandson. He said, it's already been a hot topic since they day he got married. So now, his partner and his wife are trying to figure out how to deliver a grandchild. The marriage seems very much like one of convenience, but it's hard to tell for whom. Living a lie is certainly no picnic either, but young gay people are willing to put on a charade for the sake of family peace.

Alibaba, the e-commerce mogul company in China, launched an app called "We do", which offered 10 gay couples the chance to fly to the USA and get hitched there. It was received as an innovative, contemporary, and inclusive move. Netizens openly discuss the issue of homosexuality in China, as the Internet is still the only tolerant source of information, to some extent at least. The debate was sparked by a young man who knelt down in the Beijing subway and proposed to his boyfriend. He used an engagement watch, instead of a ring. The whole situation was recorded and posted online. Of course, they can't legally get married in China, but you have got to give the young man some credit for his romantic gesture.

Sadly, although it's been over a decade since homosexuality stopped being classified as a mental illness, many hospitals still claim they have a cure for the disease, the electroshock treatments. One LGBT activist went undercover to a few hospitals to expose the aversion therapy. He was given a myriad of 'medical' advice on how to stop being gay, including taking cold showers to control his urges, jogging to release the hormone excess, or actual prescription medication. The main conclusion from his experiment was that the doctors were trying to make him scared and thus suggested the electroshock therapy, which, by the way, has been forbidden in most Western countries for over 50 years now.

Some desperate parents are known to have arranged exorcisms to free their children from what they believe is an evil spirit possession. Younger generation continues to bring innovative ways of fighting against sexual discrimination, but the process is very slow and might take ages to change the deep-rooted belief that being gay is just not right.

Would you care to rent a boyfriend? – Dating in China.

As the Chinese New Year (Spring Festival) approaches every year, peculiar sales ads can be spotted on *Taobao*. It's a must for all to go back home and spend this time with their families, no matter where they are coming from. It's the most traditionally celebrated time in China, the most awaited, the most hated by some and the longest, too. Young single people face a hard time then. They are expected to bring their partners (potential future spouses) home to meet the parents. In fact, if you are a 20+ single woman, one of the first questions whoever bumps into you would ask is: "When are you getting married?". It goes to the level of annoying nagging and I applaud my Chinese female friends for putting up with it. Many of them dread going back home and get stressed months before that time comes, just by projecting such invasive questions. Currently, lots of apps are being released to provide similar service for single men, too.

As we all know and love *Taobao*, ads offering a boyfriend to rent for RMB 600-1000 ($90-150) per day, excluding living or travel expenses, are easily found online. That's not cheap at all. Once you find the right one to play a role of your boyfriend in front of your parents and extended family, you will be charged separately for other parts of the deal, such as kissing (RMB 50=$7) or walking down the street holding hands (RMB 30=$4), etc. Prices for sticking to the charade while bumping into exes...vary. *Taobao* even hosts an official shop which promises fairness and high-quality services. Supposedly, men who are employed there aren't just doing it for the money but with hopes of finding their halves in the process.

The question arises: Why would girls go for it? Seems to be a bit too much of a hassle. Some probably want to meet their parents' expectations, while others see it as a sleek move to shut all the pestering about singlehood up. It sounds surreal to me. It strikes me as yet another perk to capitalism entangled with the communists' leftovers. To all singletons out there, stay strong! Stick to your guts! It is better to be single at 28 than divorced right after 30.

I can't share any dating in China experiences of my own because I met my husband my first year there and he's African, not Chinese. However, I will talk about a few instances of my friends dating both domestically and internationally in China. There's a catch phrase going around, "yellow fever", which basically means that almost every single foreigner who comes to China will seek a Chinese girlfriend (or a few☺), while girls won't normally share the same urge to date a Chinese guy. I have even heard my foreign female friends complain about not being able to find a boyfriend in China because they were all smitten by the Chinese beauties. Also, what I've been told, when a Chinese woman goes on a first date (with a Chinese guy), quite often set up by her mother, it can already be a serious deal, with discussions over children, marriage, and a state of bank account. My Chinese sister told me one of her dates kept talking about his luxurious estates and fancy cars for a whole hour and didn't ask her one question about herself. When a Chinese girl intends to date a foreigner, and she is not familiar with dating customs in his country, she might be up for a big surprise. He will most likely not pay for her, but suggest going Dutch (*AA zhi* = AA 制). He might be into ending the date with sex in his or her place, won't care about what her parents might think of him or will certainly not mention any future concerns. In fact, he might come across as the most unstable man in the room. Some Chinese girls will date a foreigner for the 'face factor', while others might want to polish their English. I will never forget my British friend telling me his relationship story. He had been with his Chinese girlfriend for 3 years, she moved in with him during the last year. When he final thought it would be time to go back to London, he asked her to go with him. She said, and I quote: "Do you think I would ever marry you? You are nobody. You have nothing. I will marry a rich guy my parents will find for me and enjoy a comfortable life." When he was saying this my jaw just kept dropping lower and lower. I had no idea. I met her when he brought her to my wedding as his date. She seemed sweet.

Still, don't even get me started on foreign guys playing Chinese girls. I met one who has a wife back home and still dated two Chinese ladies at the same time. Another one only practiced booty calls with his girl, while a third one was telling everyone how great it was to be married to a Chinese woman, she doesn't expect anything from him except for bringing home the bacon. Those were the kind of guys I met at work, who would openly flirt with their prettier Chinese students, always keeping an open eye for those who could benefit them with the right connections.

Apparently, the top five problems with Chinese girlfriends are: (1) her wanting to be in charge of your money, (2) her demanding an apartment, (3) her constantly nagging you to quit your teaching job and to find a more lucrative one, (4) her constantly hinting to you that all her friends are getting married, and (5) her ending every disagreement with "it's a China thing, you wouldn't understand it".

There is this phrase in Chinese, *sa jiao* (撒娇), which basically means childish behaviour of a girl who would pout and act in a coquettish way towards her partner. Interestingly, the term doesn't seem to have negative connotations in Chinese society. In actual fact, my friends say that's how a boy knows a girl really cares for him. It is considered cute and feminine, and a woman who does not engage in it might be seen as too harsh and not womanly enough. The phenomenon isn't just limited to persuading your boyfriend to buy you things (although these are the only instances of *sajiao* I witnessed). It also involves protecting you, much like having a private bodyguard, so to speak. The girl is likely to pretend to be incapable of doing certain things by herself. Very often Chinese ladies would ask their boyfriends to *pei* (陪), accompany, them to places, always carrying their handbags (tried to get my husband to do so when he was visiting me in China but he wouldn't budge 😊). My Chinese female friends told me that Chinese men are big fans of such behaviour, as it makes them feel needed, strong and manly. It is also deeply ingrained in the contemporary Chinese culture. Apparently, it has to do with traditional gender roles as well as Chinese concepts of obligation. *Sajiao* is there to ensure that everyone is playing their expected role. If the relationship progresses, a man is expected to provide for his wife, which most often means providing an apartment, a car and a steady job before a woman will ever think of marrying him. Even if a woman is perfectly capable of taking care of herself, she will still expect her husband to support her, look after her material needs while she does her part and cares for him physically and emotionally. I have seen one of my colleagues go ballistic on her husband (a foreigner), because instead of buying her a new (countless!) pair of designer shoes (on top of the many other pairs she already owned), he bought himself an iPad. Never saw such a bizarre fight in my life. According to my cultural advisor, there's an even hotter term these days, 作, *zuo*, which describes a worse version of *sajiao*. That is when a woman drives a guy crazy with no particular reason just to test how much he cares about her. Oh dear...

My foreign friends married to Chinese ladies, who do practice *sajiao* on them, quickly grow frustrated with the jealously, constant love and commitment tests, demands for gifts and clinginess. Western society generally prefers independence and self-confidence in both males and females. If I become too clingy, I'd be seen as high maintenance and a threat to my partner's freedom. I think *sajiao* is the epitome of an overly needy girlfriend and while it's a Chinese phenomenon, I am sure other cultures also share similar occurrences. After all, every culture has its own idiosyncrasies.

As one in a multicultural marriage, I understand the challenges such relationships face, or at least I'm living them on a daily basis. Not any differently, for a lot of mixed couples in China language is a barrier, different expectations are a problem, reference points in conversations don't meet and philosophies clash. But for some reason the interracial marriage is on the rise in China, presumably mixed babies are super cute. My German friend in China had a big issue explaining to his Chinese fiancé why his parents insisted on a prenup, while she tried to ease his anger when her parents demanded he paid off her brother's gambling dues and bought her mum a new washing machine in order to marry her. They did sort it out in the end, but it certainly put unnecessary stress on their relationship.

Now, let's talk about *shengnv* (剩女), or "leftover women" in China. Literally the term means "left on the shelf". Any woman over 30 who is still searching for her soul mate will be tagged a leftover one. My Chinese sister even calls herself that name. Today, many ladies in their 30s are successful businesswomen and can handle any aspect of life without male's assistance. Chinese men also rarely consider an older woman as a potential wife. This goes against the old Chinese saying: "With a wife three years your senior, you're in for a fortune". Maybe it meant her financial capital?

If you find yourself in the midst of kins' talks about your pathetic lonely life, your parents can come to your rescue. In Shanghai, a matchmaking group was formed by parents who aimed at finding mates for their single children. Boards with matrimonial ads are placed all over parks' premises. They include one's photo, education, province of origin, bank account status and even one's health records. Parents meet with other parents to matchmake their busy offsprings, which often results in the most uncomfortable blind dates moments. There are matchmaking companies that offer polygraph tests to determine if a potential candidate is lying or not. The requirements for a match are sky-high, too. Age difference, specific university graduate, matching height, and civil servant jobs are just a few of them. So, if you can't find the one, your parents will!

I never had a TV while living in China, but the Internet served me as its glorified substitute. Dating shows took Chinese mass media by storm. The most famous one is certainly *Feicheng Wurao* (非诚勿扰), which translates as "If you are the one". Its format is similar to the US classic *The Dating Game*. Twenty-four single beauties assess one suitor, who is gradually introduced to them as the show progresses. Every woman stands behind a podium equipped with a light – which signifies their passion for the candidate – which they turn on or off at the end of each round. Videos about the guy are shown, giving details of his job, hobbies, past relationships and depicting his friends revealing their opinions of him. The show ends when all 24 women have turned off their lights. It is full of twists and turns and its host has become one of the most likeable and popular TV personalities. All 24 women are talented and pretty. One would think they should have no problem finding 'the one' in male outnumbered China. Sadly, they are a part of a very demanding generation, made up of privileged urban women with great education. The competition is stiff, even in the marriage race!

Finding the right (business) mate – Money and relationships in China.

Every week in China new observations would come to me. The university I was teaching at provided me with a textbook for the course. One lesson included the pictures depicted below and asked students to create a story based on them. To my great surprise, what the students came up with was totally different from what I had had in mind.

All groups followed the same pattern in which the man in the picture is popping the question while explaining how he's lost his fortune. The woman is very sad and confused because she loves him very much but asks for more time to give him an answer, as she wishes to consult with her mother. When the mum learns that the man is no longer rich, she decidedly forbids her daughter from marrying him. The girl walks away sad but reconciled with her mum's decision. I asked my students why that was the scenario they all chose, they explained that it would be the way their mothers would react if the man usurping to be their husband was skint. One girl said: "My mum would want me to have a better life than she had with my father. So, ever since I was little she has always been telling me if I ever had a choice between having money and having love I should not think twice and select the comfort of life rather than some silly emotions". Another one said: "If my parents don't agree, no matter how much I love the man, I'll not object to their wishes". And a male student concluded: "That's why it's so hard to be a boy in China. One needs to buy a house and a car and show a very thick bank account before talking to the potential wife's parents". I was gobsmacked!

I snapped a photo of the task when my students were paring up to create their stories.
Image by Karolina Achirri.

Many a time the concept of marriage in China reminded me of a business transaction. Surely, there are couples that are together out of genuine affection, but only a small percent can be so lucky. Having a luxurious lifestyle and being comfortable surpasses the need of being loved and emotionally satisfied. Who comes to mind is a girl from one of the popular TV dating programmes, who said *she'd rather cry in a BMW than smile on a bicycle.* Some people won't even go for the relationship if the two come from different provinces. Others (right after having a kid) would immediately seek for mistresses and lovers (openly, if you catch my drift😊) but stay in the marriage claiming it's for the sake of the child. In my building alone, there were quite a few beautiful young girls who lived their dream by providing sexual services to highly ranked businessmen or government officials. Those girls made their clients' nights interesting and in return received a comfy flat, not seldom a car and a monthly allowance for shopping in brand malls. Their clients were of course married but used the receipts from their companions' shopping escapades to cover their companies' expenses or get reimbursed by the government.

You might be wondering why someone would agree to live a lie. The way I see it is that if one grew up in a society where status is everything, one would do whatever it takes to reach as high a social stratum as humanly possible. Obedience and respect towards parents leads people to drastic, but in their eyes victorious choices.

The pressure to marry in China reaches hovering levels. The strong desire to maintain family lineage and to continue the family name is still very much present in today's Chinese society. However, in first tier cities – like Beijing and Shanghai – traditional ideas about marriage are changing. As well as 'leftover women', who chose different goals for their lives than having their own families, many Chinese men decide not to get married at a young age in favour of education, career or individuality. The government's move to undo one-child policy might bring some relief to those who are facing pressure to tie the knot.

Can a Westerner fully understand the financial motives behind Chinese relationships? I don't think so. I remember the first time I learnt it the hard way was when I was invited to a Chinese wedding of my colleague and I was the only one who brought an actual gift. Everyone else handed them a red envelope full of cash. So, is it greed or need that drive young people in China these days? Medical bills alone can ruin one's life. The habit of saving for that "rainy day" is a very solid one and hence enforces the requirements placed on a potential spouse. Also, many couples with children see their personal sacrifices as educational opportunities for their kids. I don't think we should ever see Chinese people as greedy, rather as adept at grasping opportunities. Those who save harder and sacrifice more will see their children reap the benefits.

While love's priceless, a wedding can be a highway robbery in China. Even if the youth want a simple but stylish ceremony, parents are likely to object. A traditional Chinese wedding of their only child is a one and only opportunity to show off to their friends and family. At my previously mentioned friend's wedding, 2/3 of guests were her father's business partners whom she had never met before. Newlyweds (and their parents) end up spending a fortune on wedding planning companies that compete with each other over the most original ideas. A video displaying the young people's love will be played at the screen behind the stage, the bride or groom might perform for the guests, but the multiple sets of wedding gowns are an absolute must. My friend changed three times into three different styles dresses from three different eras. If one shows reluctance when talking to a wedding planner, he or she is definitely going to pressurize one even more, saying that one should never skimp on their big day.

As the word would have it, wives keep and manage family's money. Since Chinese people live closely with their parents, their family budget would often be combined. One friend of mine married rich and his wife's mother keeps belittling his lack of humongous savings. She bought them a fancy flat in the middle of a hectic city and now shows up unannounced as she pleases. He is on the verge of a mental breakdown!

Husband and wife wanted – The nuts and bolts of being married in China.

Since the day I stepped foot in China, I have been hearing the same questions over and over again: "Are you married?" It was not just asked by people I knew but also by complete strangers. At first, it was shocking; then, it became annoying. For the record, I wasn't married my first four years in China. I did get married in my fifth year. Not Chinese style, though. Being constantly asked this most private question stopped bothering me when I understood why tying the knot was so important to Chinese people.

I have heard so many stories that can make one's hair stand on end. One article I read in a newspaper, however, stayed with me to this day. It shed light on Chinese 'husband and wife' wanted practices. First, wealthy only bachelors are in demand. It's no secret that most women seek well-off husbands. There are a number of agencies specializing in delivering the best of the best. Funnily enough, also established women can be found in such agencies' catalogues. Special galas are organized to create opportunities to find love for who are willing to pay. One guy became famous overnight for offering RMB 50000 ($7400) to the matchmaker who can find him a virgin wife-to-be. Next, if nature hasn't blessed you with breath-taking looks, not to worry, there's a way to fix that, too. There are appearance consultants willing to advise you on how to change a bit here and there to become a perfect wife. There was a big lawsuit three years ago, in which a guy sued his wife after she had given birth to an ugly son. It came to light that the woman had had a plastic surgery before finalizing the deal with the man. A judge ruled in favour of the disappointed husband, granting him RMB 75000 (over $11000) in damages.

In addition, a 'poster buys' phenomenon caught my attention. "Telegraph" featured a story of three bachelors in Beijing, who due to their inability to find the time to go through normal channels to find the one, advertised themselves on a huge billboard for a bargain price of RMB 50000 ($7400). Desperation or inspiration? Oh well. Facing huge pressure back home, some resourceful young gentlemen started looking outside their hometowns and expanded the search to include foreign girls, too. Russian blondes seem to be in demand. Chinese guys seem to believe that foreign ladies are more open minded and straight-forward than their local counterparts, and that they would not insist on holding on to traditional marital roles.

Better still, a mother desperate to find her daughter a boo filmed her naked in a shower and posted the clip online. Motherly love knows no boundaries? Lastly, toy boys and trophy wives (who often become mistresses, anyways) seem to be gaining more and more popularity. There was even a mistress village in the south of China; and another *er nai cun* (二奶村), mistress village, was discovered in Southern California, USA, in 2014. It got exposed online when well-heeled Chinese businessmen were buying luxury compounds with suitcases full of cash. But hey, if one doesn't care about affection, such friends with benefits could do.

So, how has the concept of love and marriage changed over three decades in China? In the 1980s, most people were entering arranged marriages. China was just emerging from the shadows of the politicized marriage, and singles were less concerned with family background or material conditions. Being an upright, good-natured citizen was enough to find a mate. 1980s are also known for their "literary youth" evolution, so being fond of literature and art was a perk that could place one ahead of the mate race. It was then that Chinese couples could officially get divorced, legally, for reasons that could be proven in court. Then, the 90s substituted romantic desires for practicalities of daily life. Women were now looking for business managers, economically strong or those who returned from overseas. A pun was created of "rich man-beautiful woman". It was no longer a taboo for a wealthy man to marry a young woman for her looks rather than her wits. Finally, as the 21st century approached, matrimonial ads started mentioning a house, no debt, money liking, humour and affection. Seems the women started to want it all. Financial stability and hence bright future became every woman's dream. However, "naked couples" tried to defy this stereotype and claimed that they'd marry for love only even if there was no flat, car or a fat bank account. Currently, couples can be divided into those who follow traditional view of marital bliss and those who prefer a more contemporary take on the vows. Oh well, so many people, so many minds.

As I was told, Chinese men can be very protective of their wives and their looks. They dislike their wives attracting attention from other men. Many typical married ladies would dress in a conservative fashion to please their husbands. Also, long distance relationships don't bother anyone. It's commonly found that a couple works and lives miles apart. Being apart for months isn't unusual for them. Career development and chances to make good money outweigh being physically together. While many would stay faithful, some would succumb to affairs. MBA, anecdotally, supposedly means "married but available" in China.

Infidelity and divorce rates are rising alarmingly fast in China. College girls offer mistresses' services to wealthy businessmen and politicians. One Zhejiang official was outed when all of his 26 concubines showed up at the hospital he was admitted to. Apparently, Beijing's divorce rate is 39%, Shanghai's 38% and my very own Hangzhou's 29%. Getting a quick divorce is a very simple procedure too and a couple is usually able to be done with it on the same day. I don't know how much truth there is to it, but I've heard it costs almost nothing, too, we're talking RMB 10 ($1.5). Normally, there are no property battles in China. Couples try to make it clear from the very beginning what belongs to whom and nothing ever belongs to both of them. That certainly makes things easier. A few cities, like *Xi 'an* for instance, decided to limit the number of daily divorces to 15 a day. Since the marriage crisis in China hit 5000 divorces a day in 2011, the central government has been trying to prevent marriages from splitting up. The rate usually sees its peak after *gaokao* is over. I guess once the kid is out of the woods in terms of education, the truth can come out and parents can finally take care of their own affairs, without having to worry that their personal struggles would hinder their child's performance.

Couples in every culture have their own marital issues. I always felt like after my husband and I got married in China, my position got elevated in some people's eyes. We were still doing the long-distance thing for two years, but nobody was shocked by that. Instead, everyone was sympathetic and understanding about my making money in China while my husband was working on his PhD in the US.

CHAPTER 11

EVERYDAY LIFE IN CHINA

*Write it on your heart that every day
is the best day in the year.
(R. W. Emerson)*

Apple fad, selfies, Facebook war and online addictions.

Image from GFWcomic. Wikimedia Commons. Web.
09-02-2016.
<https://upload.wikimedia.org/wikipedia/commons/d/de/GFWcomic.jpg>

Every time I needed to travel on a train in China, I got a wee bit antsy. Not only was it due to the ridiculous crowds of passengers completely unaware of the presence of others beside them, but mostly due to the noise. Even if one listened to music, or attempted to, its loudness would have to reach dangerous levels approaching the threshold of deafness. Otherwise, you could hear everything around. Seems to me that some people have stopped using earphones. Once a guy sitting next to me on a train from Wenzhou to Hangzhou was watching his soap opera on the state-of-the-art iPhone and wasn't bothered a tiny bit that everybody in his vicinity could also hear those wooden dialogues. Two seats away a chubby kid was watching something that seemed to have been a talk show and at the same time made slurping noises every now and then, munching on his instant noodles. The world in the public areas in China is mad. Everything is noise. How can we understand it? Is it a way of calling attention to oneself, letting everyone know that one's alive and connected to the moving cosmos? Add up all, and it looks like complete chaos, or perhaps controlled chaos.

If I am to blame it all on something, I'd surely choose technology. You walk into a café, say to work quietly on your computer, and if you're lucky enough you'd be able to spot how families communicate. A dad is on his phone non-stop, probably scrolling down through social media sites, the mum is either chatting with people on *WeChat* (an instant communicator) or taking selfies (more on this lovely invention later), and a kid is playing games on another device. It's a common scene. No one is talking to anyone. The media are concerned that smartphones mania is widening the gap between generations in families. After all, 63% of Chinese people use their phones in bed every night.

Don't get me wrong, I am a big *WeChat* fan. I even have a QQ installed on my phone (mostly for the purpose of being able to send large files and join the work group chats). I made my sister download *WeChat* too and now she could contact me directly from Poland. The funniest things are those emotes. Two years ago, a new collection of Chinese New Year Stickers appeared in that app, and instantly went viral. Why? Well, check them out for yourself (courtesy of *Thatsmags.com*):

Luxury car, luxury mansion: BUY, BUY, BUY!

Become a CEO, marry a white, rich, beautiful woman!

Marry a rich guy!

Make a lot of money, be pig-headed every day!

Some critics claimed these stickers represent an insanely materialistic culture in China, and I'd say that's true to a huge extent. Having things and buying even more things does add to one's social status in China. So, at the beginning of 2015 (Chinese New Year) I also received a few of those presented above and chuckled.

Oftentimes I saw second-hand computers and phones advertised online, but nobody went for them. Chinese people don't trust used items. Everything needs to be new, as new things bring good luck, they believe. Everyone seems to be doing business on their phones these days. *WeChat Wallet* substituted a real one, *Alipay (zhifubao)* works as an electronic one. You can't imagine my shock when one day at the supermarket five people queuing to pay in front of me all used their phone. No paper was exchanged and I turned out to be the only one actually carrying cash. That made me feel really old. As I was told lately, Hangzhou is planning to go cashless soon.

The understanding of social media in China is also different from its purpose in the West. Chinese netizens are actively creating content as well as sharing their opinions on the products available to buy online (also adding to the consumption fashion). Everybody knows that to become famous in China one needs to be spotted online and then gain a significant number of followers (you can also buy fake followers). Even I advertised and marketed my last two books only via social media. Can't complain about the sales numbers.

When I looked around I felt a day might come when a mother in labour would be live-tweeting her delivery and it will not be official until it gets a like or two. After all, if it is not on social media it simply isn't, ehh? I belong to a more old-fashioned bunch, who would be the happiest if could live without phones. But I do recognize their obvious merits. They do save time, are a great educational tool, boost one's efficiency and shape lives into more convenient ones. We are speedily reaching times when technology is a necessity, not a luxury. Think water, food, roof over one's head and an iPhone. New people I would meet never asked me for my name card anymore. They all wanted to add me to their *WeChat* contacts.

Now, some scary but true info from China. Almost 45% of urban Chinese kids have a smart phone and nearly 68% have access to tablets. A substantial portion of those kids have been able to use high-tech devices since they were 5. These kids don't know what an encyclopaedia is unless it's digitalized. There's even a phrase 'to baidu' something, which is basically a Chinese equivalent of Uncle Google. According to the new law in Taiwan, children under two years old are banned from using tablets, smart phones and other gizmos. Since internet addiction has become a problem there, the government is trying to avoid deaths caused by long binges online.

As a teacher in China, I also faced another issue. Students couldn't do their homework without access to the Internet, and very often tried to play games or chat underneath their desks, gullibly thinking that I couldn't see that. One Chinese professor, annoyed with students using phones in class, threw three of them out the window. Well, I taught on the ground floor, so that wouldn't work, would it? I enjoyed his explanation though, when he told the students they should open their eyes to experience the real world instead of indulging in the mobile one.

Sina Weibo (Chinese sister of Facebook), found out that being disconnected from the Internet ranks Number 1 torture in China. Now, how does the Great Firewall of China fit into all this? First thing a foreigner misses when they step into this amazing world of rice and tea, is free access to Google, Facebook, Twitter, etc. I guess it is true what they say: we do not truly appreciate something until we lose it. The only way to regain access to the world, is to buy yourself a reliable VPN, which basically redirects your connection to places where any page can be opened. For me, this was not such a big issue until I needed to check my mail (Gmail is blocked, too) or search for teaching materials (Baidu dislikes English phrases). This whole Internet war had been a droll, really. The government knows that most foreigners are using various vpns, while I had been seeing more and more Chinese friends buying themselves a subscription, too.

Last but not least, the mighty selfie sticks. I was not convinced in the beginning, but I grew warmer to them as I was travelling alone. It's just so great to be able to capture yourself on top of the mountain with a breath-taking scenery all around you. You don't need to ask for anyone's help, either. And then this thing went bananas. People were taking selfies on the bus, surgeons were taking selfies in the operating rooms, smart-asses were trying to take a selfie with me on the bus. My biggest blow came as I learnt that if you want to be one of the 'cool kids' you have to foot-selfie. It might sound easier said than done, but it allows one to photograph themselves as they sleep. Oh dear! More and more narcissists are being groomed. Nonetheless, places banning selfie sticks are currently on the rise. Beijing's Forbidden City followed the example of London's National Gallery and implemented a partial ban. Way to go, ehh? It is really exasperating to be surrounded by hundreds of visitors cramped in a tiny exhibition room, all trying to capture themselves, the artefacts, and ideally you on their beloved phone.

Can we stop technological growth? Of course not. What we can do, however, is to be reasonable and more utilitarian when it comes to gadgets. Smart phones are supposed to make us smarter but funnily enough every time I try to think (which does require a certain amount of peace and quiet) my phone goes off. I don't know what China and its doohickeys market will look like in 10 years, but I'm sure I'll be able to find out online☺.

What personal space? – On crowds in China.

I don't know why I never stopped being stunned by Chinese crowds. After all, it is a country of 1.4 billion faces and Hangzhou shares 10 million of this population. You can see crowds every day, everywhere. They are especially common when there is a fender-bender of e-bikers. People just stop whatever they were doing and stand still wherever they were standing, pretty much like mimes, to observe what's going on. So, if you want to be a true part of the Chinese community, wander up to the side of an argument and look on! Feel like a local. Nothing is a secret in China, so you might even engage in a very private-made-public kind of conversation that would allow you to practise your Chinese lines.

This is just one example, a perfect epitome of 'people mountain, people sea' (人山人海):

Crowds of people on the Broken Bridge on Qing Ming Jie (Tomb Sweeping Day) in Hangzhou. Image by Karolina Achirri.

Everywhere I go, I see a sea of humanity. I am never alone and always being watched. I don't even dare thinking of travelling on national holidays. The train stations remind me of a swarm of confused ants who got lost and are desperately trying to find their way back home.

With numbers comes the bizarre concept of personal space, rather non-existent. People jump queues all the time! While they're on it, once they spot a foreigner, they still somehow manage to stop and ask you: "Where are you from?", "Do you have QQ/WeChat? (Chinese instant messengers), you get the picture. There's absolutely no societal norm for keeping any sort of distance from others in public places. I have experienced the closest encounters with complete strangers in Chinese queues. I think us, Westerners, have this uncanny ability to avoid touching others, even in the most squeezed kinds of places. We can navigate a tiny space without coming into physical contact with anyone. It just comes naturally, I guess. The same busy street in China comes as a very different experience, though. People bump into you constantly and mercilessly. Nobody bothers to say: "excuse me" or "sorry". They just keep on walking. I conducted an experiment once. I was in the middle of a hectic street, surrounded by people, but I decided not to bulge. I stood firm until someone told me to move. It was the moment I understood how it works in China. You are supposed to 'bump with the flow'.

The study of personal space is called *proxemics* and it was coined by an anthropologist Edward T. Hall. By studying what my comfort zone is, I've concluded that I need at least 1.2-2.1 metres between me and somebody else to feel comfortable. Hugs are also scarce in China. I used to always forget that my Chinese friends don't like to hug and made them really stiff a few good times when we met. So, when lining up, don't leave any space in front of you or else you can be sure someone will jump right into the gap.

Crowds are also pervasive in supermarkets in China. I don't mean small corner shops. I mean big supermarkets that offer all sorts of products. It was a huge deal for me at the beginning, when I could not read or speak Chinese. I had to pause at every shelf trying to decipher if a bottle contained shampoo, mouthwash or a deodorant. People would box me in and try to help me out. What we often ended up with was the priceless assistance of body language. I was always amused by the onlookers at the tilt. They would be most interested in this foreigner's basket's items. Do we really buy such contrastive products? My foreign friend who also lives in China (a Polish girl, thus with fair complexion) once told me there was one time she was in a supermarket buying some cosmetics. At some point, she approached the aisle with facial masks, in front of which stood a Chinese woman, hesitant about which mask to choose. When my friend picked a few masks for herself and then moved away, she spotted the woman put a few masks of the same type into her shopping basket. Surely, if a foreign (i.e. white) woman used them, they had to be good! 😊

Never ending bureaucracy – On Chinese red tape.

I used to always consider Polish bureaucratic practices as elaborate and ludicrous. But I think China beats my country in this regard.

One thing every foreigner needs to learn is that any legal document without a chop is not lawful. While most Western countries require a signature of a senior executive or a company officer to make a contract binding, in China signatures by themselves don't make anything legal. If you don't get the chop, a stamp with a person's or a company's name on, you have nothing, my friend. Each company has only one chop and one person is authorized to handle it, the most important man or woman in the building.

One smart thing I noticed is the practicality of the chop (*qi feng zhang* = 骑缝章). To make sure no pages are removed or missing from a long multi-page document, one will fan out the pages, and then chop them in a way that each page has a slice of the seal on them. When you spread the pages out, you can tell if any pages are missing. If everything is intact, you should be able to see the complete seal on the edge of the pages. Smart, right?

Chops also make for a great souvenir. I got mine as a gift from a student and I have been using it for official letters in China ever since. It stamps my Chinese name in ink, which must be red, by the way, if I want it to mean anything. I love it to bits! This is its imprint:

My chop is made of jade and reads Li Nana, which is my Chinese name.
Image by Karolina Achirri.

Chinese red tape had a lot to do with my worst day in China, which happened on April 20th, 2016. It was supposed to be a lovely day, I had everything planned out. I was to meet one of my Chinese friends who would go to the police station with me. We were trying to obtain a criminal record check for my stay in China. Then, I'd have a quick lunch and go to the city to meet another Chinese friend who had agreed to help me transfer a significant amount of money to my US bank account. Little did I know that things would go south from the minute I stepped out of the door.

I did not sleep well the night before, so I woke up half an hour late and hence needed to push my first appointment with my friend (let's call him Jack for the purpose of this story). Getting things done in China, especially if a visit to a public office is required, always calls for help of a local. It's not only the language barrier that makes it impossible to communicate smoothly, but also the 'face factor'. Basically, if the Chinese can get past the idea that you can, indeed, speak Chinese, they'll need a minute (or two) to comprehend that it's actually a foreigner trying to be heard. I've experienced this many times on a taxi. I would get on and sit at the front while my Chinese friend would sit at the back. I would then say the address of our destination in perfect Chinese (or at least that's what I'm told). The taxi driver would look at me puzzled, then make a face, turn to my Chinese friend and ask them: "Where does she want to go?". Some of my local friends would like to play along and pretend they can only speak English. It usually resulted in uncontrollable bursts of laughter from everyone, including the gobsmacked driver.

So, I took the subway to where I was supposed to meet Jack. We grabbed a morning Starbucks coffee on the way and hopped into his car. We drove to the police station, which I had been directed to by the Notary Office beforehand. The rain was coming down in buckets. We entered the police station and were shuffled from window to window, as nobody wanted to deal with a foreigner. It's just 'too much trouble' (太麻烦了 = tai ma fan le), as they like to say it here. When we finally found the person assigned to 'talk to foreigners', we were told they had no clue what we wanted and that we should go to another police station (a 15-minute-drive).

Without any other options, we went back into the rain, jumped back into the car and jollily drove off totally oblivious to what was about to come next.

When we got to the next police station, we were told that 'a person assigned to deal with foreigners' was in a meeting. We waited for about 30 minutes and then asked them to call the right guy up. Then, we waited for another hour and a half until he showed up, not having a clue of how to issue a criminal record check. Surprise, surprise. He told us to wait again while he disappeared to make a phone call to someone who was presumably better informed. We just stood there, observing other people come in with crime reports. Two ladies were having a fistfight and a lot of people tried to get their IDs renewed. There was also one other lady there, sitting in front of a computer screen. From her conversation with an officer, we gathered that her husband had left the house that morning around 7am and she was looking for him. I was a bit confused because I thought one needs to be missing for over 24hours for the police to even start the case, but then Jack told me her husband had left a suicide note on a table. He had planned to end his life. The CCTV cameras kept a very thorough footage of all angles of the streets, so she was looking through those trying to spot her hubby. I was definitely admiring her composure as I could not imagine myself in her shoes, keeping it together so well. Suddenly, she saw her husband and so did we. He was walking along the riverbank as the rain was draining him through. The look in his eyes (yes, those cameras can catch every little detail) said it all: "I'm going to end my misery". When he reached the barriers between the path and the river, he jumped over them and then the camera froze. The woman asked to have it zoomed in but the policeman said he couldn't do that since it's the closest view the device offered. From such a distance it wasn't clear whether he threw himself into the water or not, so the woman frantically stated she was going to that very spot to look for him. The policeman coldly said they were 'too busy' to go with her and wished her good luck. I was appalled. Not only did the officer let a woman, who was obviously in despair, go all the way to the river to possibly find her husband's body, but he continued sitting behind that computer for another good half hour (we were still there) doing absolutely zip. The complete lack of empathy and the smirks on the policemen's faces added to my disgust. How could a public servant be so heartless? I quickly remembered such situations from Poland years before when one was treated like a piece of dirt by public clerks. It was dreadful to even think of dealing with any governmental offices back then. Don't people become pencil pushers to actually serve the public? It was only 10am and we were both already quite low on energy, hope and faith in humanity.

After two and a half hours at the station, 'our' policeman emerged with a piece of paper, which not only had a wrong date on it but also was of no use to me. I needed a certificate stating I hadn't committed any crimes in China from the day I arrived (which was almost six years before) till that very moment. That paper didn't cover it all. Jack asked the guy if he could change it and (of course) the answer was 'no', since any thinking outside the box or altering the common mould is never met with a 'yes' in China. From that station, we moved on to the visa bureau, as we had been told visa officers might be able to help us with that particular predicament. Off we went, back to the car in a torrential (by then) rain, heading for another public office.

It was exactly 10 to midday when we got there. Everyone was ready to leave for lunch, and so was the person we had been eager to see. When we located the man in question, he was scolding a bunch of African students, who were patiently listening to his rant and obediently kept saying: 'Yes sir!' When he noticed us, he had already known what we came for, because the previously involved policeman called him with the heads-up. Jack asked him whether obtaining another document, a more comprehensive criminal record check, would be possible. Out of the blue, the clerk went into a rage, turned to me and shouted: "Ladys (sic!), you should know China law, yes? This is China, we have law. Ladys, that's the only paper you will get. That's the law." The first thing that made me see red was the fact he kept calling me 'Ladys' in a very aggressive manner, but the second thing was his finger pointed right at my face, so close he could almost stick it into my eye. I calmly said: "Sir, please don't call me Ladys, that's not my name. Also, take your finger off my face if you don't want to lose it". I really didn't care he was an official responsible for my visa and all. His attitude was very inappropriate and I felt very uncomfortable over there. Without an actual answer to our question (except for: "You should know China law!"), we headed towards the door. Then, when we were about to exit the building, the guy followed us. He screamed at Jack, in Chinese this time, and started pointing his finger at him. Now, you should know that Jack is as calm as a lamb and never loses his cool. Till then. When the man said: "What kind of a Chinese are you helping this foreigner? Which school do you work for? I can cancel your teachers' visas, I have the power. I know China law". Jack was fuming and it was the first time, in my knowing him for over 4 years, that I had seen him vexed. I tried to calm them both down because at that point in time they were screaming at the top of their lungs and everyone else was keeping tabs on what was going on. I said to the clerk: "You are being very rude. Your attitude is unacceptable. If you speak the language and your job requires you to deal with foreigners, you should know how to be more cultured". He answered angrily: "OK, I apologize". I reposted: "Have a good day, sir". And we left.

We sat in Jack's car for a few minutes just to cool down, when my boss sent me a message saying that very official had called my school complaining about OUR behaviour. Can you believe his nerve? We simply asked a question, he jumped at us without a reason and now he was claiming WE attacked him. I couldn't believe my ears. Sadly, such treatment is not a single case in China. Due to the communist system, many government workers feel empowered and know that no matter how badly they mess up, no punishment will come to them. Basically, if you work for the government you are untouchable. This attitude was so visible in that man's behaviour, it made me feel downhearted. I imagined my Chinese friends being mistreated like that on a daily basis and felt so outraged. The truth is they are trained since a very early age to take it and keep silent, but no human being should ever be deprived of their dignity.

We gave up. We took subway to the city and stayed there in defeat for the next half an hour.

Later that day I had a meeting with another Chinese friend (let's call her Amy). Amy and I arranged for my money to be transferred from her Chinese bank to my American bank on that Wednesday afternoon. By the time I got to our rendezvous point, I was drenched.

We took the number, queued again, filled out all the forms and then it was our turn at the counter. They lady took Amy's card and said she regretted to inform us that Amy got blacklisted. She said she could see in the system that it was me who had sent the money to Amy's account and as she was trying to send it to my American bank now we must have been laundering money. We were both sickened, so I asked to speak with the manager. The manager explained that the Chinese government was trying to restrict people from sending money out of China, because the economy had been going down for a while and China needed money in. She also said I could make the transfer myself but for that she'd need to see my tax returns, which I didn't have on me. Not because I forgot to bring them, but simply due to the fact that none of the schools I had worked for had ever given me any taxation proof. Clearly, it was impossible to complete our plan, which we realized as we heard the most annoying statement: 'Mei ban fa' (没办法), meaning 'there's no way'. We went to another bank to cross check the story because things have different versions in China depending on whom you ask. They also said I needed my tax returns and that I would be able to send only $500 anyways. Our plan was to transfer $15000 on that day. The system won again. We were the victims of the red tape.

Soaking wet, we left the bank and tried to get a taxi to go and meet Jack and his friend for dinner (for me) and for Amy to go back home.

I had never felt more hopeless in my life. From that very morning, when the policeman asked me: "Why are all Polish women so fat?" and another trying to snap a photo of me explaining 'they would like to show the public how excellent their service is', the day was officially marked as the worst day in China. Till that day I'd lived in Hangzhou for almost 6 years. I had gone through things and dealt with issues I had never previously even remotely imagined.

Even after I came back home, I could not get that lady and her suicidal husband's out of my head. I needed a drink, or two.

I posted the summary of the day on *WeChat* later in the evening and it sparkled a huge debate among my friends, both Chinese and expats. The Chinese were mostly saying 'that's the way it is in China and we can't change it', while the foreigners ranted something needed to be done. I believe that visa bureau clerk needs to be reprimanded and the only way to make him listen and reflect would be to have a higher-placed official give him a call and tell him off. I wished I had establish better 'guanxi' (关系), connections, in China. I know the police must have seen it all, but I wish they had compulsory empathy training sessions every now and then just to remind them that their mission is to protect and serve the public, who are human beings.

I also understand that it's hard for one person to change the system, but that's how a change happens. When communism went down in Poland, it started with an electrician, and then the crowd followed. Someone needs to be the first one to exhibit an intrepid spirit.

I love China, and most importantly I love Chinese people, but that day made me realize how tough it is for them to bear unfair sadistic treatment from the authorities. Some people on WeChat accused me of only pointing out the negative side of China. Some took my posts very personally, saying I should not speak badly about their beloved country. I did no such thing. I simply stated the facts of that day's happenings, without expressing my own opinion.

That day traumatized me and as I'm writing it the day after, seventeen of my students and colleagues came to apologize to me for what I had gone through. The 'collective - I - spirit' in China probably made them feel ashamed and perhaps even made them lose face. They did not do anything wrong, they are the good guys. They are also often mishandled by the power. I will make it my mission to reveal any abuse of power till my days in China are over and even afterwards (when I regain the freedom of speech) I'll always encourage the Chinese to stay compassionate to one another and never lose heart. If they do, the system wins. It will have created a human robot.

I am looking forward to better days for China. I woke up today with optimism that it is going to be a great day. The rain continues to fall, but my hopes are up.

Crazy for real estate? – Buying a house and renting a flat in China.

The slave of the home mortgage, or *fang nu* (房奴), is an actual phrase in Chinese describing those who pay colossal amounts of money as mortgage loans (above 70% their disposable income). They work to pay the mortgage and have almost no social life. According to traditional Chinese thinking, one needs to own a real estate to have a good life. The uncertain expectations of the future make people resort to their real estate property as the last resort for pension.

I cannot tell you how many of my Chinese landlords had more than one flat to lease. The record holder was from Wenzhou, which is considered the Chinese real estate capital of tycoons, held the property rights to 7 apartments in my building. Never saw the guy, even when I was signing my lease, I communicated with the agent he appointed to handle his affairs.

The Chinese property market has been a talk of social discussions for years now. Where to buy, where not to buy, how to buy, how much credit to take, etc. are only a few things one needs to take into account when planning to put down roots on a Chinese soil. The idea of property rights is very murky. Private ownership of land is not an option, since it belongs to the government (the remains of socialist system). One can only 'rent' it from the authorities. So, in reality you can own the space between the walls of your apartment, but not the land it stands on. Currently, all properties are bought on a 70-year lease and so far nobody knows what's going to happen when your 70 years are up. In a nutshell, you can buy as many places as you want and even develop them into whatever you want (legally) but you will not own them per se. This whole unclear arrangement motivated wealthy Chinese businessmen to invest in real estate abroad. There is a street I pass every day on my way to the university here in the U.S. 60% of houses there belong to Chinese families. And that's a small street in a small town in the Midwest. Imagine what's happening in American metropolises?

One of my colleagues, Chloe, was in the process of buying her first flat (after she got married). She agreed to give me an interview explaining the ins and outs of buying a place in China, as well as the intricacies of a Chinese wedding.

Chloe, who came back to China after studying and working in the US for two and a half years. Just got married after finding her Mr. Right. The interview was taken on November 18, 2015 in a crowded Starbucks in Xiasha District of Hangzhou City, China.

K: Hello Chloe!

C: Hello Karolina!

K: So, today we will talk about two things. Number one is how young people can get their own house in China. And number two is wedding preparations in China, ok?

Let's start with the first one. If you could give me an idea, when young people are thinking about buying a house, step by step, what would they do? Would they look for an agent, would they look online? What's the first step? How can you start?

C: I think nowadays young people would usually go to an agent, if they want to buy a second-hand apartment. Otherwise, it's really difficult to find the information.

K: By second-hand you mean a place where someone has already lived, right?

C: Yeah.

K: How old are usually such apartments?

C: As long as a person lives there for a week it is called second-hand.

K: So, would you say more people buy second-hand flats or new ones?

C: It depends on where you live. Usually in big cities, where there are not many new apartments built, people tend to look for a second-hand apartment. In areas like ours (outskirts of Hangzhou), previously the government had some tax policies to lower tax rates if tenants occupied the place for over five years. Now, it's only two years, which makes it more appealing to people to sell their house after living there for one or two years only.

K: So, have you decided to buy a new house?

C: Yeah, because I don't need to pay taxes because usually the tax is paid by the buyers. Even though the seller should pay the tax, they'll ask the buyer to do so.

K: If it's a second-hand house, do you get the furniture and the appliances?

C: Sometimes people just buy a house, then wait for the price to go up and then sell it, without actually living in it. In such case, there's no decoration, no furniture, nothing at all. Even though it's a new apartment, it's considered second-hand because it was bought from the real estate company.

K: When you are looking for a real estate company, are there any rankings you can refer to?

C: There are some famous brands. It also depends on the quality of their service. Some of them are very enthusiastic about their work, so they will show you around to find the place that would meet your requirements. Others would be more laid back and not so active when consulting.

K: Some of my friends bought a house that is not yet built. Is that a special case?

C: Not at all. That's a common case. When the housing prices are going up, the company wants to get back the money as soon as possible, because they have already borrowed a lot of money from the bank to construct the place. So, they'd want to use your money to finish off. Lately, the government, however, came up with a new policy which states that a company cannot sell an apartment if its ceiling hasn't been built yet.

K: *I see. I didn't know that. I have a friend who literally bought a house on paper.*

C: Yeah, some people sell those houses without them actually standing.

K: *How about the ownership? If you're buying it with your husband, who does the house belong to?*

C: It belongs to both of us. Both of our names are on the deed. It's fifty-fifty.

K: *What about if you're not married?*

C: Actually, we bought a house before we registered our marriage. But it's still the same case.

K: *So, I can buy a house with a friend?*

C: Yeah, you can. But some problems will arise as the two of you are not going to get married.

K: *Did you buy a second-hand house or a first-hand house?*

C: First-hand house.

K: *Talking about your house. Why did you decide to stay in Xiasha (a district on the outskirts of Hangzhou)?*

C: Because both me and my husband are working in Xiasha and I don't want to get up early in the morning and then commute. Even if I consider changing jobs later, I can always sell the place and get a new one. We treat this apartment as convenient for the wedding purposes and suitable for the time being.

K: *What do you mean by 'convenient for wedding'?*

C: Because in Chinese tradition, before your wedding ceremony is held, it is better for the young couple to have an apartment.

K: *Is it a common belief?*

C: Yeah, but of course, nowadays, many people don't follow this tradition. They only rent a place, because they know they might move to a different city, for instance.

K: *Can you give me an estimate of your flat's price?*

C: One million thirty-nine hundred yuan (approximately $213,000).

K: *How big is it?*

C: 136 square meters.

K: *How many rooms?*

C: Three bedrooms, one living room, a kitchen and two bathrooms.

K: *That is a lot of money, so what can young people, who don't have so much, do to buy their own house?*

C: Borrow money from the parents and then get a mortgage from the bank.

K: *Which one is more common?*

C: In coastal provinces in China, it is often the husband who will buy the apartment. It is sometimes required of him if he wants to marry a woman.

K: *Like a bargain chip, to marry him (laughter).*

C: Yeah, exactly.

K: *Is the woman required to buy something as well?*

C: Yes, the house furnishings.

K: *That's not very fair, is it?*

C: Not at all. That's why in China when people have a son, they consider having financial burdens for which they need to prepare. The parents need to prepare way in advance.

K: *So, do you think that most Chinese parents actually have so many* *savings to give to their kids? It really sounds like a lot of money. If the average salary is RMB 5000 (app. $768), then that's a lot of money to be saved over many many years.*

C: Yes, that's the case. That's why mortgages are becoming more and more frequent.

K: *What's the interest rate?*

C: It is changing every year. Now China Central Bank needs to stimulate the economy, so they are lowering the interest rate. So every year, one's monthly payment is based on that year's interest rate.

K: *Do you have an option to get a mortgage in a foreign currency in China?*

C: No, we can only get it in RMB.

K: *When is the key given to you then?*

C: In my case, when I was trying to buy this house, it was already completed. So I was able to see the house.

K: *What about those paper houses?*

C: Their owners need to wait for one or two years to get the keys. It also takes more time for the bank to approve their loan. Also, there's a public pension fund from which they can get a loan with a lower interest rate, compared with the commercial banks.

K: *That would only apply to people who are already employed, right? And does it need to be a national company? A governmental post?*

C: It doesn't. Private companies also have those kinds of funds.

K: *Could you use such a loan from our school?*

C: Every month the school is depositing some money to the government so that we would be able to get a loan from the government.

K: *Did you use that?*

C: I didn't use that, but my husband did.

K: *Oh, I see.*

C: He used the loan because the interest rate is much lower than that in the commercial bank.

K: *In my country, we have something similar where you can borrow money from the school with no interest rate. I remember my mother always taking loans for refurbishing the flat and there was always zero interest rate.*

C: That's so much better.

K: *Why would you buy a three-bedroom apartment for just you and your husband?*

C: Because we are thinking of having a baby in the near future and then our parents might come to stay with us and take care of the baby. Or perhaps our parents just want to come for a visit and stay with us.

K: *How far are your hometowns from Hangzhou?*

C: Mine is closer, about one hour from here. But my husband's is really far. You'd need to stay overnight on the train. Different provinces.

K: *So, when you got together, did either of your parents have a problem with you being from different provinces? I've heard stories that sometimes parents disapprove of the marriage because the distance between the couple's hometowns is too far, and it creates inconveniences.*

C: Yeah. That's because the Chinese have a tradition of getting together for some traditional festivals, in which case, my husband and I need to make a choice of whose parents we would visit.

K: *Did you have this problem with your parents?*

C: I think my parents are more open to this issue. And they live closer so they probably thought that they'd always win in this dilemma.

K: *Going back to the house. What is the time frame between the minute you get the keys and the minute you can actually move in?*

C: Half a year.

K: *How much money do you estimate you'll spend on decoration and appliances?*

C: I think more than RMB 300,000 (approximately $46,000).

K: *And where is this money coming from? Savings? Another loan?*

C: Mainly from savings. Also, my husband has two sisters with whom he's very close, so they will also help out.

K: *Is it common in your culture for siblings to contribute to house buying?*

C: It depends on the relationship. If you are very close, then yes. I also heard that my husband had lent them some money when they were decorating their houses.

K: *Is it lending or giving?*

C: It's called lending but I don't know if they had truly agreed as to when to return the money. I think as soon as we start making more money, we will give it back to them.

K: *I see. How do you furnish your place? Do you buy all items by yourselves or use the help of a company to do so?*

C: When it comes to the furniture, we buy everything ourselves. These days online shopping is popular and you can get everything sent to your place, as long as the building has an elevator.

K: *What about the hard work? Painting, laying tiles, etc?*

C: We hired a private company to do all the labour. We only decide what goes where. We have a designer who decides on the layout and the location of things. Of course, we have to approve of their ideas.

K: *This person must be a type of an artist? I assume they are expensive, too?*

C: Well, he works for the same construction company. The company has interior designers and project managers responsible for the whole process.

K: *So, it's a very well-rounded service?*

C: Yeah.

K: *Do you buy more stuff online or in a real shop?*

C: Online. The only things we bought from the physical store are two beds. The rest is from online shops, but we had visited physical shops beforehand.

K: *Do you care more about functionality or aesthetics of the place?*

C: Both. Since we suffered in the last place we were renting, we want to make sure this home is comfortable and handy.

K: *Wedding preparations and all this sounds really hectic. How do you cope with it?*

C: I think my husband has done a lot of work. He is a very organized person, so he has spreadsheets where he records all our spendings and budget. He's trying to figure out where some money can be saved and where we are exceeding the budget.

K: *Like your private accountant?* ☺

C: Ha-ha. Yeah, since he's very good at it.

K: *Another question. I have heard that even if you buy an apartment in China, it is actually never yours.*

C: That's true, for seventy years.

K: *So, what happens after 70 years?*

C: Actually, since the foundation of the New China (after 1949), no one has reached this period yet. So, problems haven't occurred.

K: *Does it say in your act of ownership that it only belongs to you for 70 years?*

C: Yes, it does. In fact, the law claims that all land belongs to the people. And I'm one of them and I'm still paying for what is actually mine.

K: *That's so true. There's also a question of wuye (maintenance), for which we have to pay monthly depending on the size of the flat. Since your building is brand new, that fee must be quite high, isn't it?*

C: Yeah. It also depends on different property managements. If their service is a bit better, that fee will also be higher.

K: *In a Chinese tradition, is there a custom of having a housewarming party?*

C: We would normally invite some friends and burn firecrackers. This is to get rid of bad spirits.

K: *According to the Western tradition, one needs to bring a gift that you can use in the house.*

C: Oh, that's interesting.

K: *On quite a few doors, I've seen a special sign (福 = fu) but upside down. Why?*

C: It's called *fudao. Dao* mean arrival, so good luck has arrived at your door.

K: *When you decorate a house, do you follow the rules of feng shui?*

C: Yeah, usually we believe that if in front of the apartment there is a river, there will be a flow of money passing through this apartment. At the back of the apartment, on the other hand, it's better to have a hill or a mountain, so that you can have support.

K: *Is there anything inside the house that would be considered superstitious?*

C: We care about the ventilation system. I think *feng shui* also divides the place according to different functions, such as the living room to entertain guests, kitchen to cook, etc.

K: *Did you decide to paint your walls or put the wallpaper up?*

C: We went with the wallpaper.

K: *Why? I'm asking because in my culture people believe that if the wallpaper is on the wall, the house cannot breathe.*

C: Oh. Previously people preferred to paint their walls, because it was cheaper. Nowadays, I think the wallpaper is almost at the same price as the paint. If you put up a wallpaper you can have different patterns. It is more artistic.

K: *Any special colours that you guys chose?*

C: Blue and stripes for a study, in the bedroom we will have purple colour because it looks more romantic, in the spare bedroom we decided on darker colours.

K: *When will you move in?*

C: After the Spring Festival (about three months from the time of the interview), because we need to make sure the smell of the paint is no longer there. Perhaps we will buy some 活性炭 (*huo xing tan*), which are bags with active carbon, to help eradicate the smell.

K: *I hadn't seen this invention before I came to China, but I think they actually work.*

C: So what do you use in Poland?

K: *Nothing, we don't wait for the paint's smell to go away, as soon as the walls are dry you can go and sleep in there.*

C: Really? In China, we believe that paints may contain some toxic substances that might be harmful, especially to women who want to get pregnant.

K: *Oh, I see. If you were to advise other young couples on buying an apartment, would you tell them to buy it before or after the wedding?*

C: I think the answer is: It depends. If they want to stay in a place for a few years, then I'd definitely suggest they buy a flat. Simply because the rent is going up together with housing prices. So, it's better to pay the money to the bank and own the place than to pay a landlord for a place that will never be yours.

K: *So, if two young people both work, with the total income of RMB 10,000 (around $1500), what percentage would their mortgage be?*

C: It also depends on the period of time for which you've taken the loan. The longest is 30 years. But you can always sell it and have the next person pay off your mortgage. We are paying about RMB 4500 (equivalent of $690). Places in downtown or in a metropolis are naturally a lot more expensive.

K: *Why is it so important in Chinese culture to actually own a place?*

C: We like to settle down, to have this feeling of belonging somewhere. There's also pressure from the other people and we want to keep face (*mianzi*). Having a new apartment shows the confidence that the new couple is about to start a happy life together. It's like a nest. A moment when you finally have something. However, my parents' generation would usually rent a place before the wedding, they did not own anything.

K: But could they?

C: They could, but it was too expensive for most people. Usually your workplace would provide housing at a really low price, back in the day.

K: Ok. Let's move on to the second topic and discuss wedding preparations. Do you already have a headache? (Chloe was due to get married three months later)

C: Ha-ha. I think my parents have a headache, because many of my parents' friends will be invited to the wedding ceremony. They care a lot about their *mianzi* (the concept of "face"). My father wants to know the exact number of my friends who will be coming to the wedding. We are also preparing little gifts for guests. Even though it's a small town, people always compare the size of the candy bag. We also have a tradition of giving dates and peanuts to our guests. That's because we have a saying: 早生贵子 (*zao sheng gui zi*). It reflects a wish for the newlyweds to have a baby soon.

K: Can you actually give birth without being married in China?

C: You can and then the baby belongs to the mother. However, you may lose your job afterwards, 'cause you will have no one to take care of you and you will have to breastfeed the baby. It's also very expensive to provide for a new-born.

K: Why is getting married in China so closely related to having a baby? It differs greatly from Western cultures.

C: I think it's because your parents also want to have grandchildren. They feel that they are aging so they want to help out with their grandsons or daughters as soon as possible.

K: Doesn't it add to the culture of the so called "little emperors" in China? (When the child is extremely spoilt by its grandparents.) It seems there is a lot of pressure on young couples these days in China.

C: I think if people are more independent, they might be able to persuade their parents to have a baby in a year or two after they get married. There's some scientific research showing that it's better for a woman to have a baby at an early age, because you can recover faster. Also, you will live long enough to see your child get married, etc.

K: *Now, since we have lately had a second-child policy implemented, would you guys be willing to have two children?*

C: I think so. Actually, even with one-child policy, we were not restricted to one offspring. That's because I'm an only child, so I was still allowed to have two babies. So, this new policy hasn't affected me and my husband that much.

K: *Let's go back to the wedding. Whose parents (who are very much involved) are responsible for what?*

C: Actually, we will have two wedding ceremonies. It's because we come from two different cities, also quite far from each other. Here, my parents will be responsible for the ceremony and in my husband's hometown it's going to be his parents who will take care of things. One is on January 9th and the other one is on January 21st. I'm not sure how I'm going to handle two ceremonies.

K: *Wouldn't it be easier to simply invite your husband's side to come here? Isn't that cheaper?*

C: Actually, the wedding in my hometown already has many people on a guest list, more than 200.

K: *Oh my goodness! What's the percentage of your friends compared with your parents' invitees?*

C: Both me and my husband will have around 30 people coming (60 altogether). My parents invited my relatives and their friends.

K: *It seems like a social event, too?*

C: Yes, because people have already heard that I'm getting married and they've been asking my parents when they can toast to us. I'm also hiring a company to handle decorations, because I'm not an expert at that.

K: *I see. The whole idea of giving little presents to guests is also very different from a wedding in my culture. These days, the newlyweds would either post their preferable gifts list online or send it with their invitations. This is to avoid getting six microwaves or three identical sets of china.*

C: So once a present idea is taken you can see what's available?

K: Yes. It's a very common practice. I also heard of some cases in China where people would give away very pricey gifts, such as iPhones.

C: They are probably trying to make their guests stay a bit longer during the reception. Because if you give expensive things, everyone will wait until the wedding is over. Otherwise, after giving *hongbao* (a red envelope full of cash) to the newlyweds and consuming the food, people will leave before the wedding is actually finished.

K: If you could give me a summary of the actual wedding day? What's gonna happen?

C: In the morning, I'll have help with make-up. Then, my husband will come with his best men.

K: How many best men is he having?

C: Two.

K: And you? Bridesmaids?

C: Also, two. And in China you have to be single to take on a role of a best man or a bridesmaid. In some provinces, if all your friends are married, then you have no choice but to have married bridesmaids. So, they come to my house and will try to get me to the car. They will play some tricks, too, and my bridesmaids will ask for some money in order to release me.

Then, we will head for the wedding ceremony. My father will walk me down the aisle. The ceremony is happening in a hotel where there will be a host, instead of the priest.

K: So there are no vows?

C: We don't call them vows, but rather promises. We promise to take care of each other in sickness and in health. Similar to vows. There will also be a video showing our history, how we met, etc.

K: How long will the ceremony last?

C: Nearly two hours.

K: *Will there be any performances?*

C: My husband is thinking of performing, dancing actually.

K: *Oh! How exciting!*

C: Yeah.

K: *Will you guys have a band?*

C: Probably not. Our reception will take place at lunchtime and we don't want to make it too long as there is another wedding ceremony in the same place in the evening.

K: *That's pretty short. Is there anything else happening afterwards?*

C: The host will organize some activities and games after the ceremony. He will give out some gifts and set a lucky draw. Each table has a different number.

K: *You should tell me where to sit. (laughter)*

C: He will also invite some kids to the stage to express their wishes. They can also get some toys.

K: *Compared with Western intimate ceremony, Chinese wedding seems more like a show, correct?*

C: Yes, absolutely. My husband and I will also walk around the tables and toast with our guests.

K: *Obviously, because you invited us (a few colleagues), there will be foreigners at your wedding. What is your parents' stand on that?*

C: Now that I'm working at the international school they want to see you guys and say Hi. They cannot speak English very well. My father interestingly has learnt a few words and is always trying to show them off in front of his friends who can speak no English.

K: *I see.*

C: For example, I taught him: *no smoking.* Because I know he likes to smoke. Or *men can't conquer nature* and he will always repeat them.

K: *That's pretty smart. I have also heard there are some specific items you are supposed to give to your guests, like cigarettes for guys. Are you going to follow? If so, what will it be?*

C: Dried dates, peanuts, candy, chocolate, biscuits, maybe other little gifts.

K: *That's a lot of gifts. How about the menu? On one of the weddings I attended, we were told that baijiu (rice wine) needs to be really expensive or else you'll lose face.*

C: Actually, not so many people would drink *baijiu*.

K: *That's another thing. They'd just put it on the table and then take it away if it's unopened. Then people will say that wedding was so lavish.*

C: I don't think many people care about that.

K: *Your generation, perhaps not. How about your parents' generation?*

C: Yeah, they might. My father will also choose the dishes.

K: *So preparations are very heavy on the parents' side.*

C: Yes, but the company I'm hiring is going to find a photographer, host, and video crew.

K: *In your case, and I assume in most cases, who's paying for the wedding?*

C: As far as the wedding ceremony in my hometown is concerned, my parents will cover the cost of the hotel (so lunch and seats) and I will pay the wedding planning company.

K: *What about the second wedding in your husband's place?*

C: His parents will pay.

K: *So you're actually getting married three times: you got married when you registered, and now there will be two more wedding ceremonies.*

C: This traditional ceremony is really important in my culture.

K: *So, if you had decided not to have it (just a formal registration), then people would consider you unmarried?*

C: Yeah. And they would ask lots of questions, like if I got married why weren't they invited to the ceremony, etc. They would think I'm too shrewd and care about saving money too much. If we invited you to our wedding, you should have invited us to yours.

K: *That's my other question. When I was getting married in China, some of my Chinese friends gave us quite a big amount of money. I was taken aback, but it was explained to me that when it's their turn to get married I'm going to be invited and expected to give as much or even more. How can one remember how much money you've given to people?*

C: That's why people write this down. Also, on the back of the envelope containing money you should write your name.

K: *In your case, do you guys prefer to get hongbaos (the red envelopes) or gifts?*

C: I think either way, it depends on the person. Sometimes it is troublesome to find a good gift for someone whom you don't know so well. That's why lots of people prefer to give money. It's just easier.

K: *That's right. Can the money you receive cover the cost of the wedding?*

C: It depends how much you spend. Sometimes it covers your expenses but often it doesn't.

K: *What about some wedding superstitions? Do you have any in your culture?*

C: Oh, I think we don't have any specific traditions, like those I've seen in American movies (something new, something blue, something borrowed). Nowadays, we are actually following the Western style of weddings. So my dress is white. I'm going to change several times.

K: *Oh yes, that's another very important part, particular to Chinese culture.*

C: I will have traditional Chinese clothes because the wedding will take place in winter. And then, for the reception I will be wearing a white dress. I rented that dress, because I will never wear it again.

K: *How many outfits are you going to have altogether?*

C: Three. All rented.

K: *How about some typical phrases Chinese people use at weddings to express their wishes?*

C: 百年好合 (*bai nian hao he*) which translates as: May you live happily and harmoniously ever after. There are also some other fixed phrases.

K: *I think you're the first person I've known who is getting married three times every time to the same man ☺. Your wedding (the one that I'm going to attend) is on a Saturday. Does this day have any special meaning?*

C: Of course, we don't want to invite people on a weekday because everyone is busy with work. Also, based on both of our birthdays, a fortune teller figured out the best day for us to get married. The numbers in the lunar calendar are important. We want our wedding to include an even number.

K: *So, according to the Gregorian calendar, your wedding is set for January 9th. What's its date in the lunar calendar?*

C: November 30th.

K: *Oh dear! Well, in my country it is a common belief that people should not get married in a month with a letter 'r' in its name.*

C: We have the lunar calendar which says that on each day there is something that you should do and something you should avoid doing. It's good for traveling, building a new house, seeing a doctor, etc.

K: *In your case, did you guys follow the Western tradition of a proposal? How did you decide to get married?*

C: In a Chinese tradition, there's a matchmaker. But we didn't meet that way. I think I could feel that he loved me a lot so I started observing him and considering whether he was a trustworthy person to marry. He also proposed to me. Of course I gave him a hint by asking: When will you propose to me? (laughter).

K: *I see. In general, you don't wear the ring, so people don't know.*

C: I plan to wear it after the wedding.

K: *What made you certain that your husband is the person you want to marry?*

C: He's a very organized person and I wanted someone like that and someone who is willing to take some initiative, instead of always being told to do something. He's also been out of his hometown for quite a while so he is quite independent. He can take care of himself. I wanted to marry someone who is not dependent on his parents. He also has a very tender heart. He is very nice to people, kind-hearted. Someone who doesn't try to take advantage of people. My relatives told me that when you're trying to find a partner, you should look for a benevolent man, not aggressive.

K: If you were to give some advice for people looking for a husband, what would you say to them, regarding this belief in your culture that if one doesn't get married by 25 they are considered second-hand? So many people are under pressure and hence tend to get married without any affection, just looking for comfort.

C: Be patient. Believe that this person will come. Before I found my husband, I had tried to find a man. But my friends told me that if I could stay patient the right person would finally come. Be pro-active. Don't shut yourself in your little comfort zone and isolate yourself from people. We actually met at an event organized by our university. Be open to adventures, get to know more people.

(Chloe got married as planned on January 9th, 2016. I was there to experience the joys and bliss of a new beginning.)

The New York Times published an interesting story on companies in China that hire foreigners to help them sell their products, including real estate. Many developers decided to build apartment complexes in the suburbs, which resulted in "ghost towns" full of ritzy buildings all vacant. So, such developers came up with an idea. They started hiring white foreign faces to advertise their properties, which is supposed to underline the notion of internationalization. They would be normal expats who are asked to pretend to be celebrities, business people or diplomats. A few friends of mine boosted up their ESL teaching income through being such models.

Now, when it comes to renting a flat as a foreigner I have been through it all. Or at least I feel like I have. My first apartment in China was a pocket-sized, cruddy, whiffy room in a flat shared with two Chinese couples. I had no idea what I was getting into, because the place was arranged by my school so I had no say in it. It was dirt-cheap, though. It was the first time I saw a shower in a form of a pole sticking out of the walls and the floor having a hole through which one could literally see the downstairs neighbour pee. The kitchen was unusable. There were cockroaches everywhere and I even developed nightmares of them crawling over me at night. Might be they actually were. I was so afraid to fall asleep. The apartment was on the 6th floor with no lift and there was no workable AC, and I arrived in the middle of scorching hot June. I got a foot infection that made me use crutches for months due to heat and the conditions I was living in. My room had a bed and a chair. There was no space for a wardrobe or a table, so for the entire month I managed to survive there before I found another (more liveable) place, I had to keep my stuff in the suitcase.

One thing many foreigners don't know when they move to China is that one is required to pay at least a 3-month rent plus a month of deposit to even start thinking of renting a place. The second apartment I moved into after that first-flat traumatic experience was a studio for which I had to borrow money from my boss who would then extract it from my salary each month. The contract being just a piece of paper is another thing worth bearing in mind. It means nothing and it's almost always written in Chinese. Even when you have someone translate it for you, you might not quite grasp the intricacies behind the language those things use. It's best to take pictures or videos of your communication with the agent.

When I came to China in 2010, there were still a few websites where landlords could advertise their own flats for rent. When I was leaving China in 2016, there were apps where agents put up adverts for the landlords. Omitting the middle man was not possible. And these guys are trained to get on your nerves. When you walk through the door, they begin to see dollars and even if you tell them your budget is RMB 2500 ($370), they will take you to places that far outdo this price and lie that that's the only flats that meet your (apparently shy high) foreign requirements! I started bringing Chinese friends with me each time I had to move, but sometimes even they weren't able to tackle the greedy hands of the go-between.

Also, be aware that some landlords can refuse to rent you their precious place once they hear you are a foreigner. I don't know if that's because they had previously had bad experiences with expats demolishing their apartment or if it's simple racism, but it happened to me a few times. Then, there is maintenance fee. If you choose to reside in a relatively new apartment building, be aware of the additional maintenance fees. Till this day I am unclear about what they actually include, since I've only seen cleaning ladies in the elevators and the people from the front desk downstairs are almost always absent. There is a maintenance office, but you can lose all hope of getting them to actually help you with any issue in this lifetime.

I had to move six times during my six years in China. And I tell you, my friend, it is no fun. The first time I only had one suitcase so it was as simple as ABC. I just rolled it down the street from one complex to another. Every other time, however, I had accumulated stuff, especially kitchen equipment – since my next kitchens were actually usable – and books. So, I was forced to hire movers. These guys are the toughest dealers in the business. They must have practised bargaining since their tender age. It basically goes like this. First, you have to bother your Chinese friend to look these guys up and give them a call. Then, they will ask you two addresses to supposedly base their price estimation on the distance between them. Next, the fun part begins when they start asking how much stuff you've got, if there's a lift in both buildings and if there's anything super heavy. Once I was moving quite a distance and I had a piano to take with me – I had a short-life desire to become a Chinese pianist then. My friend told them everything and even exaggerated the amount of stuff I've got and they agreed on the price (around RMB 300 = $45). Once the guys arrived with my things at the new location, they started puffing and huffing about how much more I had than my friend had told them and that the piano was heavier than expected. Obviously, they wanted more money and it was their plan to complain to me all along. I pretended I could not speak Chinese and got my friend on the phone. Luckily, she was able to talk them down. My point is: nothing is like it seems in China. No agreement is ever set in stone and everyone will try to milk the (rich!) foreigner.

So, a few tips to stay sane when renting a place to live:

(1) Always bring a Chinese friend with you, to both property viewing and contract signing! There WILL be hidden tiny font closures you will not be able to spot otherwise.
(2) Check every corner of the flat and make sure all the power switches work. If anything is broken, snap a photo of it for the future records.
(3) If you're moving into a new and empty apartment, the landlord has a responsibility to furnish the place. Make sure you can have a say in what he/she's buying for you.

(4) Check out your neighbours! You don't want to end up having a brothel upstairs like I did my last year in China.

(5) Make sure your deposit won't be held for months after you move out. Most agents will try to eagerly find some flaws in the state you're leaving the flat in, just to get some extra money into their pockets.

(6) Introduce yourself to the maintenance people. They might not be of much help, but it's good they know a foreign tenant moved in. (Don't expect any notices or announcements to be in English, though).

Make good friends with patient people. My Chinese friends have been a godsend to me in times of moving. If it hadn't been for their patience, friendship and determination I might have ended up being homeless 6 times in China!

Do you dare to trust your hairdresser? – Having your hair done in China.

It took me 6 months to brave up to go to the hairdresser's in Hangzhou. My Chinese was still very basic so I asked my Chinese sister to accompany me. She asked me which level of barbers I'd prefer and not knowing what that meant, I said the cheapest one. What I wanted was really very simple, or so I thought. Just trim my hair and keep in in shape exactly as it is now. However, when we stepped into two salons, they told us they don't cut foreigners' hair, because "your hair is so different". The third one was a charm but... the whole process of getting a (simple, sic!) trim lasted over three hours. First, you get your hair shampooed, then it is conditioned. Next, your scalp will be massaged for about 20 minutes and then you'll finally await your final service. All of these are normally done by 4 different people. Also, the price of your service will depend on the level of skills your hairdresser will have. You should get to choose that before starting. This place shocked me when a guy started cleaning my ears with a cotton bud. Apparently, they also shave men's nose hair as a part of their service. I thought the guy did a good job, but I hated the fact I was seated right by the window where everyone (including the shop's staff) was taking photos of me. I learnt my lesson and from then on, every time I needed a trim I'd ask them at the door if they had private rooms.

Of course, in big cities one can find very modern kinds of salons, but the price there would match that of similar places in New York City or London. Plus, you can always judge if your hair will survive the visit by looking at the stylists' own hairdos. Some of them are not the best adverts of their skills.

Also, if you like to dye your hair, you might want to do yourself a favour and stock up on those genuine dyes from abroad. Most brands sold in Chinese shops would have colours only applicable to Chinese dark hair or very bright blonds. If you decide to leave the colour in the hands of a hairdresser, be prepared to have a long price list stating which dye costs what. German brands are usually the most expensive, then the Japanese follow and the Chinese come in last. You might pay even around RMB 600 ($100) to have your hair dyed, though. I always found it cheaper to just do it myself.

Finally, when my Chinese got better and as I got more comfortable communicating my needs to the hairdressers, I would go to see them by myself. I even had my hair permed a few times, in different places, though. The photos below depict the scary process of having your hair almost electrocuted. The result, however, was actually quite good. The thing is, with foreigners most hairdressers would shoot in the dark, praying to achieve the desired outcome. It's more like the Russian Roulette than a nice, pampering experience.

This whole process took about 5 hours and lots of nervous butterflies in my stomach.

Does China need a toilet revolution? – On squat toilets.

Are Chinese squat toilets really that bad? I don't think so. I encountered them the first time in Kiev, Ukraine, when I travelled there in 2011. So, it is not only China that has those infamous inventions.

So, toilets are on the floor, big deal! Are they smelly and dirty? Most of the time, yes. They never seem to provide toilet paper, either. Nor does anyone care about soap and hot water to allow you to wash your hands afterwards. Of course, if you live in a huge city near westernized buildings then you certainly won't face this issue. You will be sitting on a porcelain toilet in no time while listening to soothing music. Not all of us are so lucky, though!

I'll admit that successful squatting requires a few trails before one masters it. The floor is usually slippery (from other people's urine) and it's not easy to make the target. Oh, and for some reason the light is almost always annoyingly out, too. When I travelled to small towns outside big Chinese cities, they only offered holes in the floor, anyways. Oftentimes there would be three stations with no dividing door and a bucket right underneath them to collect the waste. Very Wild Wild West kind of thing!

So, why do I stand out in a crowd of foreigners who always complain about China's squats and actually prefer those to their Western counterparts? There are a few reasons. First, using a squat toilet eases on your digestion. Apparently, haemorrhoids can be prevented by squatting instead of sitting while peeing. Second, they seem much more hygienic to me than Western toilets with seats. You don't have to come into contact with the seat, so nasty diseases have fewer chances of transmission. Also, according to the medical research info, our posture when we squat is actually the most recommended one.

I noticed Chinese women often leave the door open when they tinkle. I thought there must have been a reason behind that so finally someone explained to me that it is due to their concept of cleanliness. They don't touch the door handle or the toilet handle. She is in the clear. Also, not many people like to wash their hands after weeing in China. That's simply because they don't want cold water on their hands to make them sick. As long as they haven't touched anything or anyone, they are good to go.

A typical squat toilet in one of the schools I worked for in Hangzhou, China. Image by Karolina Achirri.

Of course, squat toilets have their drawbacks. The biggest one, I see, is the fact they splash back. Men don't have this problem with urinals, obviously, but us, women have to be really careful not to get flushed in our private regions. Also, your shoes might get ruined the same way. So, be mindful of that and learn to navigate smoothly in a Chinese squatter. I also saw a few Chinese ladies standing on the toilet seats in McDonald's or KFC (since these venues offer a more Western style of toilet seats). They simply don't want to touch the seat. I should try it someday☺.

Now, there are lots of people commenting on and criticizing Chinese squat toilets. I think it's more of a prejudice thing than and actual problem. If you don't like what you see, find a more comfortable place for yourself to use. Problem solved. But, what I personally do find a problem is seeing 3-5-year-olds peeing right on the floor, be it the street or bus. As was explained to me, buses have plastic buckets by the door for the little ones to use in case of an emergency. However, lots of care takers allow them to wizz on the floor. Just like this little guy:

I simply feel that children should be taught to signal when they have to go.
Image by Karolina Achirri.

Whoever lived in a Chinese building at least for a day would know about the omnipresent plumbing issues. Toilet paper does not go into the toilet. You are to place it in the basket next to it. It puzzled me for a while but when my own toilet kept getting clogged all the time, I learnt my lesson. Finally, one friend invited me to check out his new flat. When I went to the bathroom I was taken aback by his state-of-the-art toilet. The cover lifted itself before I even got to it, music was playing while I was...you know, and water got illuminated before flushing (also automatically). I was so scared to wash my hands, afraid that water might just splash itself on me, directed by an invisible hand.

So, all in all, whatever you say about Chinese squat toilets, they are not so bad and quite smart when you think of it. It's all a matter of perspective. You might want to practise your squatting skills before moving to China, though!

Safety in China and "dangerous" foreigners.

I have never lived anywhere in the world that would offer a sense of security on par with the one offered by China. You can be a woman, going back home in the middle of the night in the darkest of streets and no one will touch you. I felt extremely safe in China, always. Someone told me there's no point in stealing cars there because there are cameras everywhere and you'd be caught red-handed before you manage to take a spin.

However, when travelling, there are a few tips one should bear in mind. Firstly, beware of pickpockets, especially in chaotic traffic or crowded places. Apparently, pickpockets in China have such sophisticated methods to lift your wallet you'd not feel a thing. I can't tell you how many times I've heard people complain about their iPhones having been stolen from their back pockets (not the smartest place to keep a phone in, though!) and their backpacks. Secondly, steer clear of any public demonstrations or protests. You might be tempted to go and fight for Tibet's freedom, but reality is brutal. The foreigner in the crowd will always be spotted and oftentimes chosen as a scapegoat. Also, I always had a feeling that once an expat gets arrested, his or her family will never see or hear of them again. Next, make sure you party in peace. Chinese people are not used to loud bashes. They barely ever organize any parties, in the Western understanding of the word. They like to get together to share a meal and chat but it's never anything that wakes the dead. Lastly, don't try to play an arbitrary in random disputes. You might feel like Batman from time to time, but China is not the place to demonstrate your superpowers. Be watchful but don't get involved. It's the "dumb" and oblivious foreigner that always gets blamed, anyway. Lastly, triple check your luggage. There are horror stories of careless foreign tourists who got jailed or even sentenced to death for carrying kilos of heroin across the borders. They all claimed it did not belong to them, but to no avail. Guilty beyond a reasonable doubt!

Just before I left China, namely in April 2016, China marked National Security Education Day with a poster campaign, warning young female government workers against dating handsome foreigners whose intention could be to turn the innocent ladies into spies. I thought it was such a vile move. The posters were everywhere and some of my male foreign friends felt really uncomfortable. Just to give you the campaign's background: it's a 16-piece cartoon titled *Dangerous Love*, which tells the story of an attractive young Chinese civil servant named Xiao Li (Little Li, in English). She meets a red-headed foreign man at a dinner party and they begin dating. The guy claims to be a visiting scholar but in fact is a foreign spy who courts Little Li complimenting her beauty, taking her to fancy dinners, bringing her flowers and luring her with romantic walks in the park. Long story short: she reveals state secrets to him and they both get arrested. In the end, Xiao Li is shown to be sitting in handcuffs at the police station, being rebuked for her "shallow understanding of secrecy". Honestly, I wasn't sure if I should laugh or cry when I saw these posters. Even though it's no secret that propaganda is alive and well in China, such an openly aggressive move from the government took everyone by surprise.

I was lucky enough to save them on my *WeChat*, and so here they are, followed by an English translation.

01

Friend: One of my foreign friends asked me to hang out today. Do you want to improve your English? Come with me.

Xiao Li: I'd love to.

02

David: My name is David. I'm a China tourism major. I'm doing research on the subject now. I want to share my thoughts about it with you.

03

David: Please introduce your own job experience. Let's start with you, beauty.

Xiao Li: Sure.

Xiao Li: My name is Xiao Li. I've been working for the government since I graduated from university. I'm handling foreign relations.

David: Ok.

Narrator: After the dinner party, David and Xiao Li start dating. He showers her with gifts.

David: You are so beautiful, so sweet and awesome. I fell in love at first sight.

Xiao Li's thinking: To have a handsome, romantic, talented foreign boyfriend would be great.

Narrator: They become an official couple...

David: Honey, what exactly do you do at work?

Xiao Li: I'm responsible for writing reports for decision making unit in the government.

David: Great! Can you show it to me? It can really help me in my studies and with my essays.

Xiao Li: Sorry, I'm afraid I can't. We have rules.

David: Honey, are you going to keep secrets from me? I would just use it to write academic articles.

Xiao Li: Okay.

Xiao Li: This is a copy, but you need to give it back to me when you're done.

David: Sure, my sweetheart!

11

Xiao Li: What's going on with David? He's been out of touch with me and his phone is off.

12

Police: You're Xiao Li, right? We're from the National Security Agency. Please come with us.

Xiao Li: What? What's wrong?

13

Police: David is a foreign spy. He stole political and military information from our country. We have arrested him. You gave him these classified documents, right?

Xiao Li: What!?

14

Police: You are a state employee but have no confidential consciousness. You are accused of violating our country's laws.

Xiao Li: I didn't know he was a spy. I've been deceived!

The common reaction to the posters among the Chinese was ignorance. Perhaps the story of David and Xiaoli wasn't *so* convincing, training-wise, after all?

Chinese split-crotch pants, or baby butts.

In case you're wondering what those look like, here you go:

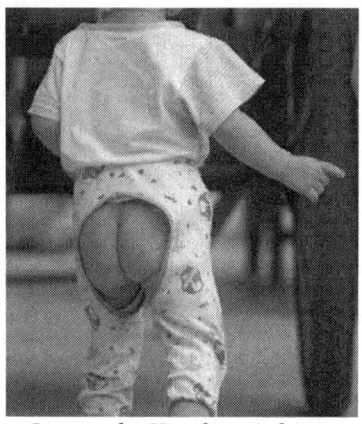

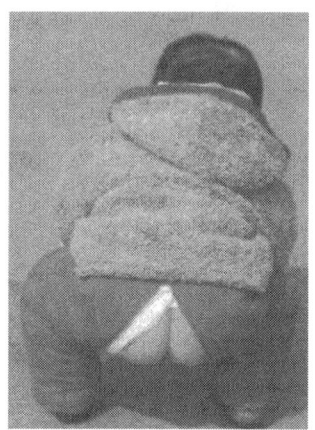

Images by Karolina Achirri.

I have been amazed at these pants for a long time. Kids peeing on the street. Toddlers flashing their bases at curious tourists. Parents not worried about changing diapers. Known in Chinese as *kai dang ku* (开裆裤), literally "open crotch trousers", have been a basic item in every baby's wardrobe for a long time.

When I did some research on where these lovely fashion icons came from, I found out that they had emerged as early as the Six Dynasties, i.e. around 220 to 589 AD. Back then, children wore white silk pants in a form of two trouser legs with a top tied together with a waist belt. Later in the 12th century (Song Dynasty), the pants took on a form of two trouser legs but connected by an apron-like string also attached to a child's shirt.

The reason for inventing those was simple: easy to use and no need to clean up. Children were able to quickly wee without having to tackle their bottom garments and parents were happy about not having to train their tadpoles to call when they needed to go.

However, these days there are a lot of debates circling around regarding *kai dang ku's* hygiene and safety. Many people claim such open clothes can make little girls prone to UTIs and other infections. Also, just before the Beijing Olympics in 2008, the central government launched a widespread campaign aiming at convincing Chinese parents to drop the split-crotch pants for the time of the games. They did not want foreign guests to be shocked or disrespected by the view of Chinese babies' butts.

Then, in 1998 *Pampers* came to China. They started their fame in big cities only to gradually spread to the rural areas. Since that moment the urban elites perceived these pants as something from the countryside, hence rural, dirty, classless and primitive.

I don't know if these amazing togs will ever go out of style in China, though. I lived in a 10-million city and had the (doubtful) pleasure of seeing them on a daily basis.

Brands, fashion fads, fakes and China's obsession with "ke ai".

As China continues to grow into becoming the world's economic superpower, its fixation with top brands simultaneously increases. The Internet is full of "top 10 brands" consumers' websites. But what actually decides whether a brand becomes an elite one? Most often, the price. Experts compare prices and create a ranking based on those. Vicious circle?

I was asked: "Where did you buy... [a particular item]?" When I replied that I got it from *Taobao*, I could sense a deep sight of disappointment in my interlocutor's voice. Most Chinese people like to shop in luxurious, extremely overpriced places, such as gigantic malls with brand goods. I never did. Many of my Chinese friends have told me they do so because the place of your purchase adds to its value. They wouldn't care that a *Louis Vitton* bag cost an arm and a leg as long as they could tell their friends that they got it from the hottest store in town. I never quite grasped that notion. It seemed to me as another form of showing off one's wealth and since I was never wealthy while in China (neither am I now☺) I couldn't follow suit.

Why are the Chinese so smitten by these plush brands? Well... In fact, 20% of Italy's *Prada* collections are currently made in China. Luxury isn't absent from Chinese products, either. Silk, jade and porcelain have been around for centuries. Funnily, many famous brands don't want to admit they produce their fancy stuff in China so they often add a tag in Europe, shortly before releasing the products. In reality, showing one's wealth is a common element of contemporary Chinese society. You should express how much you make through the way you dress, where you shop and travel. Anecdotally, as my Chinese friends who have experiences with foreign travels reported to me, the majority of the Chinese prefer to go abroad with travel agencies, on package tours. They only pay the final price and all is organized and taken care of for them. Also, the tour guides lead them to the best places to shop. I will never forget when one of my students went to Paris and the only exciting thing she was talking about was shopping for luxury brands there. Not the Eiffel Tower or croissants, *Louis Vitton* was her favourite spot.

Then, the question of fake products comes to mind. Granted, China can fake literally anything. And, to be honest with you, oftentimes the phony things look better than the original. Pricey watches, iPhones, Adidas products (with an "l" instead of an "i"), car makes, computers, you name it. Everybody knows it. Everybody at some point buys it. I don't think it should be considered bad taste or tackles. If I want to buy copy-cat art, let me! It's my money, after all. Actually, I hear people complain about fakes from China all the time. But no one can escape them. One German designer, in 2007, decided to voice his anger and created a T-shirt brand called "FUCK YOU CHINA". Must be a rich man.

Just one example of the crazy T-shirts you can find in China. Image by Karolina Achirri.

In terms of fashion I'm no expert, but some of the things people wore on the streets of Hangzhou... well... one doesn't need to be a fashionista to see that invention taken too far doesn't really match the latest trends. I was shocked at first to see people walk the streets in their pyjamas (see photo below). Mostly at the weekends, but nonetheless in public places, such as a supermarket. As I was told, it's comfortable and they want to relax after work.

Fancy a stroll in your PJ's? No problem. Image by Karolina Achirri.

Another weird fashion fad lately has been a faceskini. It's a real thing. I'm not making this up. Chinese beachgoers sport these masks in order not to get tanned. If the umbrella isn't enough, try a mask on your face. In my opinion, it makes one look like a burglar.

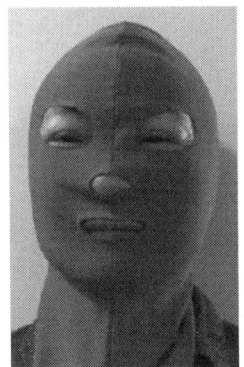

A woman should always have fair skin in China. Otherwise, people will see her as a peasant. Image from https://commons.wikimedia.org/wiki/File:Facekini.jpg.

Lastly, the cuteness (可爱 = *ke ai*). I cannot tell you how many times I heard: "Karolina, you look so cute" from my students (adults as well). It doesn't matter how hard I've tried to explain to them that a grown-up woman like me doesn't want to be "cute". That's at least not what I was going for. In China, cuteness is everywhere. Being cute equals being pretty and hip. This isn't confined to teenagers and children, as you might think, but also to mature women and even men. The trend came from Japan, naturally, the everlasting guru of cute stuff. There's *Hello Kitty*, penguin *Badtz Maru*, *Chococat*, and many others. As I've learnt, in the 70s in Tokyo, teenage girls started using a new type of a pencil, mechanical one. The lines for characters became rounder as they started adding flowers, smiles, hearts and other adornments. It was quickly banned in Japanese schools, known as "Anomalous Female Teenage Handwriting", but the style persevered in magazines and comic books. The company that produces all the dainty things mentioned above, *Sanrio*, makes about $1 billion per year.

CHAPTER 12

CHINESE FESTIVALS

Everything being a constant carnival,
there is no carnival left.

(Victor Hugo)

Merry China Christmas.

I spent six Christmases in China. I tell you this. There might not be a lot of Christ in Christmas in China, but there sure are a lot of lights, trees, gifts and shopping sales. Christmas and its commercial side has certainly arrived in China. People were asking me for years: Do they celebrate Christmas in China? I would say: They do, but probably not like you do.

Coming from Poland, I am used to elaborate pre-Christmas preparations. We have 12 meatless dishes on Christmas Eve, for instance. My mum would start shopping for food as early as at the beginning of December. Also, in Poland it's a long holiday. Schools are closed, people get time off-work to spend time with their families. In China, you work as if nothing ever happened. Three years in, my contracts started recognizing Christmas as a legitimate day-off, but only for foreigners. My Chinese colleagues had to work, while we could stay home on Dec 25th. In one of the schools I worked for, they put me in charge of organizing an activity for Christmas. That's what Chinese people like best: making a show out of something. I decided to go with "Christmas around the world" theme and asked my colleagues to introduce Christmas traditions from their countries. I even put up a Christmas tree, Polish style, ha-ha.

Me and my Christmas tree☺. Image by Karolina Achirri.

We had lots of fun discussing Christmas traditions and its background. In fact, I think it was the one time any Chinese school let me openly talk about Jesus. I even taught them some carols:

Image by Karolina Achirri.

The school's managers provided us with a huge turkey, so Chinese students were happy. Because in China nothing attracts as much attention as free food.

Of course, Christians in China are still in minority, but their numbers are growing rapidly. The catholic church in Hangzhou that became my oasis since the first time I saw it, provided Christmas services. But... they were all in Chinese. I went only once (my first year) and after 4 hours of being squashed like a sardine, not understanding a word and becoming a model for random people's photos (snapped of course to document having foreign friends on *WeChat*), I had enough. Since then I spent Christmas with friends or simply by myself, video chatting with my family.

So, I can't really give you any shocking facts about how the Chinese flipped Christmas. However, I always did wonder why people gave apples to each other on Christmas Eve in China. Large cities, with significant expat population, had been seeing a surge in interest regarding Christmas. Every year, I'd go home from work with a few apples that had *ping an* (平安), which means *peace*, either curved on or drawn on them. I didn't know why until I started learning Chinese. It was then when I realized that Christmas Eve in Chinese is *Ping'an Ye* (平安夜), literally a peaceful night. The word apple (*pingguo* = 苹果) sounds like *peace* in Mandarin. That's how Chinese people invented their one and only Christmas tradition.

If you happen to be in China around Christmas time, you'll definitely still experience its spirit. Might not be *the* spirit you're used to or are looking for, but it will surely try to imitate Christmas. Merchants will try to rip you off on impulsive purchases. Girls will use

Christmas as an excuse to nab gifts from their boyfriends. Young people don't mind adapting to Western traditions, the more the merrier!

Heads-up: Chinese students love cultural classes, so they'd enjoy a lesson on Christmas anytime.

Fancy a holiday? – Unusual Chinese celebrations and days-off.

Days off in China are arranged according to 传统节日 (*chuan tong jie ri*), which is a traditional Chinese calendar. Chinese vacations resemble mass migrations, especially during the golden week (黄金周 = *huang jin zhou*) in October (Oct 1-Oct 7 is the National Day celebration in China). Most public holidays are secular and whenever 1.4 billion people try to travel at the same time, chaos unravels. If you are brave enough to take a train, be ready for standing tickets only, which are oversold as well. So, you might end up waiting for 5 hours to board a train that won't take you anyway.

Since my employment experiences in China are limited to working only in different types of schools, I can offer insight into what these offer as days-off. Training schools I worked for stipulated between 5 and 15 days of actual holidays per contractual year, while public schools offered more time off. But, every time a bank holiday would approach, the public schools I worked for would practise mysterious manoeuvres of shuffling these days. In reality, we would have three days-off in a row (including weekend) just to work it off later in the month (at the weekend). Thus, Monday would become Thursday on schedule, creating widespread havoc in terms of keeping to a timetable. I never quite grasped why they did that, but someone told me they wanted you to have more days off together (like in groups of 2 or 3) instead of having to enjoy only one single day free of work. Oh well, it didn't make much difference to me.

The weirdest thing was the requirement to *always* apply for a day-off beforehand, even when it was a sick leave. How was I supposed to know that I would fall sick in advance? Five people would have to approve such request, so I ended up taking sick days with financial penalties more often than applying for them. Also, one school would make me re-do missed classes once I was back, so I didn't see the point of submitting any applications to anyone. I was a rebel, ha-ha.

China also celebrates some unique (weird!) festivals, like The Festival of Hungry Ghosts (中元节 = *zhong yuan jie*). Your eyes did not trick you, they actually celebrate it, usually at the end of August. If you hear or see noisy crowds of people running around to burn fake money on the streets, you've found it. The money is burnt to appease the ghosts. Actually, other fake representations of the things ghosts could potentially like in the real world, such as fake houses, cars or women, are also sacrificed. Lanterns are burning and fireworks are whooshing to scare away the ghosts. Especially seniors still celebrate this day, praying for peace in their lives.

Another weird occasion to honour is Dog Eating Festival. Even though it was officially banned by the government in 2011, it is still happening in some remote places. Prior to the ban, the Chinese were chopping up, cooking and eating dogs to commemorate a Ming dynasty military victory from 600 years back. Apparently, the army was able to succeed because they killed all dogs in the area, so that the animals could not warn the enemy. Their meat was served at a feast that followed. Luckily, phones and social media made this festival infamous and hence created a public outcry among animal lovers around the world.

However, my favourite strange jubilee has been Yunnan Province's Monihei Carnival. They celebrate the discovery of a miraculous herb that grants immortality. It is made into powder and is to be mixed with water to make a paste. Then, one needs to rub his/her body with it. These days mud is used as a replacement. So, what actually happens is that people have an official day to get dirty in public. According to tradition, mud on a child's face means peace, on an elderly person's face represents longevity; and on a woman's face beauty. This one actually sounds like fun.

A blasting Spring Festival.

When the Chinese Year comes, firework explosions are so loud that the blaring TV with the CCTV Spring Festival Gala can't be heard.

(As I am told by this book's cultural consultant, the government has banned fireworks in China during this festival). It is the one time of the year when the sky is so illuminated, one can forget it's still polluted. Spring Festival, *chun jie* (春节), also known as the Lunar New Year, falls on the first day of the lunar calendar. It was 1912 that marked the beginning of China following the Gregorian calendar, though. January 1st became Solar New Year, or *yuan dan* (元旦), and the Lunar New Year got the name of *chun jie*. I always found it funny that they called it Spring Festival, since it usually happens in January of February when the weather is still freezing cold.

There are numerous traditions related to the Chinese New Year. The last week of the ending lunar year is marked with thorough house cleanings, "dirt-cleaning days", to make room for the new. Many people would also buy new clothes to welcome the new year fresh and shiny. Food plays an important role, too. I would never go shopping around that time because the crowds reached their peak then. Families stock up on chicken, duck, fish, veggies, tea, wine, nuts, sweats, etc. Basically, anything that one can possibly want to eat will be in their shopping baskets. Everyone wants to honour visiting family members with a luscious feast. Pigging out is a common problem during that period of time. The Chinese make sure traditional New Year food is not overlooked either. *Nian gao* (年糕), rice cake, is made of glutinous rice and eating it is supposed to bring good luck, since its name is the homophone of "higher year". It symbolizes self-improvement and supping it can make one taller and better in the following year. No table would also lack *tang yuan* (汤圆), ball-shaped dumplings made of glutinous rice, served in boiling water. Its name sounds like "union" and symbolizes togetherness. Of course, perhaps the most famous food associated with Chinese New Year is *jiaozi* (饺子), traditional dumplings. They are believed to bring prosperity, because they supposedly look like the gold ingots (*yuan bao* = 元宝), which were used as currency during the Ming Dynasty. Also, their name sounds like the word for the earliest paper money. Normally, they would be stuffed with meat and/or vegetables, cooked in boiling water, steamed or fried. As for a dessert, *ba bao fan* (八宝饭) is probably the most common. Its name translates into "eight-treasures rice" and it is served on New Year's Eve. It is made of glutinous rice steamed and mixed with lard, sugar and eight kinds of fruits and nuts, such as red dates, lotus seeds, longan, raisins, walnuts or peanuts to name a few. Each ingredient of this sweet dessert has its own meaning. The lotus seeds (莲子 = *lian zi*) represent a harmonious married life or a wish for many children, longan signifies reunion, red dates stand for wishes to have a healthy baby and pumpkin seeds mean "safe and sound". I found it scrumptious.

Around the New Year time, doors are decorated with red paper that has yellow welcome wishes inscribed on it. Red lanterns hung by the entrances, glowing the character for happiness and prosperity, *fu* (福). This character is often turned upside down (福到 = *fu dao*), because it means "luck arrives" in Chinese, so it indicates that happiness is on its way. Some houses also have the gods of wealth guarding their door.

Found on my neighbours' door at New Year's in 2015.
Image by Karolina Achirri.

As for tradition, Spring Festival has another name, i.e. "leaving of the Nian". Nian was an animal who dragged bad luck around. If Nian (whose name shares both the character and pronunciation with "year") stopped by, the grass would shrivel back to the ground and the trees would wither. Only when it left were the flowers blooming again. So, people decided to try and keep Nian away. They came up with firecrackers. That's why today people set them off in such numbers.

For Chinese people, New Year is the time for family reunions. It is full of happiness and peace. Since many people migrate to big cities for work, *chun jie* might be the only time they get to go back to their home town to see their family. It is certainly very different from a typically spent New Year by most Westerners. Sharing food and spending time together beat getting drunk and partying all night.

It was estimated that in 2015, 2.8 billion people travelled during Spring Festival in China. No wonder I always tried to stay home at that time. Every year, media report horror stories of New Year's travel. Seven people got fit into a 5-person car by putting two of them in the boot. People camp in ticket halls at the railway stations for days to purchase their tickets back home. Travellers disappointed by either ticket's price or the fact that tickets have just been sold out, faint in front of the ticket windows. Sometimes waiting in line might also be longer than the actual train ride home. The saddest news I saw, however, was a piece on a man who spent 36 hours in a queue to buy a ticket to see his family who lived miles away. He was a worker in the south of China and they lived in the north. He only saw his family once a year for Spring Festival. When he finally reached the window, the tickets were gone. He jumped off the station's roof out of desperation.

Festive clothes are worn, elders' long lives are celebrated and red envelopes (filled with cash) are given to children. Dinners are eaten and then more dinners are eaten. On the second and third day of the New Year, visits are paid to relatives and friends. Ancestors are commemorated as well. The festal atmosphere spills out to the streets where traditional lion or dragon dances entertain everyone.

Image from https://commons.wikimedia.org/.

The end of Spring Festival is marked two weeks later, on the Lantern Festival (元宵节 = *yuan xiao jie*). This time of year is the most important celebration not only to China's Han majority, but also to the other 55 ethnic minorities. If you're lucky enough to experience this time with a Chinese family, bear a few tips in mind.

1. Bring gifts. You don't have to go crazy. A gift box of fruit that are in season or a nice bottle of local spirits will certainly suffice.
2. Don't forget the *hong bao* (red envelope) full of money for the younger family members. RMB 100 ($15) will do, since you're a foreign guest who just try to be polite.

3. Try a little bit of every dish on the table. But, be sure to warn the hosts of any food allergies you might have. I learnt the hard way that I was allergic to soy sauce at the hospital the next day.

4. Be prepared to watch TV. After the big meal, most families would gather around their TV to watch the Chinese New Year's TV Gala. It might be challenging to comprehend what's being said, but it will certainly make your hosts happy.

5. Wear new clothes and compliment your hosts on their new outfits. You might wear something clean if you don't want to buy anything new, but a New Year shopping trip is always a good idea if you're a woman.

Observing Spring Festival in China left me amazed at Chinese people's devotion to the family, their hard work throughout the year and their jovial spirit around that time. I think I can only compare it to Christmas in Poland. No matter where you are, don't forget to greet your Chinese friends with *xin nian kuai le* (新年快乐) or *ci jiu ying xin* (辞旧迎新), out with the old, in with the new.

Celebrating suicide anyone? – Dragon Boat Festival.

Dragon Boat Festival, or *duan wu jie* (端午节), falls on the 5th day of the 5th lunar month, according to the Chinese lunar calendar. Normally it would be at the end of May or beginning of June, according to our (Gregorian) calendar. You can't miss it if you live near a river, because colourful boats, with traditional dragonheads attached to the front of the boat, carrying different teams who race each other won't let you sleep.

The races originated over 2000 years ago to commemorate Qu Yuan (屈原), a poet who lived during the Warring States period (475-221 B.C.). He was greatly respected for his wisdom and open fight against corruption. So, as history would have it, he was exiled. But people kept loving his patriotic poems even more. He loved the Chu state (楚国 = *chu guo*) and praised it in his mesmeric poems. When he heard of its defeat by neighbouring Qin state (秦国 = *qin guo*), he was so distraught that he drowned himself in the Mi Luo River (汨罗江 = *mi luo jiang*). In his moment of despair, the villagers jumped into their fishing boats and raced to his rescue. To no avail. In order to save his body from the fish, they threw sticky *zong zi* (粽子), triangular rice pieces, into the river to distract the fish. Some people also poured rice wine into the river to intoxicate the fish.

The tradition of eating *zong zi* survived till this day. They are made of glutinous sticky rice stuffed with a wide range of fillings and wrapped in bamboo, reed or Nimtree leaves. Different types of leaves bring different flavours: bamboo, lotus, banana, corn, to name a few. They are steamed or boiled for a few hours until the rice fillings are thoroughly cooked. Sweet fillings include red beans, mung beans, jujubes; savoury ones might be filled with pork, Chinese sausage or preserved duck eggs (these are my least favourite). I guess if you try and don't like them, you can always feed the fish😊.

Zong zi. Image from https://commons.wikimedia.org/wiki/File:Zongzi.jpg.

For the dragon boat races, there are usually about 22 people in one boat. 20 of them would paddle, 1 would be a designated drummer, and 1 would sit at the tail of the dragon. The drummer has a job of conveying the dragon's heartbeat and hence is responsible for setting the stroke timing for when the paddles hit the water. Of course, the race symbolizes the many unsuccessful attempts to rescue Qu's body. I personally found them a bit loud and each time I would go to watch them, it would rain. These days, there are also international dragon boat competitions, especially in places with dense Chinese diaspora.

Dragon boat racing. Image from http://www.kadena.af.mil/News/Commentaries/Display/Article/419976/unleash -your-inner-dragon/.

Interestingly, some more superstitious Chinese people would wear talismans to fend off evil spirits around that time. Children might be carrying fragrant silk pouches, while adults might enjoy Xiong Huang wine (雄黄酒 = *xiong huang jiu*); all of which are believed to have protective powers. Interestingly, residents of Hangzhou prepare "five yellow-coloured dishes" (*wu huang* = 五黄). The dishes comprise of wine, cucumbers, eels, slated duck eggs and a type of a sea fish. All of these types of food contain either a yellow colour or a character that coincides with the word *yellow*.

The less common festivals of China.

Water-Sprinkling Festival (泼水节 = *po shui jie*) in Yunnan Province.

Every year in April, residents of China's Yunnan Province, which I consider the most picturesque part of the country, get very wet. The Dai ethnic group (傣族 = *dai zu*), one of the 55 ethnic minorities in China, celebrates this day to mark the beginning of the Dai calendar's new year. They share this tradition with people in Thailand, Cambodia and Myanmar. They basically splash water at each other to pray for good fortune and safety. It lasts about three days and is accompanied by boat races and lanterns flying.

Image from https://c1.staticflickr.com/4/3556/3443344503_d61c7cff85_b.jpg.

The first day is marked by amazing boat races, which often take on a form of canoe races. Before the competition starts, team members gather on the river bank. Captains light incense and then sprinkle the flames with *baijiu* (rice wine) to assure good luck to the boats. Ships are decorated with good luck charms; team members wear traditional minority clothes. Races go on the whole day and they are culminated by evening lantern flying. Releasing those to the sky is a way of bringing good fortune for the new year.

The second day circles around a visit to a temple, as most Dai people practise Theravada Buddhism. They wash the Buddha in a ceremonial manner and some people collect drops that have touched the statue, as holy water. This ritual is supposed to guarantee prosperity in the new year. Also, many temple goers bring food as an offering to the monks.

On the last day of the festival, the public drenching begins. Anything goes: buckets, water guns, cans. Anywhere is also a place where one can get wet. There are no limits. From dusk to dawn, there is water everywhere. Special polls full of water are usually prepared ahead of time in parks. If, by the end of the day, you're still dry, you did not celebrate Water-sprinkling the right way.

Chinese Valentine's Day, aka *Qixi* (七夕).

On the seventh day of the seventh month in the Chinese lunar calendar, the Chinese celebrate their own Valentine's Day. This day is also observed in Japan, interestingly. There are several versions of the legend behind this day that circulate around. The oldest one comes from a poem (2600 years old) that depicts a forbidden romance between a weaver girl – *Zhinv* (织女) and a cowherd – *Niulang* (牛郎).

The beautiful 7th daughter of the Goddess of heaven abandons her duties to weave clouds and decides to spend one frolic day on earth. She bathes in a lake when *Niulang* falls in love with her. They get married, have two children and have their almost perfect ever after. With one little detail. *Zhinv's* mother conspires to break them up. She calls *Zhinv* back to heaven to perform her monotonous clouds weaving chores. *Niulang* is left alone on earth with their children. Then, his ox (that can talk) offers to sacrifice itself for *Niulang* and his children to be transported to heaven. But, the Goddess banishes her daughter to the eastern star Vega and *Niulang* to the western star Altair; and creates the Milky Way to keep the two separate forever.

As the tale has it, every year on the 7th night of the 7th month, the magpies of the world make a bridge (鹊桥= *que qiao*) so that the couple can be re-united for one night only. I found this story much more fascinating that the one behind the Western Valentine's Day. And eh, who doesn't like yet another opportunity to celebrate love.

Dead people's day – Qingming Festival.

The *Qingming* Festival (清明节 = *qing ming jie*), or a Tomb-Sweeping Day, is a traditional Chinese celebration that falls on the 104th day after the winter solstice, so usually around April 5th of the Gregorian calendar.

In the early 12th century, Zhang Zeduan (张择端) painted "China's Mona Lisa", a massive panorama (over 16 feet), called *Along the River During the Qingming Festival (*清明上河图 = *Qing Ming Shang He Tu)*. It captured the hectic nature of Kaifeng's holiday market. Back then, that market had a huge community of Jewish traders. Then, in the 1950s, when by accident the remains of 7 dead Chinese soldiers were discovered in Hawaii, the government decided to pay for the burial of those soldiers at the Manoa Chinese Cemetery. Then later in 2000, with mandatory cremation in China, the Chinese figured the only logical place to honour their ancestors was in fact the Internet. Websites started selling virtual memorial halls to replace actual burial plots. So, in 2008, the Chinese government officially reinstated *Qingming*.

It originated from Hanshi Day (寒食), a day with cold food only and prohibited fire), as a memorial day for Jie Zitui (介子推). It has continued since Ancient China. Linguistically, *Qingming* means "pure brightness". The name refers to the time for people to go outside and enjoy the greenery of springtime. Normally, people would burn up the sweepings from the graves and then ignite paper offerings and joss sticks. It's a very important day in China.

Today, it's a chance for the Chinese to remember and honour their ancestors at graveyards and cemeteries in a new (slightly modern) way. While entire families still pray to their forefathers, sweep the tombs and offer food, tea, wine and chopsticks; the items that are getting burnt certainly reflect contemporary societal trends. I was to learn that people burn paper iPhones, luxurious cars and cut-outs of houses. Someone told me that food is understandable, because ghosts need to eat (duh!), but those modern hi-tech devices might also prove to be useful to them in the afterlife world...

I think I envy Chinese people the togetherness of this day. Many of my friends would travel back home for this occasion, even though it is just a one day-off holiday. Luckily, those who can't go back may join their loved ones on *FaceTime* these days.

Moon Cake Day, or Mid-Autumn Festival.

Zhong Qiu Jie (中秋节), falls on the 15th day of the 8th month of the lunar calendar. It is named Mid-Autumn Festival because it literally falls in the middle of autumn, which happens to be China's shortest season. The full moon is supposed to be the brightest and the roundest at this time. Because families like to sit down around a round table, this festival is also called "gathering holiday" (团圆节 = *tuan yuan jie*). It is one of the most important traditions to Chinese people.

I've heard many legends surrounding the origins of Moon Cake day, but one seems to be the most widespread. It's about *Chang E* (嫦娥), who flew to the Moon. Long long time ago, when the sky had 10 suns, the crops would get burned to the ground by them. One hero, named *Hou Yi* (后羿), sensitive to people's suffering, decided to climb *Kun Lun Mountain* (昆仑山). When he reached its peak, he used his divine bow to shoot down 9 suns. The remaining sun was from then on forced to rise and set according to his schedule. *Hou* Yi took *Chang E* as his wife. She was beautiful and kind. Everyone admired the couple's love and devotion. Unfortunately, as in every story, there was a villain named *Feng Meng* (逢蒙). One day he decided to steal from them the medicine that could make everyone divine. *Chang E* was alone in the house that day, so knowing she could not fight *Feng Meng* by herself, she drank the medicine. Immediately, she flew off to heaven. However, she wasn't able to bear being separated with her beloved husband, so she landed on the moon instead. When *Hou Yi* learnt about what had happened, he tried to kill *Feng Meng*. Overcome by grief, he began calling his wife's name to the sky. Suddenly, he noticed that the moon swayed on the shadow that looked exactly like *Chang E's* figurine. He tried running towards the moon, but with every step he took, the moon would move further away from him. Having realized he couldn't get to her, he set up a table with incense, fruit and sweets as an offering to *Chang E*. When others heard that she had flown to the moon, they also wanted to honour her by setting up tables with offerings. And that's how Mid-Autumn Day began.

There are also other, less-known stories about how it all started. There's one about Wu Gang (吴刚), who was punished by a god to cut the sweet osmanthus tree. He has to cut it forever, without rest, as it regrows each year. This story reminds me of a Sisyphean task. Another story recalls a little rabbit who lived on the moon. Its body was white like a jade stone, so its name was Jade Rabbit (玉兔). The rabbit would use a jade stick to kneel down and blend the herbs for a magic pill. Whoever ate such a pill, would become an angel.

Today, China commemorates this day by familiar get-togethers, large festive meals with family and friends and soaking in the moon's light. Some more traditional people would make wishes to the moon, hoping for happiness, health and prosperity. This festival wouldn't be complete without moon cakes. They are basically cakes shaped like a moon, with thick oily pastry on the outside and fillings of red bean or lotus paste. There are also other varieties, including my least favourite ones, filled with meat. They are the most popular gift around that time. It's also common to find a salted egg yolk in the middle of a moon cake, as it symbolizes the full moon.

Image from https://pixabay.com/en/mooncake-lotus-filling-pastry-2409860/.

Singles' Day.

In the spirit of "any occasion is good enough for a celebration", China gave November 11 a capitalist makeover. 24 hours of frantic sales online are the main feature of *Shuang ShiYi* (双十一), or Double 11. There's a Chinese term, *guanggun* (光棍), which means "bare branches" and refers to single men. If 11/11 is written like that, it comprises four singletons or four leafless trees.

Innocently, four single students of Nanjing University decided to create a day for single men in 1993. They simply wanted to make their lives more colourful with activities like KTV-singing. Their idea quickly grew into a national day of celebrating singlehood.

Then, *Alibaba* saw a business opportunity and turned this day into a shopping madness. Black Friday would have to be on steroids to match the scale of the online sales magnitude. I know people who stayed up, just to click first thing after midnight to buy heavily under-priced home amenities, brand shoes and clothes or even cars. The first time *Taobao* launched this sales campaign, within the first 90 minutes they earned $5 million. These days the 11/11 sales are going down even faster as more and more people are using this service on their mobile phones.

Even though the 11/11 online sales originated as only one day, over time they have grown into a week of shopping bonanza. Millions of products are offered at lower prices, *kuaidi* guys (delivery men) don't sleep for weeks after 11/11 to make sure all goods find their rightful owners. People obsess about this day months in advance. Now, even *Alibaba*'s global app offers similar services around the time of 11/11.

Why not buy something 10 times cheaper, ehh? Quoting Bo Derek: *Whoever said money can't buy happiness simply didn't know where to go shopping.*

CHAPTER 13

Love-hate relationship with China

We love the ones we hate.

(Jessica Shirvington)

Stereotyping foreigners in China.

I am not a fan of stereotypes, but they are inevitably present in every society. Chinese people stereotype foreigners as well as foreigners stereotype other foreigners in China. I'm going to describe a few types of foreigners I met and interacted with during my stay in China.

1. The Sinophile: somebody who came to China for the love of its culture. Such a person has been most probably living in China for a few good years and might even stay longer. They would be motivated to learn the language well with hopes of getting a non-expat kind of job, for example as a journalist or a translator. They would love traditional places and would often visit historical sites.

2. The international school teacher: somebody who gets angry when confused with a TEFL teacher. Paid well and with opportunities for promotion, such expats live more comfortably in China than they would ever in their home countries. They would most likely eat in luxurious restaurants and travel abroad every chance they get. They would use taxis as their main means of transport. They would also (quite possibly) not be into Chinese culture or language.

3. The expat business person: somebody who was sent to China by their company back home. They would struggle with cultural differences (especially in their workplace) but would surely enjoy thick financial benefits their job brings them. They usually live luxuriously, oftentimes in posh hotels that their company pays for. They have no reason to learn the language and hence aren't that much into the cultural side of the job. Quite often their families would be with them, too, of course fully financed by the employer. Kids would attend an extremely expensive international school while the wife would be a homemaker. They would have a chauffeur at their disposal.

4. The writer turned teacher: somebody who came to China with lofty ideas of writing a book or a screenplay but ended up teaching as much as possible to make ends meet. These guys are easy to spot in cafes with their fancy *Macbooks*, energetically typing everything and everywhere. Due to their financial restrictions, they would share a flat with other expats and regularly attend gatherings of foreigners (in pubs) to show off their barely alive dream of becoming the next J.K. Rowling.

They would wear glasses to look smart and use an e-bike or a bike to move around.

5. The fake English teacher: somebody who found nothing better to do and so decided to have a go at teaching. They are native speakers of English and they think that is *all* that it takes to teach a language. Looked down on by other more professional expats. They like to call themselves: English specialists or experts. Chinese people respect them, since teachers are generally respected in the culture. They have no clue how to teach a language or what it takes to be a teacher, but they proudly wave their passports from English native-speaking countries as they collect their fat pay checks. Being white and handsome usually suffices as "job qualifications". So it also happens, that male English teachers would find themselves a young and pretty Chinese wife. That's how they survive. The wife serves as a translator and cultural mediator. They aspire to blend into Chinese culture, but also pride themselves on being foreigners (see: better than the locals).

6. The Chinese language student: somebody who comes to China on a student visa and aims at learning some Chinese. These guys often live in dormitories for international students, eat in tiny local joints and ride bikes or e-bikes. To make any kind of income, they teach illegally at the weekends. If you are a young, slim, white and blond girl with some command of English, you will be swarming in teaching job offers (especially from kids' schools). They would normally be regular pub goers and beer-pong players.

7. The hippie traveller: somebody who lives a pretty frivolous lifestyle and one day just randomly decided to explore China. With scruffy looks and a musical instrument, such a person travels around China making a living by street performing or hustling. They have a wanderlust in their eyes as they nomad from place to place, often sleeping on other people's couches. They travel on foot and live frugally. They find China fascinating and don't plan anything anytime. They are true explorers, whose spirit of adventurous determines their next destination.

8. The real English teacher: somebody who actually knows how to teach English, holds a reputable diploma (not just a 20-hour online certificate), and came to China for the passion of teaching. Chinese students are the best. Such a person might learn Chinese on the way. They would live in various types of

accommodation, depending on their income level. Oftentimes too professional for the school they work for. A person with a mission: to enlighten young Chinese minds.

What people back home think about those of us who decided to move to China is another story. I observed two types of people. Those who chose to come to China and those who were forced to. The former wanted to learn about the culture, pick up some Chinese and generally experience life abroad. The latter are often running away from something (or someone!) back home. Most male expatriates are expected to find a Chinese girlfriend (or two!), embodying the notorious "yellow fever". People back home often feel like our lives in China are either full of horror (of the unknown and different) or bliss (marked with exotic travels and adventures). While it might be true for some, most of us live a simple, routine kind of life in China. One must adjust to the system in order to survive. I think one way to help our family and friends get rid of stereotypes about China is to fill them in on what's going on in our daily lives. Or you can write a book about it, like I did😊.

How far can being white get you in China? – The types of jobs available to foreigners.

So, it hardly matters where you come from, China is a very, very, very different place from whence you are from. The Chinese workplace is no exception in that regard.

Hiring based on one's looks is a very common practice. Not just for foreigners but also for the Chinese. I still remember when one headmaster of a school I worked for said at the staff meeting: *We need a new assistant but the last one we interviewed was too ugly.* I think foreigners in the room were much more gobsmacked than our Chinese colleagues. Some young Chinese girls are even willing to undergo pricey and painful surgical altering to be seen as more competitive in a workplace. Some college majors still have appearance and height requirements in China (e.g. flight attendants). Well, I am yet to meet a foreigner who would be that desperate, though. In our case, being white gets you places. Especially if you are blond, tall, slim and pretty.

Your country of origin stops being important the second you enter an interview. But to be fair, America has its own share of lawsuits based on discrimination related to looks.

Another thing to remember when working in China is the fact that intellectual property is pretty much non-existent there. I was developing three language courses for one very famous training school in Hangzhou. When I left the job, the curricula stayed with them. People in China will steal your ideas in broad daylight. Just go on *Taobao* and see how well knockoffs are made. Sometimes it's even hard to tell them apart from the originals. If you work as a part of a team, and in 1.4 billion country you always are, expect the whole team to share your successes and failures.

Additionally, you might have co-workers who would openly smoke in the office or right outside its door. Getting paid under the table isn't uncommon, either. If you don't care, fair enough, but wait till you need a bank statement with your earnings. And of course, the *guanxi*, hiring people who are completely unqualified based on personal relationships. I cannot tell you how many times I was introduced to someone new at work, who couldn't even write a simple lesson plan. Ehh... Finally, meetings in Chinese companies (and schools are also businesses there) are endless and oftentimes conducted in Chinese. If they designate someone to translate for you, chances are he/she will get tired after the first hour and then retrieve to online shopping on their smartphone leaving you clueless and bored to death.

So, what *can* foreigners do in China? They can be a model. Ha-ha. I know it sounds silly, but many people you and I would consider ugly, the Chinese - love. The skinnier and paler, the better. If you see a vaguely-worded job ad in broken English says things like: *assist boss* or *Caucasians only*, you found yourself a *face job*. Car companies are always looking for pretty girls to parade around their vehicles. Even corporations seek handsome white males to pretend they are the CEOs at the grand openings. Hotels pay top dollar for just hanging around their lounge and looking white. So, if you're smart and not too ugly, you will never go hungry in China.

Other jobs include the infamous English teaching, translation (if your Mandarin is proficient enough), consultancy (mainly for study abroad programs), childcare (most often done by experienced Filipino ladies), or stardom. Yes, you can become an actor/actress. Qualifications? Talent? Nobody cares. One friend of mine played a role of a priest in a Chinese telenovela and called me from the set asking: *How do I baptize a baby?* One day of shooting can earn you even RMB 1500 ($230). Not to mention all the fame you may gain. There are also those who get hired as DJs or managers in music clubs. This happens mostly because the clubs' owners want to attract more guests. Another version of a "face job". Sadly, because these guys work mostly at night, and often have a day job, I have worked at schools with them and experienced their morning hangovers first-hand, when they would call in sick 10 minutes before the class or worse - come to class smelling of booze.

Sadly, if you are of a different ethnicity or skin colour, you will likely meet multiple roadblocks, even if you are the most qualified person for the job. One friend of mine was interviewing for a position of an ESL adult teacher at my training school. He's an African American from D.C. The manager told him the parents wouldn't accept him, first justifying it by "parents only want native speakers", and then "you're not tall enough". He didn't want to tell him that the school prides itself on hiring Whites only.

To recap, before you depart on this exciting journey of moving across the ocean, make sure you're pretty/handsome enough, slim enough, pale enough and flexible enough to jump through all the hoops the Chinese job market might have for you.

Mutual (mis)conceptions - What the Chinese think about us and what we think about them.

Let's face it. We all stereotype others, especially those who are so different than us, it's in our human nature. The Chinese have their own ideas about foreigners and so do we, before our eyes are opened to the reality. Quoting Chimamanda Ngozi Adichie, one of my favourite African writers, "The problem with stereotypes is not that they are untrue, but that they are incomplete. They make one story become the only story".

So, what are the common misconceptions about foreigners in China?

1. *All foreigners are rich.* Couldn't be further from the truth. In fact, most foreigners come to China to make some money. For Chinese people, the fact that one was born in America or Australia accounts for having money. That's why foreigners are often overcharged. Truth be told, many foreigners in China live from pay check to pay check, always scrambling money to travel. I personally know only one person who has managed to save during her stay in China. Everyone else simply spends what they earn.

2. *Foreigners can't speak Chinese.* Oh well... Every time I opened my mouth and greeted someone with a simple *Ni hao*, I'd hear *Your Chinese is so good!* I think it's really difficult for most Chinese people to grasp the idea of a foreigner commanding their language. Granted, it is the hardest language I have studied so far, but it's not impossible to learn. Every now and then another foreigner becomes famous on a TV show for his or her exceptional Chinese skills. However, *the face thing* does truly exist. When I was on a taxi and told the driver where to take me in close-to-fluent Chinese, he or she would always awkwardly pause for a moment before they could process that a foreigner just gave them directions in Chinese.

3. *Foreigners can't handle hardships and need luxury in life.* This is most visible in types of flats the estate agents take one to. No matter how many times I'd bring a friend to help me out, explain my budget and expectations, they would always take me to the most expensive (far beyond my budget) places first. As for the hardship part, my dentist told me he didn't like to treat foreigners because they always demand anaesthetics, while the Chinese just handle the pain gracefully.

4. *Foreign women aren't into Chinese guys.* The number of foreign girls dating Chinese guys is significantly lower than that of Chinese girls with foreign boyfriends. So, while this might be true to some extend (I belong to this stereotyped group), I have a few friends who dated or even married Chinese men. All depends on personal preference.

5. *English men are all gentlemen.* I can assure you from my own personal experience of living in England in my early 20s, that this one is totally untrue. In fact, I find most British guys swearing like a sailor.

6. *Westerners can't use chopsticks.* Couple of waitresses in China did bring me a fork before I even ordered, but I took it as a mere

concern. Were I not able to use chopsticks, they were simply trying to save me from losing face.

7. *Everyone in America owns a gun.* Well... Surely not everyone, but one must admit that recent news doesn't do much to convince one otherwise.

8. *All Americans are fat.* Not all, but many. To be honest, I have never seen so many obese people in my life before I moved to the U.S. They just don't take care of themselves, living off fast foods and leading a sedentary lifestyle.

9. *How do you get your skin to be so white?* This one is reflected in cosmetics. Whitening creams and all sorts of goodies with the word *whiten* on them, make many Chinese women spend money like water.

10. *Why don't you have blue eyes?* I just don't and stop asking me this question. This vision of a perfect foreigner having blond hair and blue eyes is truly an overstretch.

11. *Paris is the most romantic city on the planet!* God no! You have no idea how many times I heard this sentence as the main reason for someone's travel to France.

12. *You're so cute!* This is the compliment I heard for years. Not that I'm not cute 😊, but this might not be the thing a grown-up woman longs to hear.

As a riposte, foreigners also carry all sorts of preconceptions that are corrected fast when reality of living in China strikes them. Here are some I've heard:

1. *Chinese people are small.* That's a fact if you compare the majority of them with the majority of, say, Americans. Sizes can even go as low as XXXXS. Once I was shopping in a mall (I don't remember what for), and as I entered one of their boutiques, the clerk came up to me and said in Chinese: *You won't find anything here. You're too fat.* I didn't know if I should laugh or cry but instead I decided to answer her back with all my repertoire of Chinese swearings, ha-ha!

2. *Chinese people are quiet.* Your first night in the place you'll be renting will quickly teach you otherwise. Nobody cares about being quiet in public places in China. People even listen to music without headphones on the subway.

3. *The Chinese youth is critical of the government.* That depends. Some students of mine were forced to join the communist party as they were college students, with threats that their father

would lose his job if they didn't. Many young people in China travel abroad extensively and from there they bring a more critical look at the politics, but whether they express how they truly feel or not is another story.

4. *Chinese people can't wait to leave China and live abroad.* Many of them would like an opportunity to experience life in what they call more developed countries, but nobody is willing to jump on the first plane with a one-way ticket to Europe. Their cultural heritage is very important to them.

5. *Chinese women only want your money.* Again, while this is true for many gold-diggers, I know quite a few mixed marriages where a woman is the most frugal person you'd ever meet.

6. *Chinese people have low salaries.* I think this can be exemplified when one compares a foreign teacher salary with a Chinese English salary at a typical training school. It is usually three times higher than what they pay the locals. I never knew why this was the case, but always felt a sense of injustice when my Chinese colleagues would work double but earn less.

7. *Chinese people just want to use you to practise English.* Yes, that's true to some extent. But, to their defence, that's how they start small talk with foreigners, so it is not a premeditated technique to use and abuse you but rather a common strategy to overcome shyness in speaking English.

8. *Chinese people work really hard.* Yes, that's true I'd say, but in more and more instances (especially when young people begin their careers) people in China are looking for ways to make good money fast and with minimum sweat. It's the new generation that takes wealth for granted, though.

9. *All Chinese people must know kung-fu.* Ha-ha. I think this is one of the most hated statements by the Chinese. Just as not all Swiss love cheese and not all Brits love tea, not all Chinese know how to practise *kung-fu*. It's a very meticulous martial art that requires hours of training and devotion.

There are also some cultural *no-no's* that every foreigner needs to know.

1. *Don't get angry.* Just calm down and walk away. Chances are your problem won't be solved anyway. You might as well save yourself some stress.

2. *Don't embarrass anyone, especially in the presence of others.* Losing and saving face are still very much present in today's China. It's humiliating to them.

3. *Don't let your visa expire.* Many people hope that the Chinese government won't notice or won't care that you've overstayed your visa. But trust me, they do care. So, make sure all your ducks are in order before you find yourself in a conundrum.

4. *Make an effort to learn something about China.* It is just common sense to want to know as much as humanly possible about your new home. It will grant you some brownie points with your Chinese friends.

5. *Don't get first and last names mixed up.* In China, the family name always comes first. Remember that before you commit a social faux pas.

6. *Don't talk about Chinese government to Chinese people.* Although they might share your concerns and opinions, they will likely feel very uncomfortable discussing it with you. After all, you are just the Other and they have to live there till they die.

7. *Don't be too picky about how your food is prepared or served.* You know what they say: don't look a given horse in the mouth. Just be grateful you can afford a nice meal in a restaurant (something that maybe was always out of your reach back home) and appreciate the time someone devoted to cooking for you.

8. *Wear pyjamas in public if you feel like it.* And don't stare at those who do. It's a socially accepted practice, so don't be surprised next time you shop in your neighbourhood supermarket and you meet your businessman neighbour in his jammies.

9. *Don't compare everything to back home.* There's no point. You are missing out on a beautiful adventure of conquering the new, the unknown, the wild. Embrace it!

Making friends in China and more cultural peculiarities.

Everyone who moves to live abroad needs people. Sure, you can hang out with other foreigners and feel like you never left home, but then what's the point of going to China? Yet, making friends with the Chinese is quite a complex endeavour.

Many a time young Chinese would come up to me in Starbucks and ask: *Can I be your friend?* While this might seem overreaching to you, I found it amusing. Most of them wanted to practise their English. Also, it's okay to say that to a Chinese person. Be careful about one thing. Once you do establish any sort of friendly relationship with a Chinese person, they'll go out of their way to treat you to meals. It's just in their blood. Sometimes I wouldn't even know that my friend had paid the bill, as he or she did so secretly when I went to the loo. It's really hard to win this game with them. In Chinese culture, treating friends is very important and so the next time you invite your Chinese colleagues to dinner, be aware that you're paying. Splitting the bill is slowly entering today's China, but isn't yet too widespread.

One way the Chinese make friends is through going to KTV (karaoke club). This seems to be their most favourite pastime. I like singing, so it never bothered me, but I know people who dreaded every time their friendly outing finished with a round of serenading. Your friends, as were mine, will be super proud of you if you can sing a song in Chinese. Your phone might come in handy because most KTVs display traditional Chinese characters, so you might need to look up the good old *pinyin* or simplified Mandarin.

Before we box locals in China as insincere opportunists, we should understand the concept of friendship in their culture. The word *friend* (朋友 = p*eng you*) is used for everyone from a colleague to an acquaintance. Since the society is based on having good connections (关系 = *guan xi*), your contact details might be asked for within the first minutes of an encounter. So, don't judge them too hard. And try not to apply your own understanding of friendship onto the Chinese scene.

As in every multinational friendship, different senses of humour, different views of world politics and basically everything different make it harder to establish a deep relationship and even harder to maintain it. My personal feeling is that when I was in China, most of my Chinese friends stayed in touch with me on a regular basis. Once I left, the messages stopped. I felt like since they don't need me anymore to either teach their friends' kids English, teach in their own language schools or help them with IELTS, I was no longer needed. Hence, my feeling is that many Chinese people, not all though, liked me when I was able to benefit them somehow. I have to say that a few of my Chinese friends stayed and I know they will always be there. But a few really disappointed me.

Many young Chinese people would like to learn from you about the world. They'd be curious about your country and its customs. But, this interest often is not reciprocated. Not many foreigners have a real desire to learn about China. And that's very unfair. And then of course the language barrier. It's one thing to have survival Chinese skills and another thing to be able to conduct a deep at-length conversation with a Chinese national. Too much is being said between the lines.

You cannot survive in China without the help of your Chinese friends. I cannot stress this enough. When I first moved to China, I spoke literally zero Chinese. I had to ask people to go shopping with me (to help me read the labels), to help me take the bus, to go to the doctor with me. I felt so uncomfortable with asking people for help ALL THE TIME, I decided to learn Chinese to be able to take care of myself. All of my friends were extremely helpful and very often eager and willing to help, but I just felt that's not what friendship should be about. From finding an apartment and starting your own business to buying stuff on *Taobao* and arranging a wedding, you will need help. I have always tried to repay my friends in some ways, but I can never say THANK YOU enough to all those who made my life in China liveable and enjoyable.

Someone once told me that in order to fit into the Chinese society one needs to speak like the locals, eat like the locals, live where the locals do and travel like the locals. Bearing that in mind, I always liked to visit small rural areas outside the metropolis, just to get the sense of what the REAL CHINA looks like. To experience the local flavours and to interact with the local people. These trips are the most memorable days for me.

Every culture has its own peculiarities. It's entirely up to us to choose how we look at them. Take eye contact as an example. In the West, it's very important to look people in the eye. Otherwise you'll come across as unsociable and dishonest. But in China it is the other way round. Direct eye contact during a conversation is often seen as being too direct. The business world is also full of such discrepancies. Always hand your business card out with both hands. It means you're respectful of the other person. A foreign friend of mine was so sick of all the beggars in Shanghai (who usually gather around bars at night) targeting foreigners. He printed business cards with 我没钱 (*wo mei qian*), which means I don't have money and gave them out each time a beggar would stop him.

Another thing that might take you by surprise is the view of people sleeping at work. They would either sleep with their arms on their desks and their head in them, or on actual portable beds. I must admit I had one of those myself in my last job. I wasn't sharing an office with anyone, so after lunch I'd lock the door and take a half an hour nap. I know now why it's called a power nap.

Some last few pieces of wisdom. Carry your own toilet paper, because chances are you won't find it in most toilets. Don't take black taxis, which actually look like normal private cars, but carry a certain degree of danger. Ask a waiter to bring extra menus if you're dining with friends. In China, commonly only one menu is given for the entire table. And don't ever bring up the Three Ts: Taiwan, Tibet and Tiananmen Square, if you value your friendships.

Is Chinese as easy as ABC? Absolutely not!

Learning Chinese was the best thing that has ever happened to me and the worst thing that has ever happened to me. It was my sixth language, but the hardest one, it seemed. It was so complicated to develop learning strategies that would work with Chinese. I think, however, that every expat who lives in China SHOULD learn Chinese. This language carries so much culture and history that without studying it one can never truly understand China.

Let's start with numbers in Chinese. I have already written about the hand system of showing numbers in China elsewhere in this book, but I didn't explain how complex the numerical system in Chinese really is. Words in Chinese are built of combinations which usually make sense. For example, if you want to say *pork*, you cluster *pig* with *meat* (猪肉 = *zhu rou*) and you're good to go. The case of numbers doesn't follow this handy rule, though. Until you get to 9999, you can still use logic and construct, say, 30 by saying 3 + 10 (三十 = *san shi*). After 9999, however, the little unit called *wan* (万) comes into play. *Wan* is worth 10 thousand, so instead of saying 10 thousand you'd say 1 10 thousand. Confused yet? A hundred thousand also doesn't exist per se, but instead 100K is replaced by 10 10 thousands. So, in fact, it is possible to count to one million with just 13 characters. Here's how:

10,000 = 一万 = *yi wan* = (1 x 10,000) = ten thousand (1,0000, Chinese style)

100,000 = 十万 = *shi wan* = (10 x 10,000) = one hundred thousand (10,0000, Chinese style)

1,000,000 = 一百万 = *yi bai wan* = (100 x 10,000) = one million (100,0000, Chinese style)

10,000,000 = 一千万 = *yi qian wan* = (1000 x 10,000) = ten million (1000,0000, Chinese style)

100,000,000 = 一亿 = *yi yi* = (1 x 100,000,000) = one hundred million (1,0000,0000, Chinese style)

1,000,000,000 = 十亿 = *shi yi* = (10 x 100,000,000) = one billion (10,0000,0000, Chinese style)

So, China' 1.4 billion population is expressed as 14 hundred millions = 十四亿. No wonder all my Chinese friends come across as mathematical geniuses!

Another part of learning Chinese that gave me many sleepless nights are the characters. It's one thing to speak Chinese and even read *pinyin*, but characters are a game changer. You can, surely, survive without ever learning them but your experience will definitely be deprived. And you'll still need help reading your bus timetable 😊. Characters are tricky as many of them differ by just one tiny (almost invisible) stroke and hence mean something utterly different. I honestly don't know how my Chinese friends have learnt all of them. They told me it's only possible through repetition and memorization. I got to being able to recognize about 2000 characters, which is what I needed for my HSK4 (a Chinese proficiency exam), which, I'm happy to brag, I passed with flying colours. But being able to recognize Chinese characters and being able to write them by hand are poles apart. I even know some Chinese friends of mine who, due to excessive use of smartphones that predict characters based on *pinyin*, forgot how to hand-write certain things. Don't be discouraged! Be imaginative! I used to imagine that a character represented some visual form and that helped me a lot with improving my reading speed and comprehension rate.

Dictionaries don't help much. Looking up Chinese words is another hurdle. It takes ages to find something and requires quite a complex training first. Also, just like in English, Chinese comes with a myriad of fonts in print. So, you may be able to read one while not able to decipher another one at all. You shouldn't expect to learn Chinese overnight. It takes time and commitment. However, do practise as often as you can. I used to chat with cleaning ladies, security guards, taxi drivers and shopkeepers just to get the conversation going. Now, tones. Are they really that important? Honestly, I never paid too much attention to them, because I took a shortcut to speaking as fast as I could. This way everyone thought I was fluent (fooled them all😊) and my tones were not so crucial. As long as I could maintain certain musicality of the sentence, I was fine. And so will you be. Do get a teacher! I started off eagerly learning by myself only to realize at a certain point that I couldn't move forward alone. My teacher had to scratch all the wrongly-learnt structures and it took a lot of explaining for her to get me to follow Chinese grammar patterns. So, hire someone who knows what they are doing, not just a Chinese native speaker who wants to practise their English while supposedly teaching you.

I even taught a class of College English from a Chinese/English textbook once. I think by the time I was leaving China, the percentage of my using Chinese in comparison to English was about 60 to 40%. Even now, a year after I left China, I still find myself use a few Chinese phrases in daily life. I'd often smuggle: *suibian* (随便), which means *whatever*; *meiwenti* (没问题) = *no problem* or *wasai* (哇塞), which means *wow!* into my daily conversations in the U.S. It cracks my husband up each time.

In addition, you probably already know quite a few Chinese words without even realizing it, since English borrowed a whole lot of those. Here's my own list:

- Kowtow = from the Chinese word *ke tou* (磕头), bump heads, representing an action of respect, usually bowing;
- Tea = from the Chinese word *cha* (茶), which infiltrated many languages;
- Typhoon = from the Chinese word *taifeng* (台风);
- Ketchup = from the Chinese word *koechiap* (in the Amoy dialect);
- Brainwash = from the Chinese phrase *gei... xinao* (给...洗脑), which literally means *to wash somebody's brain*;
- Silk = from the Chinese word *sichou* (丝绸), created from Chinese transliteration;

- Fengshui = from the Chinese *fengshui* (风水), adapted by the English language almost sound-by-sound and word-by-word;
- Dimsum = from the Cantonese *chadian* (茶点), which means *something sweet* for the tea;
- Paper tiger = from the Chinese *zhilaohu* (纸老虎), signifying something that looks threatening but is in fact harmless;
- Mah-jong = from the Chinese game of *majiang* (麻将);
- Ginseng = from the Chinese phrase *renshen* (人参), which can be broken down into person+herb;
- No can do = from the Chinese phrase *bu neng zuo* (不能做);
- Hacker = from the Chinese *heike* (黑客) that literally means *black guest*;

And of course, many many other words I could fill another book with.

Chinese language is also progressing and evolving as the world does. Hence, it has quite a few widespread words for wealth and being rich. *Fu'erdai* (富二代), translates to *rich second generation*. It refers to Chinese born into wealthy families after the 1980s. These kids are eligible to inherit tons of money and assets from their parents. Then, they are broken into a few categories of *guan'erdai* (官二代) as kids of government officials, *xing'erdai* (星二代) as children of celebrities, and *hong'erdai* (红二代) as children whose parents have strong connections in the Communist Party. Born with silver spoons in their mouths, these kids grow up financially pampered and often sent away abroad for education. Another relatively new word everyone in China knows and uses seems to be *tuhao* (土豪), which described China's nouveau riche who got rich overnight but aren't much educated. You might still remember the special edition of the Apple gold iPhone 5s, anecdotally called *tuhao gold watch* (土豪金). "Spoiled brats with a deep sense of entitlement" are the best words describing this group.

Lastly, let's talk about Chinese insults. As is the case with every language, acquiring a solid command of swearings is a must. It helps you survive and, more importantly, know when someone is cursing you. I must admit I used my entire repertoire of those when I was driving in Hangzhou. It helped relieve my stress and frustration, ha-ha. So, a few of those here:

- *wang ba dan* (王八蛋) = a person who doesn't know his or her father;

- *ni hen taoyan* (你很讨厌) = you're a nuisance;
- *goupi* (狗屁) = dogfart, what you say is a lot of crap;
- *dai lv mao zi* (戴绿帽子) = you're a cuckold;
- *er bai wu* (二百五) = you're a fool;
- *san ba* (三八) = to a woman, she's a witch, only spelled with 'b'  or "big mouth";
- *ni mei jiao yang* (你没教养) = you're uneducated;
- *tu baozi* (土包子) = dirt dumpling, a hickish person;
- *sha gua* (傻瓜) & *ben dan* (笨蛋) = stupid, moron;
- *yang guizi* (洋鬼子) = 'foreign devil', an evil foreigner;
- *shenjing bing* (神经病) = 'sick in the head';
- *dian deng pao* (电灯泡) = a light bulb, a third wheel;
- lan chong (懒虫) = lazy bones;
- shamao (傻冒) = dumb;
- *nao bei lv ti le* (脑被驴踢了) = kicked in the head by a donkey, stupid (This one is my favourite!).

I would like to encourage you to learn Chinese. It is going to overtake the world. Many countries in Africa are already teaching it as a second language. It is so much fun!

My love-hate relationship with China.

Every foreigner who lives in China has their good and bad days. The key to stay sane is to make sure the good days outweigh the worse ones. There are so many things I miss about China now that I left. There are also those that never grew on me. So, I decided to conclude this chapter by listing both.

Things I love about China (but never expected to):

- *Soya bean milk.* Not only did I use to buy it whenever I got a chance, but also bought a soya milk machine. How Chinese is that! Every morning, instead of a traditional and highly overrated cup of coffee, I would make a jar of soya bean milk and enjoy it with about half a billion Chinese.

- *KTV*. Well, I have always liked karaoke clubs as I enjoy singing now and then, but the Chinese version of these places really rocks. They remind me of small clique clubs for the chosen ones. You should book a room in advance because this type of entertainment is extremely popular at all times in China. It's also very different from the Western version of karaoke I had visited. You don't need to sing in front of the whole audience, but instead you get to stay with your people in a separate room. Most Chinese people love singing and I must admit some of my friends are very good at it. They get passionate and the entire thing ends up riveting.
- *Rice*. In my country rice is mainly eaten on Fridays (for the purpose of fasting) with marmalade or some kind of fruity juice. In China, rice is everywhere and it comes in all forms and colours. My Chinese sister also taught me how to distinguish the good rice from the close-to-non-edible one. To make our lives easier, there are rice cookers available for close to nothing, so that nobody has to worry about the smelly results of burnt pots.
- *Food*. China has the richest plater of foods available at very affordable prices. It doesn't matter what your favourite is, you can be sure to find it in China. I was brave enough to try some challenging dishes but never had the guts to go for a snake, scorpion or lizard.
- *People*. Chinese people are the nicest, the most friendly and helpful people I ever had the pleasure to befriend. With exceptions, of course. My students were a pleasure to teach and my colleagues taught me more than I ever thought I could learn.
- *Chatting with taxi drivers*. I just loved practising my Chinese with these guys. They'd always teach me a handful of new (bad!) words.
- *Public transportation*. Despite its crowds and unpleasant smells, China has an extremely developed public transport system. In the U.S., you can't get around without a car. Buses here come and go as they please. I miss my comfortable train rides!
- *Conveniences*. In China, everything is accessible to you. It doesn't matter what you need, chances are *Taobao* will have it. The delivery services are simply fantastic. I could practically spend a month indoors and have everything I needed delivered to my doorsteps.
- *Cost of living*. I long for the days where I could comfortably live in a two-bedroom flat for RMB 1800 ($300). Right now, my rent is $900 (RMB 6000) for a pretty much the same size place. And I

used to make money, as a teacher in China; while now I'm a poor PhD student in the U.S.

- *Cheap options*. Everything comes in cheaper versions in China. You can buy beautiful knockoffs of things and use them happily for years. I loved the varieties of prices and the fact everything was open for bargain.
- *Perks of being a foreigner*. People were always willing to help me, strangers on the street. You don't find the same level of involvement anywhere else.
- *Language*. Even though I'm currently conducting research related to Chinese students in the U.S., my chances to use Chinese are very limited. It's a shame.
- *Traditional Chinese Medicine*. You have probably already figured that I'm a big proponent of acupuncture. It helped me out in so many health dilemmas. It's so expensive here in the U.S.
- *Chinese culture*. I know it's hard to see its remains in the huge developing monstrous cities, but that's why I would always travel to little remote rural places. That's where the real China is. I miss chatting with the locals there.
- *Teaching*. I truly enjoyed teaching Chinese students. They were the most curious, respectful and hard-working people I have ever taught. They were my constant inspiration to better myself.
- *Chances China gave me to discover my new identities*. I have learnt so much about myself through my stay in China. It changed the way I look at life and made me more understanding and patient.

Things I won't miss about China:

- *Honking*. It was so frustrating as there was never silence. You'd wake up at 6am to find an impatient Uber driver waiting for his passenger blaring outside your windows.
- *Staring*. Even though one gets used to it after a while, it never stopped bothering me for some reason. I did learn how to professionally stare back, though.
- *Crazy e-bikers*. These guys seemed to me as more dangerous than car drivers. They'd never look around, joyriding through the streets like they owned them. One really had to stay observant in order not to be killed by one of them.
- *Traffic*. Given that Hangzhou, where I lived the entire 6 years, has about 10 million people, it was so challenging to get from point A to point B. When subway was constructed, the jams were finally reduced. I did not like the bumping-into-people on the street.

- *MSG in food.* It's so prevalent and it's difficult to know that before one takes a bite. It used to cause all sorts of weird diseases in me.
- *Loud cell phone conversations.* When will people learn that not everyone on a train is interested in what they had for lunch? This really bothered me and I'm glad that the U.S. bans cell phone use in public places, such as hospitals.
- *Square-dancing ladies.* Although I joined them a few times myself, it was annoying having to listen to the same songs on a loop every single night. Don't they ever rest?
- *Name calling.* I developed this nightmare where I'm walking down the streets of New York City and someone calls me by my name, but I don't react. Then, they switch into shouting: *Laowai, laowai!* And that's when I turn around. Pathetic, I know.
- *Red tape.* Getting things done legally in China is painstaking, not just for foreigners but also for the Chinese.
- *Pollution.* That's the main reason I left. I'll be forever wondering how many years my life will be shorter by now because of all the inhales of whatever's in the air in China.

I reckon my balance stayed on a positive note. I really loved living in China. I had to leave because the pollution was making me ill, I got admitted to a PhD programme in the U.S. and my husband lives here. If not for these reasons, I most probably would have stayed. China is forever in my heart.

CHAPTER 14

All stories here come from Chinese news. I find them both hilarious and alarming! Sources:

www.chinadaily.com.cn

www.china-mike.com

www.amcham-shanghai.org

www.whats-your-sign.com

www.echinacities.com

Thailand isn't happy about Chinese tourists' hygiene routine.

Image from http://www.thatsmags.com/china/post/9128/thai-authorities-upset-that-chinese-tourists-keep-washing-their-feet-in-public-sinks

Thai authorities are reported to be very unhappy about Chinese tourists washing their feet in public toilets. This news follows another gross example of a baby's diarrhoea plugging the sink on a Hong Kong flight causing severe delays. The reason Thai people can't stomach this ritual is that they consider it a form of a 'cultural sin'. According to the tradition in Thailand, feet can only be washed in a separate basin. Therefore, new anti-feet-washing signs have been put up in most popular touristy spots in Thailand.

A 7-year-old designated driver spotted.

Image from http://www.thatsmags.com/china/post/8229/photos-7-year-old-in-guangxi-drives-dad-home-after-night-of-heavy-drinking

On one infamous January night, a 7-year-old designated driver was driving his drunk father back home. It is said the little one drove for over 20 km. Allegedly, his older brother was also seen sluggishly meandering the city under the influence. Let's hope the child driver wouldn't have to get acquainted with a 12-step AA programme himself in the future.

"Riding my pig saves me a lot of energy and is also quite fun".

Image from http://i.dailymail.co.uk/i/pix/2014/03/14/article-o-1C48C1D000000578-333_634x416.jpg.

A 68-year-old farmer from Chongqing rides his swine after illness left him unable to walk long distance. The pig weighs 250kg and is 3 years old. The farmer started riding his hog after bronchitis made him too weak to walk by himself. His unconventional means of transport turned him into a celebrity. Way to go, Mr Jiang! Thumbs-up for creativity!

A power nap? Yes, please!

Image from http://2.bp.blogspot.com/-MrzQj4Baimc/Td3hQ41zplI/AAAAAAAADug/GQTuEVFj6S8/s400/nap_chinese.jpg.

When I first started working in China, I was surprised to find most of my Chinese colleagues sleeping on their desks after lunch. Well, their heads would be buried in their arms and they would still be sitting in their chairs. I had no idea what that was until I discovered the power of a power nap. The midday snooze seems to be a perfect refresher, especially during cold winter days. Having a swift doze really does help one enliven the mind, boost productivity, improve memory and even lower the risk of heart disease. Apparently, there are 4 stages to napping. Firstly, you fall into a very light sleep, a state that weirdly feels like being somewhere in between being awake and asleep. Secondly, you slowly drift away from the surroundings and get ready for a deeper sleep. At this moment, your breathing is regular and your body temperature goes down. By the time you reach stages three and four, you're in deep sleep, with stage four being more acute. Your muscles are completely relaxed. The contrast between a good and a bad sleep depends on which stage you'd wake up in. To obtain a perfect power nap state, one should target stages one and two only. Ideal naps should last from 20 to 40 minutes.

Then, a new fad appeared, super cool desk sleeping pillows, looking just like these:

Ostrich pillow. Image from *http://io1.i.aliimg.com/wsphoto/vo/869379357/Free-Shipping-Ostrich-font-b-Pillow-b-font-for-Travel-Sleeping-Nap-font-b-Pillow-b.jpg.*

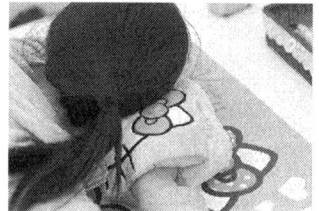

Hello Kitty pillow. Image from http://coach3.gomdesign.com/YeongHun/Auction%20File/Cushion/hellowkitty/JPEG/3.JPG.

And of course, a traditional one. Image from http://thumbs.dreamstime.com/t/tired-asian-businessman-sleeping-laptop-pillow-table-60194398.jpg.

You can even buy sperm on Taobao these days.

Ehh.... my favourite place - Taobao. For those who don't know what that is, a word of explanation. It's the biggest online platform for shop owners to sell their goods in China. It's amazing. It allows one not only to buy all the necessities without leaving the house, but delivery is super quick, too. One can pay utilities there as well as charge one's phone. It's basically a better and more convenient version of eBay.

According to *China Daily*, over 22,000 men signed up to donate sperm to be sold on Taobao. It is believed that donors were attracted by not having to meet face to face with the representatives of the physical sperm banks, which would save them embarrassment. The only three requirements are to provide one's name, last six digits of their ID card and their email address. Also, the fact that every volunteer would receive between RMB 3000 and 5000 certainly makes a nice incentive. In Shanghai, a three-hour delivery service was opened to assure folks in urgent need of some sperm. Go and multiply!

Mind your hands!

I have noticed a few times by now that the weirdest things happen in Anhui Province in China. In March 2015, a jealous husband, after discovering his beloved wife's affair, cut off both of her hands. The lady of 27 years, named Jiang, was also accused by her cross spouse of allowing their life savings to be taken by scammers in a pyramid scheme a few years back. Not only did the swindlers brainwash her, but also made her continue such evil endeavours behind her husband's back. Mrs Jiang went online and extended her relationship into the real world. When Mr Chen, the husband, confronted his wife in their kitchen, things got too far and the kitchen cleaver came to use.

Mrs Jiang was rushed to the hospital and luckily survived while her vexed hubby was detained by the police. I guess he should be thankful that *Lex talionis* (the law of retaliation) isn't taken too seriously these days.

A private hairdresser at school?
It happened in Guangxi Province!

Wuzhou, in Guangxi Province, became infamous on October 10, 2014 when a vice-principal publicly cut a few students' hair. The reason stated was them being late for class as well as their hairdos not following school's rules. Despite a strong online criticism of the event, the headmaster gained approval from several parents. Netizens claimed this public shaming was disrespectful and should not go unpunished. When the principal was interviewed a few days later, he claimed he had had good intentions because he didn't want his students to resemble Korean pop stars.

A man three-months along!

A hospital in Sichuan was fined RMB 3,000 (approximately $460) for having misdiagnosed a male patient as three months pregnant. They even gave a guy an official document stating the diagnosis. After the patient went to the hospital with excruciating abdominal pain, the doctor ordered his hospitalization. The man spent over RMB 4,000 on numerous checks and scans just to be released after six days with the shocking diagnosis. The doctor in question got punished by a month suspension along with an official letter of apology to the "lucky" patient.

No napping!

Whoever has worked in China for even a few months, recognizes the importance of an afternoon nap. But one school in Hunan wasn't happy with its students dozing off during lunch hour. They decided to charge each student found sleeping RMB 1 as a fine. Before someone reported it, the school had already managed to gather an equivalent of one employee's monthly salary. The school authorities tried to explain that with the need to cover school's management cost during lunch break.

Sexology postgraduate student
changes her vocation!

Ms Peng Lulu decided to change her career and become...a Buddhist nun. After graduating in 2011, Ms Peng struggled to find a suitable job in China. So, she decided to go for her other calling and follow Buddhist philosophy more closely. Her dream is to establish a TV programme discussing both sexology and Buddhism.

Flight or fight?

Last year (i.e. around August 2015), a plane was deflected back to Beijing. It was on its way to Toronto, Canada. A passenger in a rage attacked a flight attendant on board. The pilot tried to land in Japan first but to no avail. When they finally managed to reach Beijing, the unruly traveller was apprehended by the police. No details of the incident were released to the public. That was just the beginning of a series of stories of this kind.

Flying to and fro, I have seen my share of weird behaviour on planes handling the Chinese. People do tai-chi in the aisle making the life of the flight attendants a living hell. Some watch Korean soap operas throughout the entire journey (that's usually 10+ hours) without using their earphones. Others travel with kids and, as far as I'm concerned, these are the worst. Not only do they stare at any white face in their proximity but also uncontrollably kick, scream, sing, shout, jump and want to be on the move when the seatbelt sign is on. I always try to book the last seat in the cabin just to avoid being hoofed all the time. However, my best personal one is the scene when a middle-aged woman places a moisturizing facemask on her face and falls asleep in a seated position.

Hilariously, a friend of mine, who is a pilot and frequently flies to Asia, told me once that most aircrafts detest heading for China. For one simple reason. All toilets need replacement as the Chinese – used to using squat toilets only - typically break them by standing on the seats.

Oh well! Still, the number of international flights from China to any reputable part of the world rises like blazes.

Having a period? Take a day off.

It's no joke. A factory in Shanxi province has already begun granting its female employees menstrual leave. One is able to rest a day or two, upon providing a doctor's certificate proving painful periods. Opponents of the idea claim it would be more reasonable to allow women to take a sick leave than a paid leave, though. Well... Being a female, I reckon all jobs should implement it☺.

Pay for the ride!

One Shanghai district decided to charge patients for their ride to the hospital and so taxi meters were installed in ambulances there. Next time you are being rushed to the hospital in a critical condition, make sure you have enough cash. The meter will surely change with each kilometre.

Yours for RMB 5mln!

A university professor in Chongqing stood on a busy street holding posters auctioning himself to a wealthy woman for RMB 5mln (approximately $768,000). He claimed he wanted to continue his PhD research abroad but came from poverty and did not have enough cash. I really hope someone cashed him out☺.

Butter up the bridge!

There is a bridge in Guangzhou (called 猎德大桥 = *lie de da qiao*), notorious for people trying to commit suicides there. Authorities claimed they tried to place guards on each ends of the bridge but it didn't work. So then they put up notices pleading with people not to jump. Special barriers were also installed, also to no avail. Finally, tired of disrupted traffic and a rising number of calls for help by watchers, the police put... butter over the bridge. This way no one can get up there and hence problem solved. Go figure!

Quantity over quality.

Everyone knows that Chinese construction companies built faster than anyone can catch up with. In Changsha, Lego-style skyscraper was done in 19 days. It has 57 storeys and 800 flats. I wouldn't want to live there for the world. One day I might wake up to realize that my house is down just like Lego blocks.

Who doesn't love Apple?

Most Chinese people, and quite a few foreigners I know here, are crazy about Apple products. To them it would not be surprising that a son of Wang Jianlin (China's richest man couple of years back) bought an Apple watch for his dog. The price of the bling was over RMB 250,000 (approximately $38400) and of course it was gold. Keke, the dog, is also becoming more and more famous online for its designer clothes, bags and other stylish accessories. As famous as he might be, though, Mr Wang lost a lot of followers after his interview in which he said: "When I make friends, I don't care if they have money or not; no one's going to have more money than me anyway". Quite a charmer, huh?

I'm the only one!

A 13-year-old girl threatened to kill herself in Hubei Province if her mum didn't abort her second baby. The woman, pregnant for 13 weeks, gave into her daughter's pleads after she cut her wrists with a razor blade in an attempted suicide. Something to think about for the inventors of the one-child policy.

Horny grandma?

A 100-year-old granny was spotted with a 6 cm-long horn sticking out of her forehead. She said it had appeared a year before. According to scientists, the horn was made of the same keratin as hair and nails. Quite a keeper, that one.

IKEA is to shop, not to drop!

Ever since IKEA opened new locations, it's become obvious that some customers simply go there to catch a nap, and not to buy anything. Nannies and kids sleeping on displayed couches are an everyday picture. When asked, they said it's just so comfortable, especially with the air-conditioning on in the scorching summer time. Many shops now ban sleeping on beds and sofas, but as we all know creating a rule in China is one thing, trying to make it work – a completely different story.

He's unconscious! And he's a foreigner. RUN!

During my stay in China, I fainted on Chinese subway twice. Both times I was lucky enough to have someone call the ambulance and help me out of the carriage. Another fellow expat was not so lucky in Shanghai. When he blacked out, every single passenger rushed out. Not even one tried to help him. Lucky me, I guess!

A real player!

On March 24, 2015 a man was rushed to a hospital in Hunan Province from a car accident. What he did not expect were all his 30 lovers at his bed when he woke up. Must have been quite a welcoming. Not sure if the guy survived☺.

Hi Mum! -Bye Mum!

A man was going to visit his mother in Anhui Province. On his way, he saw an accident with an old lady lying on the side of the road. He kept going without stopping. When he reached his mum's house, the relatives told him she had already left to meet him. For one reason or another, he rushed back to the crash scene only to discover it was no one else but his own mother he had previously ignored. He rushed her to the hospital but sadly she died on the way there. Wouldn't like to see his guilt's size!

Dance it off!

A traffic accident does not need to be a bummer as "aunties and uncles" know how to turn it into a thrilling dance-off. On a highway in Yunnan Province, they left their vehicles and started to shake a leg while waiting for the jam to be resolved. Way to go!

Long distance is never easy!

A woman filled in her leave-from-work form explaining she wanted to go to see her husband (who was working in another far-away province) as she had almost forgotten what he looked like. She asked for 10 days. It was granted!

Discounts for students!

Sex scandals are quite widespread all over the Chinese media. No wonder universities don't want to fall behind. One college in Wuhan has a brothel in broad daylight. It even offers discounts for students showing their student ID cards. Since the story went viral the "hotel" has been under investigation. However, as it's owned by the university principal's brother in law, I see a bright future for it.

Making a sex tape in Uniqlo!

I think everyone who lived in China in 2015 heard the story of a couple who decided to fool around in a fitting room of a Beijing's Uniqlo. The man posted the video which depicted his partner naked in the middle of the shag. It went viral in a split second and was taken down even quicker. Some went as far as to accuse the company of posting it as a marketing stunt. Really? A fitting room? Get a room!

China's bizarre laws!

In China, I have come across a list of some of the most grotesque laws one could ever hear of. The list is below:

1. One should not stop at zebra crossings.
2. One should not keep explosives in the basement.
3. One should not eat another man's wife deliberately.
4. One should not date one's colleagues.
5. One should not give away a secret of silk production.
6. One should not give their children strange names.
7. One should salute passing vehicles (found in Elementary School).
8. One should announce the approach of a Russian.

This is China!

Don't drag your dirty laundry outside!

Recently, there has been a rise of Chinese students mailing their dirty clothes back home for their parents to wash. Many commentators rebuke this method claiming it stops the young from growing up and learning essential life skills.

As most of China residents have surely noticed, the Chinese have a way of drying their laundry outside, on poles. They believe the sun is the best drier and its ultraviolet rays kill the bacteria on one's underwear.

I'm a diva!

One Chinese teacher in Shanghai made her students carry her umbrella at all times over her head. She was photographed sitting on a bench and fanning herself with a huge fan, hiding behind a fashionable pair of sunglasses, her student holding her umbrella over her head. Ms Teacher was shocked when the photos went viral online explaining she had only agreed to her students plead to hold her umbrella, and that it was not her idea. Queen bee?

ABOUT THE AUTHOR

Karolina Achirri lived in Hangzhou, China, for six years. She taught English at a public university, private training schools and an international high school. She also tested IELTS speaking and writing for the British Council, in East China exam centres. She is the author of *IELTS Band 9: An Academic Guide for Chinese Students. Volumes I & II* and *IELTS Examiner's Tips: An Academic Guide to IELTS Speaking and Writing*, published in 2015. Currently, Karolina is working on her doctoral degree in Second Language Studies at Michigan State University, USA.

For more information visit www.karolinaachirri.com!

INDEX

Made in the USA
Columbia, SC
09 November 2022

70589709R00185